Computer Supported Cooperative Work

Springer
London
Berlin
Heidelberg
New York
Barcelona
Budapest
Hong Kong
Milan
Paris
Santa Clara
Singapore
Tokyo

Also in this series

Gerold Riempp
Wide Area Workflow Management: Creating Partnerships for the
21st Century
3-540-76243-4

Celia T. Romm and Fay Sudweeks (eds)
Doing Business Electronically: A Global Perspective of Electronic
Commerce
3-540-76159-4

Reza Hazemi, Stephen Hailes and
Steve Wilbur (Eds)

The Digital University

Reinventing the Academy

With 35 Figures

Springer

LB
2395.7
.D54
1998

Reza Hazemi, BEng, MSc, PhD
Stephen Hailes, MA, PhD
Steve Wilbur, BSc(Eng), MSc, CEng, FIEE, FBCS
Department of Computing Science, University College London,
Gower Street, London, WC1E 6BT, UK

Series Editors

Dan Diaper, PhD, MBCS
Head, Department of Computing, School of Design, Engineering and Computing,
Bournemouth University, Talbot Campus, Fern Barrow, Poole, Dorset BH12 5BB, UK

Colston Sanger
Shottersley Research Limited, Little Shottersley, Farnham Lane
Haselmere, Surrey GU27 1HA, UK

ISBN 1-85233-003-1 Springer-Verlag Berlin Heidelberg New York

British Library Cataloguing in Publication Data
The digital university : reinventing the academy. - (Computer supported cooperative work)
  1.Computer-assisted instruction 2.Universities and colleges - Data processing
  3.Education, Higher - Data processing 4.Education, higher - Computer network resources
  5.Universities and colleges - Computer network resources
  I.Hazemi, Reza II.Hailes, Stephen III.Wilbur, Steve
  378'00285
  ISBN 1852330031

Library of Congress Cataloging-in-Publication Data
The digital university : reinventing the academy / Reza Hazemi.,. Stephen Hailes, and Stephen Wilber, eds.
      p.   cm. -- (Computer supported cooperative work)
    ISBN 1-85233-003-1 (alk. paper)
    1. Education, Higher--Great Britain--data processing.   2. University cooperation--Great Britain.
  3. Education, Higher--Effect of technological innovations on--Great Britain.   4. Internet (Computer
  network) in education--Great Britain   5. computer-assisted instruction--Great Britain.   6. Distance
  education--Great Britain.   I. Hazemi, Reza, 1996-   . II. Hailes, Stephen, 1965-   .
  III. Wilbur, Steve, 1944-   . IV. Series.
  LB2395.7.D54   1998
  378'.00285--dc21   98-6346

Typesetting: Camera ready by editors
Printed and bound at the Athenæum Press Ltd., Gateshead, Tyne & Wear
34/3830-543210 Printed on acid-free paper

Contents

The Contributors

Susan Armitage

Learning Technology Support, Information Systems Services, Library Building, Lancaster University, LANCS, LA1 4YW, UK

s.armitage@lancaster.ac.uk

Mark Bryson

Learning Technology Support, Information Systems Services, Library Building, Lancaster University, LANCS, LA1 4YW, UK

m.bryson@notes.lancs.ac.uk

Mark D'Cruz

City University Business School, Frobisher Crescent, Barbican Centre, London, EC2Y 8HB, UK

s/313@city.ac.uk

Graham R. Gibbs

Department of Behavioural Sciences, University of Huddersfield, Queensgate, Huddersfield. HD1 3DH, UK

G.R.Gibbs@hud.ac.uk

Stephen Hailes

Department of Computer Science, University College London, Gower Street, London, WC1E 6BT, UK

S.Hailes@cs.ucl.ac.uk

Christopher Harris

Department of Computer Science, University College London, Gower Street, London, WC1E 6BT, UK

C.Harris@cs.ucl.ac.uk

Reza Hazemi

Department of Computer Science, University College London, Gower Street, London, WC1E 6BT, UK

R.Hazemi@cs.ucl.ac.uk

Peter J.H. Hinssen

Telematics Institute, P.O. Box 589, 7500 AN Enschede, The Netherlands

p.hinssen@wxs.nl

Clive Holtham

City University Business School, Frobisher Crescent, Barbican Centre, London, EC2Y 8HB, UK

C.W.Holtham@city.ac.uk

Ismail Ismail

Department of Computer Science, University College London, Gower Street, London, WC1E 6BT, UK

I.Ismail@cs.ucl.ac.uk

Kim Issroff

Higher Education Research and Development Unit, University College London, Gower Street, London, WC1E 6BT, U.K.

K.Issroff@ucl.ac.uk

Alain Karsenty

Institut Eurecom, 2229, route des Cretes, PB 193, 06904 Sophia Antipolis, FRANCE

karsenty@eurecom.fr

Lisa Kimball

Metasystems Design Group, Inc., 2000 North 15th St., Suite 103, Arlington, VA 22201, U.S.A.

lisa@tmn.com

J Kirakowski

Human Factors Research Group, University College, Cork, Ireland.

jzk@ucc.ie

Linda Macaulay

Department of Computation, UMIST, Sackville Street, Manchester, M60 1QD, UK

Lindam@sna.co.umict.ac.uk

Bernard Merialdo

Institut Eurecom, 2229, route des Cretes, PB 193, 06904 Sophia Antipolis, FRANCE

merialdo@eurecom.fr

Brian R Mitchell

Director, Management Systems Division, University Collage London, Gower Street, London, WC1E 6BT, UK

B.Mitchell@ucl.ac.uk

Peter Monthienvichienchai

Department of Computer Science, University College London, Gower Street, London, WC1E 6BT, UK

P.Monthienvichienchai@cs.ucl.ac.uk

Kent Norman

Department of Psychology, University of Maryland, College Park, MD 20742-4422, U.S.A.

Kent_Norman@mail.lap.umd.edu

Angela Sasse

Department of Computer Science, University College London, Gower Street, London, WC1E 6BT, UK

A.Sasse@cs.ucl.ac.uk

Abdul Naeem Shaikh

Department of Computation, UMIST, Sackville Street, Manchester, M60 1QD, UK

ans2@sna.co.umist.ac.uk

Ben Shneiderman

Dept. of Computer Science, University of Maryland, College Park, MD 20742, U.S.A.

ben@cs.umd.edu

Jacqueline Taylor

Department of Applied Psychology, Bournemouth University, Fern Barrow, POOLE, Dorset, BH12 5BB, UK.

jtaylor@bournemouth.ac.uk

Ashok Tiwari

City University Business School, Frobisher Crescent, Barbican Centre, London, EC2Y 8HB, UK

A.Tiwari@herts.ac.uk

Philip Uys

Wellington Polytechnic, Private Box 756, Wellington, New Zealand

philip.uys@wnp.ac.nz

Claude Viéville

Laboratoire Trigone, Universite des sciences et technologies de Lille 1, Batiment B6 - Cite scientifique, 59655 Villeneuve d'Ascq CEDEX - France.

Claude.Vieville@univ-lille1.fr

Steve Wilbur

Department of Computer Science, University College London, Gower Street, London, WC1E 6BT, UK

S.Wilbur@cs.ucl.ac.uk

Sylvia Wilbur

Department of Computer Science, Queen Mary and Westfield College, Mile End Road, London, EC1 4NS, UK

sylvia@dcs.qmw.ac.uk

Roger Young

Department of Computation, UMIST, Sackville Street, Manchester, M60 1QD, UK

Foreword

*Ben Shneiderman**

The turbulence generated by the integration of information technology into higher education provokes more conversations than the weather. The hot winds of hyperpromises and the cold front of angry skeptics are clouding the judgement of administrators, faculty members, and national planners. A clear forecast is not likely to appear until implementations are in place and thoughtful evaluations are conducted.

This edited collection points the way towards more clear thinking by presenting detailed reports about promising projects and a hint of the thoughtful evaluations that will be so important in the coming years. A broad range of improved tools are covered including authoring tools, course management, groupware for faculty/ students, and collaborative environments for administrators. Much of the work is shifting to the World Wide Web and this has positive implications for distance education and universal access. This collection emphasises practical approaches and case studies of implementations. The chapter authors are well past the stage of complaining about the weather, they are contributing to clearing the air.

However, we are just at the beginning of creating successful digital universities. Much work remains to be done, especially in conducting effective multi-level evaluations of these emerging technologies and philosophies. It will be necessary for developers to refine their user interfaces, for professors to adjust their teaching, and for administrators to understand how university life is being changed. The changes implied by the digital university are nicely categorised by the Dearing Report's four areas of collaborative activity: teaching, research, systems support, and administration. First generation collaborative software tools are already being applied in all areas, and they are likely to become more sophisticated, integrated, and ubiquitous. Evaluating the impact of these tools in each area will be a prime occupation for several decades.

Evaluating teaching technologies has always been a challenge because adequate theories were lacking, appropriate controls were difficult to ensure, and reliable

*Ben Shneiderman, Director, Human-Computer Interaction Laboratory, Department of Computer Science, University of Maryland, College Park, MD 20742, U.S.A.
Email: ben@cs.umd.edu

metrics were hard to identify. Furthermore, the introduction of new teaching technologies has usually resulted in changes to the curriculum, or at least the actual outcomes, thereby invalidating the existing student assessment tools. For example, the introduction of collaborative methods in software engineering courses shifts the emphasis on to teamwork and communication skills, which are rarely measured by solitary programming tasks on tests. Secondly, collaborative methods often increase student retention, making comparisons with other courses that have high drop-out rates difficult.

Each of these puzzles leads to a re-evaluation of what is the purpose of education. As the answers swing from information accumulation to process-oriented capabilities, the metrics for success change. Educators increasingly talk about learning to learn, critical thinking skills, self-awareness, and capacity to participate in work environments, neighbourhood (or on-line) communities, and democratic processes. Students need to be able to identify problems, understand existing solutions, explore creative possibilities, consult with peers and mentors, and then implement and disseminate results. This active-learning inquiry-based approach fits well with collaborative methods and service-orientation, but educators are struggling to assess collaboration.

Like several of the authors in this collection, I promote team projects to accomplish ambitious goals, and add the requirement that the projects be done for someone outside the classroom. This philosophy [Shneiderman, Ben, Relate-Create-Donate: A teaching/learning philosophy for the cyber-generation, Computers & Education 30, 3 (1998)] has been useful to me in shaping undergraduate and graduate courses, and effective for others with younger and older students. Assessments can then include the intended audience for class projects, as well as the project participants who can contribute peer reviews. Such multi-level evaluations offer richer feedback to guide teachers and students. Questionnaires and interviews with teachers and to students can include process improvement questions. On-line logging gives useful feedback about the utilisation of email, Listservs, Websites, and specialised educational software.

Documenting the benefits of Relate-Create-Donate and other novel teaching/learning/research collaborative methods will help to refine them and overcome the resistance to change in many teachers and students. Some of that resistance is appropriate, and sometimes live lectures are an excellent form of education. Rigorous evaluations of collaborative methods will help promoters of digital universities to get past their wishful thinking, develop more successful strategies, and help calm the turbulence.

Prof. Ben Shneiderman, University of Maryland

Director, Human-Computer Interaction Laboratory

http://www.cs.umd.edu/hcil

Chapter 1

Introduction

Reza Hazemi, Stephen Hailes and Steve Wilbur[*]

1.1 The Need

A recent report by Sir Ron Dearing[1] and the National Committee of Inquiry into Higher Education published recently includes recommendations on how the 'purposes, shape, structure and funding of higher education should develop to meet the needs of the United Kingdom over the next 20 years.' Whilst this review is aimed specifically at UK higher education, there is nothing particularly special about the UK system in respect of the need continually to increase efficiency. As a result, many of the report's conclusions are applicable in an international context.

In his report, Sir Ron notes that:

'A sustained effort to improve the effective and efficient use of resources by institutions is required to secure the long term future of an expanding higher education system.'

He goes on to note the importance of adopting suitable national and local Communications and Information Technology (C&IT) strategies as a major factor in achieving this aim. Already, current C&IT spending is estimated as being of the order of £1 billion (or 10% of the total higher education turnover). However, it is clear that 'the full potential of C&IT in managing institutions has also yet to be realised' but that, when it is, 'There are likely to be significant cost benefits from its increased use.'

---

[*] Department of Computer Science, University College London, Gower Street, London, WC1E 6BT, UK.
Email: {R.Hazemi, S.Hailes, S.Wilbur}@cs.ucl.ac.uk
[1] http://www.leeds.ac.uk/educol/ncihe

As can be seen from current expenditure, institutions are already recognising the importance of C&IT. Indeed, of 50 institutions responding to a survey conducted by the Universities and Colleges Information Systems Association (UCISA), 'over 75 per cent' already have in place an integrated C&IT system in each of the areas of personnel management, finance and accounting, and student registration. However, only 26 per cent of the same institutions use such systems in the management of research and consultancy and the collection of institutional statistics, amongst other important functions. They admit that they are severely underutilising system capacity, even in areas where utilisation is highest, leading to Sir Ron's conclusion that universities are 'not near to' exploiting the potential of C&IT systems.

As a result of the above considerations it is clear that not only will the absolute levels of investment in C&IT have to remain high, but that what there is will have to be spent ever more intelligently. Part of this will come through top down leadership, the setting of national and institutional goals, but these will have to be realised through the development of appropriate strategies, including the training of higher and middle management in using and developing the potential of C&IT, and consideration of open standards.

1.2   The Solution

In this book, we consider one of the major ways in which the efficiency of higher education institutions can be increased from a number of different perspectives. Specifically, we choose to address the issue of collaboration, using what are known technically as *asynchronous* collaborative techniques. In plain English, these techniques are simply those used within a C&IT setting to allow some number of people jointly to perform some task, without the requirement that those people work in parallel[2]. In its simplest form, this involves the exchange of electronic mail where one person hands over a partly completed task to another.

So, why have we chosen to look at the collaborative aspects of C&IT policy and why, specifically have we chosen to look at asynchronous collaboration? Firstly, as Sir Ron Dearing notes:

'Collaboration matters. It may, in some case, make the difference between institutional success and failure. But it needs to apply throughout institutions, from individuals to management teams.'

Many of the tasks which universities perform are inherently collaborative: the teaching and learning process involves at least two parties; the lecturer and the student; research normally involves several people, possibly split across different institutions, maybe internationally; and administration inherently involves the administrator and the subject of the administration. Thus, in seeking to increase the

[2] In contrast, *synchronous collaboration* is typified by video conferencing-type applications, where several people must simultaneously work on the same task for it to have any meaning.

efficiency of institutions, it is vital that we consider the potential for and costs of different collaborative mechanisms. In fact, we believe that the greatest scope for increase in efficiency specifically lies with asynchronous collaboration. The reason for our belief is that many of the synchronous activities within higher education institutions are currently conducted face-to-face without great difficulty, in view of the proximity of those involved. With the widening of the student base and the consequent need for distance learning, and with the increasing inter-institutional cooperation required by Dearing, this may change, though the numbers involved in such activities will remain small compared to those still engaged in face-to-face meetings. On the other hand, most of the significant and increasing administrative load borne throughout universities, for example, is inherently asynchronous in nature, with different sub-tasks being performed in a linear fashion by those with the necessary information and expertise.

We aim to show throughout this book that there is a significant role for asynchronous collaboration within higher education institutions, that its current limited exploitation can usefully be expanded, and that there are exciting technical developments which promise the potential to increase both cost effectiveness and the quality of the student experience well into the future. Although this book is (intentionally) rather forward-looking, we recognise that in order for the full potential of any form of C&IT collaborative techniques to be realised, both money and political will within HEI management, the funding bodies, and government will be required. Again, the Dearing report tends to support our view:

"There needs to be more encouragement within institutions, for example to support faculty teams to develop their ideas and evaluate the costs and potential of collaboration, and incentives to staff. At institutional level too, governing bodies should include a review of collaboration in the review of performance recommended in the Dearing Report (chapter 15). At national level, there is scope for more imaginative funding arrangements which would help institutions to get over the initial costs that can sometimes arise from collaboration before the longer term economies arise. We think that the Funding Bodies might usefully consider bringing forward part of institutions' allocations and offsetting this against future funding, where institutions make strongly-founded proposals with clear educational and financial benefits that cannot otherwise be realised. It will also be important that the new quality assurance arrangements to be developed by the Quality Assurance Agency do not discourage collaboration between institutions where this would lead to improvements in learning and teaching."

The extent to which these laudable aims are realised will largely determine the actual, rather than potential, benefits given by collaboration, and the C&IT techniques which are used to support them.

1.3   The Structure of the Book

In this book we have concentrated on asynchronous collaboration in a learning environment. The book is divided into five sections:

* Reinventing the academy

- Challenges faced by universities

- Using the technology to meet the challenges

- Using groupware for teaching and learning

- Realising the vision.

We have tried to cover policies, market and management of asynchronous collaboration and the technical section covers four main topics of principles, experiences, evaluation and benefits of asynchronous collaboration but there is an overlap between various sections.

Chapter 2 is a tutorial chapter. It examines functions of a university, which include teaching, research, support and administration and examines how these functions could be performed more efficiently. The changes in performance of these functions could result in what we term reinventing the academy. The Dearing report which will form the basis of policies made by universities for the next few years has been highly influential in writing this chapter.

Chapters 3, 4 and 5 look at the challenges faced by the universities. Kimball argues that teaching style and strategies impact the quality of learning in distance learning more than the technology itself. She argues that there is a need and a challenge to change the process of teaching and learning in distance education. Norman argues that in order to support quality education, principled models of interaction, user interface design guidelines, and policies for management of interaction and collaboration have to be used. He then presents a model and a metaphor for this purpose, and describes how the interaction between students and teachers could be managed. Uys defines the virtual class as an electronic meeting place of students and lecturers for the purpose of learning and teaching - an educational experience of real people in a virtual dimension, and looks at use of hypermedia in a virtual class.

In Chapters 6 to 14 authors present their experience of developing tools using the Web and Lotus Notes to meet the challenge. Wilbur argues that critical dimensions of successful support for collaboration are effectiveness, engagement, and flexibility and describes a Web-based system designed on these principles which supports asynchronous collaboration. In Chapter 7 Issroff and Hazemi argue that current use of Web-based tools in academia is passive and describe their efforts in familiarising academics with use of Web-based tools for teaching and learning in their institution. Viéville describes a Web-based communication system, where the users use active form to communicate with the system. He presents the functional specification and the usability matrices of the system they are designing for their institution. In Chapter 9 Gibbs describes a Web-based object oriented tool called coMentor which supports private group-work areas, role-playing, annotation and threaded discussion, concept mapping and synchronous chat. His paper looks at both synchronous and asynchronous support in a text-based virtual environment. Karsenty and Merialdo describe their work in developing a Web-based tool for joint production of documents as part of the European effort to produce a Web-based asynchronous collaboration tool. Chapter 11 presents TACO a tool used for distributed authoring and management of computer-based coursework developed by Sasse et al. TACO uses a form-based tool which enables lecturers to create Web-based self-learning exercises and assessed coursework.

In Chapter 12, Hinssen evaluates use of Lotus Notes as a collaborative tool for information exchange. Based on interviews conducted amongst Notes users he argues that Lotus Notes promotes information exchange. Armitage and Bryson illustrate, through the use of case descriptions, how Lotus Notes software is being used to support asynchronous collaboration and information sharing among staff and students in their institution. Hazemi et al. identify three categories of asynchronous collaboration in an academic environment: teaching; research; and support for teaching and research. They look at use of groupware in organisations, and at a range of groupware which supports asynchronous collaboration.

Chapters 15 to 18 evaluate groupware. Taylor describes an evaluation of student experiences using CMC tools. She discusses some of the issues and conjectures made for CMC teaching and learning and examines some of these claims. Kirakawski looks at the application of ISO standards to multimedia learning systems in Chapter 16. He looks at quality of use and practical considerations in the development of multimedia learning systems. Macaulay et al. examine the criteria for groupware success. They describe two case studies carried out to measure the effectiveness of shared workspace for document sharing, threaded discussion and email; and use of video conferencing with whiteboard, chat, video and audio and present a set of criteria for the success of groupware in universities. Holtham et al. review the support of asynchronous teams utilising Intranet-based mini-case study publication with Web-based conferencing. They report on this exercise from both pedagogic and groupware perspectives.

Finally in Chapter 19 Mitchell looks at the relevance of collaborative working to the management of Universities. He argues that a formal development of collaborative working practices, supported by appropriate technology, can make a substantial contribution to the effective running of a modern university.

Chapter 2

Reinventing the Academy

*Stephen Hailes and Reza Hazemi**

This chapter is a tutorial, with the aim of examining the ways in which asynchronous collaboration is able to benefit universities. In order to do this, we first examine the functions of a university, then look at the basic tools and techniques of asynchronous collaboration before bringing these together to show which functions of a university are susceptible to support using asynchronous systems.

The importance of this activity cannot be underestimated in the light of the Dearing [1] report's emphasis on the development of a standard approach to the acquisition and delivery of electronic information, including everything from the management of the teaching and assessment processes through to the delivery of teaching material and the student admission process.

2.1   Collaborative Tasks

There are essentially four different areas of activity within a university: teaching, research, systems support and administration. The first two of these are very high profile, and are assessed externally through HEQC and the RAE activities, the results of which can have a significant impact on the standing and income of a university. However, the ability to perform these key tasks well is affected significantly by the availability and efficiency of support and administrative services. We will, therefore, analyse all four areas independently.

*Department of Computer Science, University College London, Gower Street, London, WC1E 6BT, UK
Email: {S.Hailes, R.Hazemi}@cs.ucl.ac.uk

2.1.1   Teaching

Teaching involves considerably more than simply lecturing students. In fact, there are at least 6 different activities, which could reasonably be considered as constituting part of the teaching 'interface' between a university and its students:

1.   *The production of primary teaching material.* This involves the production of slides, notes, videotapes and, increasingly, multimedia material, and affords the primary mechanism through which students will be informed about the course content. In many cases, this material is produced jointly between multiple lecturers and it often relies on prerequisite material in earlier courses or must be complementary to material in other, related, courses.

2.   *The delivery of course material.* This can be done both through synchronous communication, if the teacher is lecturing a class or, can be used to present either primary material (OU type courses) or supporting material in an asynchronous manner. Note that this is no longer restricted to textual material, but could involve multimedia or more speculative concepts such as the 'virtual university' [2].

3.   *Small group teaching.* Almost all courses run activities when small groups of people from a course are involved at any one time. Examples of such activities are tutorials and project supervision. Often, the agenda of such meetings is defined rather more loosely than for the delivery of primary material, if at all.

4.   *Setting and marking of exams and coursework.* As part of the mechanism of obtaining a degree, there is an obvious need to assess the aptitude and progress of students. This can be done in the form of unassessed self-testing to determine what course material has not been understood clearly and hence should be revised, or in the form of formal assessed coursework or examinations.

5.   *Staff student contact.* In addition to the requirements of formal teaching, there are a number of different forms of rather more ad-hoc student contacts:

   a)   *Ad-hoc course queries.*

   b)   *Regulatory and disciplinary matters.* Students must be informed of their rights and responsibilities, and of the rules and regulations which will apply to them in taking particular courses. If they transgress then the disciplinary action taken against them and the grounds for taking it must be made clear and recorded.

   c)   *Complaints.* Occasionally, students have complaints against members of staff, the way in which courses have been taught, or the ways in which they have been examined. In such cases, details of the student complaints must be logged together with any action taken.

6.   *Peer support for students.* In many instances, students learn well when allowed to discuss matters amongst themselves. These interactions can be structured, in the form of activities like supplemental instruction (SI), or can be rather more ad-hoc, in the form of discussion databases. Such discussion databases can relate to focused activities, such as group projects, or can be wider-ranging discussions on the wider issues within a course.

It is increasingly becoming the case that formal lecturing represents only a small part of the time occupied in dealing with students in teaching related activities. More often than not, currently, many of these activities are dealt with synchronously by lecturers. As students start to pay course fees, then their expectations are likely to increase still further and they are likely to be less willing to defer requests for information until times which suit the lecturers concerned. This will negatively impact the other activities performed by lecturers and, as a result, the costs of failing to manage both the enquiries and the other activities efficiently could easily become disproportionately high.

2.1.2 Research

Like teaching, research is not a single unified activity but rather involves both the direct performance of the task, together with a series of monitoring and support activities. In short, there are a number of aspects:

1.   *Contact between researchers.* Typically, such researchers will be involved in the same project, but there are sometimes instances of collaborative activity between projects as competitive or complementary work is discovered. In the grant-giving process at present, considerable weight is put on cross disciplinary and inter-departmental work. This is especially true for large proposals (e.g. EC projects), which usually involve consortia containing 5-10 different partners. Simply keeping everyone informed of everyone else's activities is a major source of time and expense in such cases.

2.   *Generation of grant proposals.* Very little happens in the way of research without the generation of grant proposals, saying what work is to be carried out and how. Again, these proposals can and often do involve multiple partners, from a mixture of different departments within the same academic institution, a mixture of different academic institutions, and a range of industrial and commercial concerns. Although a proposal is usually a relatively short document, compared to deliverables produced during a project, it must be produced by people who are currently employed on some other activity and the process of negotiating between potential collaborators must be approached with sensitivity and in full possession of the facts.

3.   *Project management.* Once a project has been approved, staff are hired to carry out the work. Not only must those staff be kept in contact at a technical level, but it must be possible to manage them effectively. The day-to-day management of staff is usually done at the sites at which those staff reside. Even in this case there is often more than one academic involved in the management of the project and all of the so-called principal investigators need at least to be informed of the current areas of activity and the progress being made, in order to have meaningful meetings. The problem is compounded where one has a consortium in which there are several institutions involved, each of which has several people involved. Simply finding out who is doing what, never mind managing it, involves a significant amount of effort at present.

4.   *Research support activities.* There are some specific activities which must be performed by those undertaking research. For example, researchers should (even if they do not) log details of those publications they have read, together with short reviews or abstracts of them. In an ideal world, where several people working in the same area would potentially be interested in such reviews, this annotated bibliography could be held in a common format online, accessible to those who needed it.

5.   *Reviewing papers and proposals.* All academics are asked, at one time or another, to review material destined for books, journals, conferences, workshops, etc. or to review the technical and organisational content of research proposals. These reviews are often submitted by post or fax, rather than electronically, and those contributing or reviewing often need to be chased (repeatedly!), making the organisation and collation of information rather more tedious than it need otherwise be.

In view of the pressures of activities like teaching, many academics cannot be as actively involved in research as they would like, and often confine their activities to the supervision of work, writing up research for publication, applying for grants and managing projects. Those who perform the day-to-day activities are usually employed specially for that purpose, and are relieved to some extent of the need to see the bigger picture. In order to achieve the best results from the money invested, it is essential that there be fast and accurate communication between research management and those performing the tasks, as well as across management teams and between researchers.

2.1.3 Support

Academics and researchers only make up a proportion of those employed in universities. Others are employed to support their activities and to manage the finances of the university as a whole. There are two particular areas in which academics and those who want access to them interface to support staff:

1.   *Meeting/diary management.* Contrary to popular mythology, today's academics are extremely busy people, and finding slots in which several of them can meet is almost always difficult since, to do it efficiently, it relies on the simultaneous availability of the participants so that they can consult their respective diaries. Arranging meetings by successive exchanges of email is painful, if more than two people are involved. Automated diary management systems can help in this task, since they can be consulted in the absence of the people to whom they refer.

2.   *System support.* Within departments, there is often a need to request technical support (e.g. please install Windows 2000 on my machine), or to indicate that something is broken (the roof leaks), or to schedule activities that can be conducted offline (e.g. requesting NMR runs for particular samples). In the current financial climate, technical services often suffer cutbacks first, and the staff who run them are frequently hard to obtain synchronously. As a result, there is little alternative but to use asynchronous techniques. These are still often based on the exchange of pieces of paper, the information from which may need to be re-entered by the recipient at some future point.

2.1.4   Administration

Administration is awarded a section of its own because it is an activity that underlies an academic's ability to perform any task. There is a considerable range of administrative activity, from that performed by individual academics to the interaction with central administrative authorities:

1.   *Financial issues.* The most important administrative activity in universities is that which concerns money. Money in universities comes from several different sources. Much of a university's income is given directly by the government, based on the number of students in each department. Thus it is imperative that accurate records be kept, since individual departments receive funding based on the number of FTEs they teach, and some of these may be from other departments, and the university as a whole needs to know what its numbers are in each particular area. Other monies come from research funding councils, charities and industry. Clearly, all of these need to be accounted for and managed both at a departmental and college level. Furthermore, it is necessary that the principal investigators on any given grant be able to monitor precisely what has been spent, and under what budget headings. In terms of expenditure, the college has wages to pay, buildings to heat and keep in good repair, etc. At a more mundane level, expenses claims by academics and researchers need to be authorised then processed, requisitions need to be authorised, then forwarded to whoever acts as the purchasing manager, then monitored until delivery is made, invoices are processed, and the money is deducted from the appropriate account.

2.   *Personnel issues.* Academics and researchers have a career structure, which involves a sliding scale of wages, several levels of possible promotion, and all the standard personnel type information, which must be exchanged (preferably securely) between department heads and the central college authorities.

3.   *Student admissions.* Offers must be made to prospective students, usually conditional on obtaining a given set of 'A' level grades. This information must be recorded at UCAS. Once the 'A' level results are produced they need to be retrieved and matched against their offers. Problems need to be highlighted and dealt with. The same is true of postgraduate courses, though in that case, there is no central authority with which one can deal.

4.   *Student management issues.* There is a growing need to maintain precise records about students, including which courses they attended, their attendance records, their marks, medical evidence which could affect the final grade awarded to them, any disciplinary matters, and so forth.

5.   *Creating and holding student references.* Every student, when applying for a job requires references from their university. Often these requests go directly to lecturers who know the students particularly well (e.g. their project supervisors). If these lecturers leave, then it can be hard to generate references for students.

6.   *Student occupations.* We are required to keep details of first destinations of students after they have graduated. Where possible, we keep these up to date as students inform us of their movements.

7.   *Training.* All research students and research assistants who assist lecturers must be appropriately trained. Records must be kept of what courses they have attended.

Administration is often viewed as a necessary evil; however, there is a considerable amount of it in a university since there are a large number of employees, and thousands of students to be dealt with. Accurate record keeping is essential, but administration is not an end in itself; it is there to support the primary aims of a university, teaching and research. As such, it needs to be done as cheaply and with as little effort as is consistent with achieving the desired accuracy. There is a lack of coherence in the automated systems in a university (where they are actually used), and it is often the case that data is transferred on paper only to be re-entered elsewhere in a different form. Clearly, this is not consistent with obtaining the greatest efficiency possible, and funds which would otherwise go to support teaching, releasing effort for research, are being devoted to servicing this inefficiency.

2.1.5 Comment

Academics are required to perform a very wide range of tasks today and, further, to do them relatively efficiently. As university funding is squeezed, the increase in efficiency required to maintain services means that there is less time which is unaccounted for both for academics and those that support them. This is double-edged, since it means that communication between students, academics, researchers, and those that support them is extremely hard to schedule synchronously. Thus the choice lies either in delaying the communication to some future point, which can be difficult to fix in time without proper diary support, or, alternatively, in using some form of asynchronous communication. Typically this is done using email (if the department has ready access to computers and is computer literate) or paper if it is not. Both are some considerable way from being ideal.

There are numerous sources of inefficiency in a university, as in any large organisation. Furthermore, there is now more teaching, research, and administration required than a few years ago, so waste due to inefficiency has a greater impact. Crudely put, inefficiency absorbs funds which could better be used elsewhere. Whilst it used to be the case that inefficiencies which took academic's time were effectively free, since academics receive the same salary regardless of what they do, academics are now reaching saturation point, and this is no longer the case; either teaching or research standards will slip, affecting the standing of the university, or more staff will need to be employed to cover the shortfall.

As a result, we need to look at solutions which will enable academics to do what they are best at: teaching and research, and either reduce the amount of time they spend in related activities, or make it more productive. As Dearing [1] says:

15.31   "Over the next 20 years, C&IT will provide increasing opportunities to improve institutional effectiveness and efficiency. A continuing challenge to institutional managers will be to realise the potential and to ensure that the systems they introduce are used to full effect. Furthermore, there will be new and essential tasks that institutions will be unable to perform without significantly enhanced usage of their hardware and software. Some of the other developments advocated in our report will depend on institutions securing fuller benefits from C&IT in their management. For example:

- institutions and those that fund their teaching are likely to want to know more about patterns of student participation and achievement;

- tracking student progress through one institution, or several, and throughout lifelong learning, will assume a greater significance;

- the single 'learner record' which we advocated in Chapter 8 will require better exploitation of the common language capacity of C&IT across institutions, within and outside the higher education sector;

- the use of on-line registration of students and the use of 'smart cards' to secure access to facilities and, in some cases, payment for them by students, are likely to proliferate;

- the need to demonstrate maximum value for money to a wider range of stakeholders, as part of the new compact, will demand better ways of analysing costs and the way institutional resources are used;

- maximising the use of space by developing fully computerised central timetabling."

2.2   Available Tools

In this section, we will look at the tools which support asynchronous interaction. Collectively, these are known as groupware tools. Essentially there are three sources of tools.

2.2.1   WWW-based Tools

There are a number of different WWW-based tools from different suppliers. Most prominent amongst these are Netscape (Navigator/Communicator) and Microsoft's Internet Explorer. These tools tend to be free and, as such, have a very deep penetration into the academic environment. They are somewhat rough (being forms-based, for example) and require some expertise to configure effectively - one must know something about HTML, CGI, Java, etc. to create the most effective Web-based sites. This situation is changing somewhat; Web-based publishing is becoming decidedly easier.

2.2.2   Commercial Tools

The major supplier of true groupware tools is Lotus, with Lotus Notes being the clear market leader. Microsoft Exchange is somewhere behind this, with more specialised tools such as Novell's GroupWise, Collabra Share, Oracle, etc. all terming themselves 'groupware'. In a sense they do all fall into this category, although only Lotus Notes and perhaps Microsoft Exchange fall into the category of general purpose systems.

In so far as academic systems are concerned, commercial tools have two major disadvantages. They cost money, and they are new tools to the academic environment, the use of which needs to be learnt. Furthermore, they have not, until relatively recently, interfaced well with the tools already in widespread use[3], leading to the need to support dual systems. If the perceived benefits are not sufficiently great (or not sufficiently greater than, say, the Web), or the top down

---

[3] For example, in Lotus release 3 the IP support was weak, and one had to interface to the SMTP world through (expensive) gateways. Lotus have addressed many of these problems in release 4.

drive to install such systems is not strong enough then, as we have seen, there is likely to be considerable resistance to their introduction in academic circles.

2.2.3   Locally-built Tools

There are a number of tools for asynchronous collaboration designed in academic circles, together with an inevitable collection of those that have been cobbled together locally to meet some perceived need in the past. Some of these tools (e.g. WebCT [3] developed at British Columbia University) are finding their way into the commercial world.

2.2.4   Comment

In all of these cases, groupware tools have proved to be less than ideal, providing what is often a relatively poor user interface in comparison to those available from GUI builders. Furthermore, they do require time and effort to use, and writing applications which make use of their facilities is not a task to be taken on lightly since it involves considerably more effort than may at first be thought to produce something worthwhile. Sadly, aside from Web-based tools and email, little effort has gone into producing quality tools for group interaction which are free and sufficiently robust that one would entrust valuable data to them. Finally, there is no standard for information interchange between groupware products, so once a general method of solution has been decided upon, one is effectively locked into that.

2.3   Application of Tools

In the final section of this chapter, we will explore some of the ways in which the above tools can be useful in supporting some of the major issues identified in the first section. This is a general walk through these areas, looking at the realities of the university environment, since the applicability of asynchronous collaboration in most of the areas identified in (Section 2.2) is usually self evident.

2.3.1   Teaching

In terms of teaching, many departments are now distributing information on everything from course regulations through to lecture notes by using the World Wide Web. By virtue of the fact that it is moderately complex to set up Web pages, this activity has largely been restricted to those departments with the technical know-how and enthusiasm to expend the effort necessary to initiate and keep such sites up-to-date. In particular, it is often seen as a prerequisite that the students associated with a department should have the confidence and opportunity to use the sites; if not, then the effort is largely wasted.

Institutions such as the Henley Management College, which runs very disperse distance learning courses, utilise the Lotus Notes groupware products to set, mark, return, and record grades of coursework, to allow for discussion groups, and to allow the students to chat informally.

2.3.2   Research

It is clearly the case that many of the research activities which are taking place would benefit enormously from the support which can be provided by groupware tools, particularly those which are concerned with the management of research, the generation of grant proposals (which is an examplar workflow application), and the management of research finances. This potential benefit is not matched in the use of groupware tools, with the exception of the Web and email.

2.3.3   Support

Diary management systems are being introduced, albeit in rather an ad-hoc way, into academic departments, in view of their extreme usefulness and the growing need for academics to schedule their time more efficiently.

2.3.4   Administration

Many academic administrative systems still rely on paper, though specially tailored management information systems have and are being developed, often by external consultants. If anything, this is the area in which the greatest benefits are to be had by introducing groupware, provided that increased uniformity and cross-platform working between the individual and usually incompatible products can be obtained. There are large numbers of employees, and very large numbers of students, so marginal increases in efficiency per employee or per student could present a significant cumulative saving. At present, the same information is often to be found in more than one place, usually having been keyed in more than once. This is wasteful in terms of time, and leads to inconsistency, which again takes time to resolve.

2.3.5 Comment

It can be seen from the above that there is a potentially wide ranging role for asynchronous collaboration in the provision of the university of the future. However, in order for that potential to be realised, it must be recognised and acted upon by those in senior management and, in particular, those who control the allocation of funding. Fortunately, a recent and extremely influential report [1] in the UK has indeed recognised these points, and this is summarised below.

2.4 The Future of Higher Education: the Dearing Report

In this section, we will examine some of the suggestions made in the report of the National Committee of Inquiry into Higher Education (NCIHE), chaired by Sir Ron Dearing. The committee delivered its wide-ranging report on 23rd July 1997. It will have a major impact on the shape of higher education into the foreseeable future and is very forward looking. It addresses directly the impact that communications and information technology (C&IT) is having on all aspects of academic life, and foresees a future in which it is a central plank in both the delivery of material and support for that delivery in universities. In this section, we will summarise the major points of the report as they relate to C&IT, the material being drawn particularly from Chapter 13 which is the relevant part of the report.

2.4.1 Teaching

The Dearing report has a considerable amount to say about the future for teaching:

13.3 "We believe that, for the majority of students, over the next ten years the delivery of some course materials and much of the organisation and communication of course arrangements will be conducted by computer. Just as most people will come to expect to be connected to, and to make use of, world communications networks in their daily lives, all students will expect continuous access to the network of the institution(s) at which they are studying, as a crucial link into the learning environment."

13.7 "Over the next decade, higher educational services will become an internationally tradable commodity within an increasingly competitive global market. For some programmes, United Kingdom (UK) institutions will rely heavily on C&IT to teach across continents. Within the UK, by the end of the first decade of the next century, a 'knowledge economy' will have developed in which institutions collaborate in the production and transmission of educational programmes and learning materials on a 'make or buy' basis. We must expect and encourage the development and delivery of core programmes and components of programmes, and sharing and exchange of specialist provision, to become commonplace."

13.8   "The development of a world market in learning materials, based on C&IT, will
            provide scope to higher education institutions to become major participants in this
            arena. This in turn might lead to the formation of trading partnerships between
            institutions for the provision of infrastructure, services and content. Such
            partnerships could include major companies in the communications, media and
            publishing industries."

From this, it is clear that there is a view at a high level that teaching is likely to
become internationalised, partly as a result of and partly as a driver for the use of
our increasingly comprehensive high bandwidth networked infrastructure and the
adoption of both synchronous and asynchronous collaborative techniques. Without
the innovation and effective use of appropriate collaborative techniques and the
agreement of common standards, such collaborative activities will happen in a
piecemeal and disjoint fashion. This will inevitably lead to unnecessary replication
of work and indeed, in extra work in translating between the different custom
systems in use.

Given that the computerisation of UK education is seen as a priority, Dearing has
suggested concrete methods for achieving it, in terms of the necessary hardware.
By 2005-6, it will be considered compulsory for students to purchase some form of
notebook computer. Referred to by Dearing as the Student Portable Computer
(SPC), this will be capable of connecting to networks, but is not seen as a
replacement for the so-called Networked Desktop Computer (NDC). Indeed, the
penetration of NDCs is expected to increase from its current ratio of 15 students to
one machine to a ratio of 5:1 or better. Both of these machines are envisaged as
forming part of the standard mechanism for the delivery of teaching:

13.43   "Over the next ten years, all higher education institutions will, and should,
            progressively move significant aspects of administration and learning and teaching
            to the computer medium. They should be planning for this now. The development
            of powerful paperback-sized 'notebook' computers, capable of sending and
            receiving e-mail and accessing the Internet, is envisaged within the next few years.
            We expect that this technology will be harnessed by students and institutions for
            learning and teaching and administration through the development of a Student
            Portable Computer (SPC)."

13.44   "The SPC will store basic course information and enable the student to undertake a
            significant amount of work off-line (for example drafting of assignments). It will
            also allow the student, via a network connection, to access electronic information
            (such as timetables, course materials and library catalogues), to submit
            assignments, and to communicate with tutors and other students. It is possible that
            the SPC might be a fully mobile device accessing the network through wireless
            technology. We found, on our visit to the USA in January 1997, that an SPC
            (usually an industry-standard laptop computer) is already a requirement for courses
            at a number of institutions. The same requirement applies to some UK
            programmes."

13.45   "To use their SPCs effectively in this way, to communicate and send and receive
            information, students will require daily access to the network. There will,
            therefore, need to be adequate provision of network connection ports in institutions
            into which students can plug their SPCs and there should be provision of dial-up
            connectivity for off-campus students at each institution."

13.50 "Networked Desktop Computers (NDCs) need to be of a sufficiently high technical specification to make full use of the network and networked services, and permit the use of the latest interactive multimedia learning and teaching materials and other applications (whether accessed via the network or CD-ROM). They must, therefore, incorporate up-to-date sound, video and graphics technology."

13.51 "Existing evidence suggests that, at present, the ratio of students to desktop computers in higher education institutions is only slightly better than 15:1 across the UK.22 In the short term, student access to NDCs needs to be improved across the sector as a whole. The required ratio will vary from institution to institution, depending on such factors as subjects taught, types of student and learning and teaching methods. A ratio of 10:1 would be a good standard at present but this needs to improve to 8:1, particularly where an institution makes extensive use of on-line learning materials and electronic information services. We expect that, as such methods become widespread, a ratio of 5:1, or better, will be necessary for multi-faculty institutions. Students will need information about the adequacy of an institution's provision of equipment for their use and must know in advance of study what expectations there are of students providing their own access."

"Recommendation 46

We recommend that by 2000/01 higher education institutions should ensure that all students have open access to a Networked Desktop Computer, and expect that by 2005/06 all students will be required to have access to their own portable computer."

Whilst Dearing has little to say explicitly about software, it is clear that the aims stated in the above paragraphs cannot be achieved without a significant amount of development which will allow non computer expert academics to capture their knowledge and interact with their students in a relatively straightforward way. Given the salaries paid by industry to consultants who specialise in developing either Web sites or Lotus Notes applications, the process can be seen to be far from simple for the untrained at present. It is imperative that, on a very short timescale given the dates set for the introduction of hardware, the best pedagogic methodology is aggressively explored, including both the technical issues and those of social interaction between parties using the computer to teach and learn.

2.4.2   Administration

The problems and costs of administration are well known in both the academic and commercial sectors. Increasingly, the commercial sector has been turning to asynchronous collaborative techniques, as evinced by the success of systems like Lotus Notes, because they have been persuaded of the cost benefits to be had through using them. According to Dearing:

13.09 "As in other industries and businesses, C&IT is affecting the management and administration of higher education institutions, and is assisting institutions to manage increasingly complex activities and services such as finance, personnel, admissions, time-tabling, data collection, estates management, catering and conferencing. Progress in the successful use of C&IT for these purposes has been mixed but higher education institutions should aim to improve their economy and efficiency by making more effective and extensive use of C&IT (see Chapter 15)."

13.50   "While the effective adoption of C&IT in higher education requires appropriate technology, adequate resources and staff development, success depends on the effective management of change. The development and implementation of an integrated C&IT strategy will be one of the main challenges facing managers of higher education institutions."

It is clear from both the industrial experience, from our own personal experience, and from the recommendations of the Dearing report that, to achieve the successful deployment of asynchronous collaboration systems, there must be appropriate infrastructure, a clearly defined C&IT policy, and high-level will, effort, and understanding to make it happen. At present, there is technology available, even if it needs further development to be ideal for the needs of academia, but I do not think that many institutions could claim to be driving a coherent C&IT policy from the top down, with the aim of achieving the objectives Dearing has set.

2.4.3   The Changing Face of Higher Education

Increasing student numbers
Recommendation 1 reads:

"Recommendation 1

We recommend to the Government that it should have a long term strategic aim of responding to increased demand for higher education, much of which we expect to be at sub-degree level; and that to this end, the cap on full-time undergraduate places should be lifted over the next two to three years and the cap on full-time sub-degree places should be lifted immediately."

It is apparent from this recommendation that the numbers in higher education, which increased significantly under the last government, but which were then capped, will again rise. Historically, a rise in the number of students has not been accompanied with a commensurate rise in the numbers of lecturing or administrative staff. There is some saving to be had in, for example, lectures which take little extra effort to give to greater numbers. However, it has always proved to be the case that the increase in load through extra administration, project supervision, tutorial groups, etc. has more than outweighed this, and members of academic staff and those that support them have had to work harder. There is little slack in the system now, particularly as many undergraduate courses are changing from three to four years (MSci, MEng type qualifications) without greatly increased resources. This simply means that staff must work more efficiently and, as argued above, groupware has a significant role to play in this.

Widening participation

Recommendation 2 and 6 state respectively that:

"Recommendation 2

We recommend to the Government and the Funding Bodies that, when allocating funds for the expansion of higher education, they give priority to those institutions which can demonstrate a commitment to widening participation, and have in place a participation strategy, a mechanism for monitoring progress, and provision for review by the governing body of achievement."

"Recommendation 6

We recommend:

- **to the Funding Bodies that they provide funding for institutions to provide learning support for students with disabilities;**

- **to the Institute for Learning and Teaching in Higher Education (see Recommendation 14) that it includes the learning needs of students with disabilities in its research, programme accreditation and advisory activities;**

- **to the Government that it extends the scope of the Disabled Students Allowance so that it is available without a parental means test and to part-time students, postgraduate students and those who have become disabled who wish to obtain a second higher education qualification."**

In these recommendations we see a commitment to widening access to disabled and otherwise disadvantaged groups; this being backed up with funds. Dearing has something to say about the way this will be achieved though, perhaps, this is something of a statement of hope rather than of certainty:

13.4   "C&IT will overcome barriers to higher education, providing improved access and increased effectiveness, particularly in terms of lifelong learning. Physical and temporal obstacles to access for students will be overcome with the help of technology. Those from remote areas, or with work or family commitments need not be disadvantaged. Technology will also allow the particular requirements of students with disabilities to be more effectively met by institutions."

It is widely believed that all forms of C&IT have, at least potentially, something to offer to everyone. However, the 'disadvantaged' are not a homogeneous group and it is far from clear that we know exactly what the needs of individual sub-groups actually are, let alone the extent to which these specific needs can actually be addressed by application of C&IT.

Record keeping
Recommendation 7 and 20 state that:

"Recommendation 7

We recommend that further work is done over the medium term, by the further and higher education Funding Bodies, the Higher Education Statistics Agency, and relevant government departments to address the creation of a framework for data about lifelong learning, using a unique student record number."

"Recommendation 20

We recommend that institutions of higher education, over the medium term, develop a Progress File. The File should consist of two elements:

- a transcript recording student achievement which should follow a common format devised by institutions collectively through their representative bodies;

- a means by which students can monitor, build and reflect upon their personal development."

Here we see a commitment to creating and holding records over the long term. To be effective, this will require the interfacing of existing departmental and university-wide systems to wherever the relevant central information is held. Clearly, this provides an opportunity for standardisation in both the information interchange format and in the mechanisms used for keeping such information.

Staff development
Recommendation 9 states that:

"Recommendation 9

We recommend that all institutions should, over the medium term, review the changing role of staff as a result of Communications and Information Technology, and ensure that staff and students receive appropriate training and support to enable them to realise its full potential."

This is a direct realisation of the fact that universities are changing and must change in terms of the ways in which they carry out their primary tasks and that all staff need to be appropriately trained in the sorts of techniques we discuss in this book.

Strategies
Recommendations 41 and 42 state that:

"Recommendation 41

We recommend that all higher education institutions in the UK should have in place overarching communications and information strategies by 1999/2000."

"Recommendation 42

We recommend that all higher education institutions should develop managers who combine a deep understanding of Communications and Information Technology with senior management experience."

These timescales are very tight. Those implementing these recommendations will need to assess, and quickly, the current state of the art in and potential for computer-based collaborative techniques in academia. Without specific technical input from those who know about these systems, and those who have thought about their uses in relation to more than just administration, the benefits to be had will be severely curtailed. If, in fact, the wrong choices are made and implemented, simply in order to be seen to have some sort of policy, then the consequences could be very costly.

2.4.4 Comment

Recent initiatives in the developed countries and increase in the use and development of Internet tools will lead to an increase in networked computing, asynchronous collaboration and remote learning and teaching in the near future. The number of full-time students will increase and funding bodies will provide more funds for the expansion of higher education. The strategy of the higher education establishments and the commercial establishments, which provide tools for HE, should be to provide support for open and flexible learning.

2.5 Conclusion

Considerable effort has been put into support for real-time collaboration based on videoconferencing but, in the academic world, less attention has been focused on the requirements of asynchronous collaboration. While academics have continued to rely largely on email and, lately, the World Wide Web, there are also numerous groupware products now available and in use in many commercial environments. In both the commercial and academic environments, more emphasis is and has been placed on having good tools for asynchronous collaboration than for synchronous collaboration. The reason can be attributed to the fact that asynchronous tools simplify business processes, remove paper from the environment, and operate on the same items that the business itself uses. The material that once was printed on paper and posted can now be delivered via email and the World Wide Web [4]. This electronic approach increases the distribution efficiency, but it does not exploit the full potential of the technology as an enabler of reengineering of the educational process itself [2].

Synchronous collaboration is important, and likely to become increasingly so as more people move away from traditional office or campus environments in such a way that they can only be virtually present at meetings and so forth. In all of these cases, however, multimedia conferencing cannot capture the nuances present in face-to-face meetings and so is less than the ideal in this respect, though it enables those who cannot simultaneously be collocated to communicate in a cost effective way.

New tools may alleviate some of the problems of synchronous collaboration like information overload in a virtual classroom [5], however, it is likely that universities will remain structured much as they are today. Synchronous collaboration will help distance learners, but asynchronous collaboration will help both distance learners and those that are present on campus, and will also aid in the whole process of organising teaching and research, allowing those delivering the services to act more efficiently.

In this chapter we looked at teaching, research, support and administration as four main tasks of an academic environment and presented tools to support these tasks. We presented recommendations of the Dearing report regarding these tasks. We believe the time has come for reinventing the academy and a digital university.

References

1.   http://www.leeds.ac.uk/educol/ncihe

2.   Hamalainen, M., Whinston, A. and Vishik, S. (1997) Electronic markets for learning: Education brokerage on the Internet. *Communications of the ACM*, 39, 6, 51-58.

3.   Murray W. Goldberg and Salari, S. (1997) An Update on WebCT (World-Wide-Web Course Tools) - a Tool for the Creation of Sophisticated Web-Based Learning Environments. *Proceedings of NAUWeb '97 - Current Practices in Web-Based Course Development*, Flagstaff, Arizona, June 12 – 15.

4.   Chellappa, R., Barua, A. and Whinston, A.B. (1997) An Electronic Infrastructure for a Virtual University, *Communiation of ACM*, 40, 9, 56-58.

5.   Hiltz, S.R. and Wellman, B. (1997) Asynchronous Learning Networks as a Virtual Classroom, *Communications of ACM*, 40, 9, 44-49.

Chapter 3

Managing Distance Learning - New Challenges for Faculty

Lisa Kimball[*]

Although the technology of distance learning gets most of the attention, it is really teaching strategies and style which have the most impact on the quality of learning in distance programs. Facilitating learning communities at a distance requires some new approaches to the practice of managing the teaching and learning process. Effective faculty start with a completely new mind set about where technology fits into the equation. Rather than struggling to make up for qualities distance programs are perceived to lack when compared to traditional classrooms, faculty members who are most successful with distance technologies see them as actually providing some qualitative advantages. In addition to managing the delivery of the content to their courses, faculty teaching at a distance must learn to manage a new set of variables which determine the extent to which their courses are effective including: metaphor, meaning, culture, roles, time, awareness, and collaboration. Learning and practicing the skills to manage these dimensions is the key challenge for faculty development.

3.1   Introduction

What does the concept of "wait time" mean for faculty teaching students at a distance? How do you pull virtual chairs into a circle for creative dialogue?

Although the *technology* of distance learning gets most of the attention, it is really teaching strategies and style which have the most impact on the quality of learning

---

[*] Metasystems Design Group, Inc., 2000 North 15th St., Suite 103, Arlington, VA 22201, U.S.A.
Email: lisa@tmn.com

in distance programs. Facilitating learning communities at a distance requires some new approaches to the practice of managing the teaching and learning process. Effective faculty start with a completely new mind set about where technology fits into the equation. Rather than struggling to make up for qualities distance programs are perceived to lack when compared to traditional classrooms, faculty members who are most successful with distance technologies see them as actually providing some qualitative advantages.

Many institutions introducing distance learning spend a large amount of their resources (both time and money) on training faculty to manage the new technical and administrative aspects of distance courses. Instead, faculty need to learn to manage critical dimensions of the new environment in which their courses are taking place, dimensions like metaphor, meaning, culture, roles, time, awareness, and collaboration.

Distance learning can involve many different technologies used alone or in combination. Although a lot of the decisions you need to make are about which of the many possible technologies and media will work best for specific purposes, the focus of this chapter is on the role of the facilitator as distinct from the delivery system.

In some ways, distance learning is like the canary in the mine which detects life-threatening problems before anyone else realises they are in danger. The issues raised for instructors about designing and managing learning programs at a distance are really the issues which need to be raised about all learning experience including; How do you achieve the right balance between presentation and experiential activity: Between individual and collaborative learning? Between teacher-driven and learner-driven assignments?

New technology *requires* us to rethink these dynamics because we do not have the option to use familiar approaches. It gives us an opening to change the way we manage the teaching and learning process in general. The critical part of the question, "How can we engage learners via distance learning technology?" is really "How do we engage learners in more meaningful learning activities?" Facilitating distance learning is not about taking our old lesson plans and transposing them for delivery using new media. Rather, it is about expanding our available tools to create new learning dynamics aligned with the best thinking about adult learning.

3.2   A New Management Mind Set

There are some critical aspects of a learning manager's mindset which must shift in order to take full advantage of new opportunities created by distance learning technology [1].

From	To
Face-to-face is the best environment for learning and anything else is a compromise.	Different kinds of environments can support high quality learning. What matters is how you use them.
Learning is what happens when teachers interact with students at a fixed time and space.	Learning happens in an ongoing, boundaryless way and includes what learners do independently of teachers.
Being people-oriented is incompatible with using technology.	Using distance learning technology in a people-oriented way is possible and desirable.
When the learning process breaks down, blame the technology.	When the learning process breaks down, evaluate our teaching strategies, not just the technical tool.
Learning to manage distance learning is about learning how to use the technology.	Learning to manage distance learning is about understanding more about the learning process.

Table 3.1. Shift in mindset.

3.3   A New Style of Management

"The European navigator begins with a plan - a course - which he has charted according to certain universal principles, and he carries out his voyage by relating his every move to that plan. His effort throughout his voyage is directed to remaining 'on course.' If unexpected events occur, he must first alter the plan, then respond accordingly. The Trukese navigator begins with an objective and responds to conditions as they arise in an ad-hoc fashion. He utilises information provided by the wind, the waves, the tide and the current, the fauna, the stars, the clouds, the sound of the water on the side of the boat, and steers accordingly. His effort is directed to doing whatever is necessary to reach the objective." [2]

The distinction between a linear and dynamic approach to navigation could also describe a major shift from the old view to a new view of managing education. The first challenge for distance educators is to figure out how to harness the power of new media to take advantage of its capacity to support flexibility, parallel processing, and just-in-time design - not just use the new media to deliver the same old stuff.

In the old model, learning design proceeded in a linear fashion from defining objectives to lesson planning to course delivery. Educators first engaged in a comprehensive learning needs analysis process, often based on assessments done by others about competencies and learning objectives. Comprehensive course syllabi were developed. Finally, the course was delivered as planned.

Associated with this linear approach were a set of teaching strategies which matched its linear qualities. These strategies were characterised by being predominantly one-way, centralised, and broadcast-oriented. When students appeared bored and unengaged in this type of program the solution was to find ways to use new media to make the one-way broadcast more entertaining. Much early distance learning was nothing more than a way to generate a broadcast of an expert and his multi-media slides with good production values.

Distance learning was praised because of its ability to scale up to reach larger numbers of students at standardised levels of quality. But an expert lecturing to a group of passive students is engaging in didactic one-way teaching whether that lecture is delivered from a stage in an auditorium or via broadcast television to students sitting in their living rooms.

A new mindset for teaching has emerged. Teaching and learning is seen as an ongoing process rather than a program with a fixed starting and ending point and the importance of widespread participation by learners in the design of their own learning has been recognised.

Distance learning technologies are particularly well suited to a more dynamic approach to managing learning. Good teachers have always been open to changing their lesson plans based on student input. New media makes it easier. For example, it is easy to provide additional reading materials based on student interest instead of having to rely on a text book ordered weeks or months before the course began. Online environments can provide space for continuing conversation among students about what is working and what is not working in the course.

The same technology can also contribute to more participatory course design. In a masters level business course, the professor contacted most of the course members via e-mail during the summer to find out about their interests, expectations, concerns, and skills so that he could take those into consideration when designing a course offered in the Fall semester. He was able to use that information to create preliminary project teams and develop initial assignments which reflected the specific needs of course participants.

3.4   Managing Metaphor

One of the first things it is important to think about is the kind of ambience you need to create in order to have the kind of learning experience you intend. In distance learning settings, language and metaphor are primary tools to use to create the ambience because you need to help participants evoke images to put them in a mind space conducive to learning even though they are doing it at different times from different places. Many distance learning environments borrow language from traditional school settings to provide cues to learners about what to expect such as classroom, lecture hall, and library. This can be a good strategy to help learners navigate through unfamiliar environments. However, there is a danger in using language which matches the distance learning environment to the traditional environment because it may hardwire old models into the new medium. If you want to take advantage of the new media's ability to support more self-directed learning it is important to signal to participants that they are *not* entering a traditional classroom where they would expect to wait for the instructor to tell them what to do.

One way to start is to think about the kinds of interactions and experiences you need to support in terms of the feelings you want to evoke. Do you want participants to have intimate self-disclosing conversations like they might have late at night in a café? Or do you want to have teams of learners engage in lively brainstorming exchanges like might happen around a conference table? Putting the group in a virtual "classroom" does not help you evoke either of these dynamics.

The Institute for Educational Studies (TIES)[4] at Norwich University is a one year intensive Masters degree program in transforming education. The design is based around communities of teachers from around the world forming a learning community which meets in a virtual campus using asynchronous Web-conferencing. In order to help participants "feel" a sense of being part of a virtual campus components include lectures, seminars, discussions, study groups, and guest faculty. Course participants come together in a variety of virtual lecture halls, seminar rooms, and discussions. But the most important aspect of the program is to create a peer-to-peer learning community where participants share their deepest thoughts and feelings about their own personal growth and its relationship to their role as educators.

In order to support this core part of the program within the distance learning framework, TIES made use of a metaphor from the participants' experience at a face-to-face meeting which was held to kick off the program. The meeting took place in the Vermont countryside at a house which had a big front porch. Participants spent a lot of time between sessions and in the evenings sitting on the porch sharing stories about themselves. TIES created a space online called "The Porch" where that same quality of conversation could continue throughout the year. Although the online environment was new and strange for most participants, they had no trouble understanding what to do in The Porch and immediately began sharing stories and reflections there.

At Digital Equipment Corporation, a large high tech company, there was a thing called a "woods meeting" which at first actually did take place at the company founder's cabin in the woods of New England. Everyone knew that when you went to a woods meeting it meant that you would be brainstorming about the future of the company rather than doing day-to-day stuff. So, people started having "woods meetings" in conference rooms on site at the company. Just naming it put people in a different mind-frame about what would happen. So a "woods meeting" title for an on-line conference could convey something similar about what needs to happen there.

In groups which do not come with a common experience to draw from you can achieve a similar shared repertoire of metaphors by taking time to elicit ideas from

---

[4] The Institute for Educational Studies: http://www.tmn.com/ties

the participants. Have participants tell stories about previous learning experiences and engage them in dialogue about different learning dynamics and the environments where they took place. Get the group to create metaphors and names for different components of your program and use the stories yourself to provide cues, "This part of our environment is where we will have the kind of peer coaching Ted described in his story about the marketing team's white-water rafting retreat. Let us call this chat space The Raft."

Whenever possible, engage participants in choosing metaphors. Have a dialogue early in the course to talk explicitly about ambience like, "What kind of interactions do we want to have in here?" Even within the larger framework of the course environment, you can use metaphors to define spaces for different kinds of interactions. For example, many groups benefit from having at least one place in the environment which uses metaphors like *water cooler* or *break time* to serve the same social lubrication purpose as a coffee break serves in a traditional course.

Remember, there is a big difference between facsimile and metaphor. Facsimiles can trap participants into default ways of behaving. Metaphor can be evocative and help participants create a richer mental construct about what they are doing.

3.5   Managing Meaning

Distance learners can have a harder time than those in a traditional course integrating all the different course components into a focused whole. Course managers can help by providing regular summaries of where we are and where we are going next. Weaving the multiple threads of conversation together gives all members a chance to start fresh or take off in a new direction. It can help keep the group from spinning its wheels. Sometimes, you can give people a better sense of what the virtual group is all about by simply copying the topic index or a list of all the conference messages and posting it. This may remind participants of items they want to go back to or it may reveal a gap in the conversation that can be filled by starting a new item.

It is also important to integrate the study of communication and media itself into the curriculum. Developing the learner's ability to question the process of learning will make them a more effective learner.

One of the things many distance learning programs get hung up on is the tension between delivering content resources which are essentially one-way communications (articles, books, videos, expert lectures) and providing the two-way interaction around that material which makes it meaningful to learners. It is often true that the same media environment is not optimal for both needs. An environment which does a great job of storing and organising materials of various kinds is not necessarily a good place to hold the discussion stimulated by that material. It is very hard to conduct a role-playing exercise in a file cabinet. There is more to developing a relationship among a collaborative learning group than sharing access to a file folder.

PBS Mathline[5] is a professional development program delivered at a distance to classroom teachers. The content of the program consists of videos showing teachers in classrooms using the new ideas about teaching maths and the lesson plans and associated materials being used by the teachers in the videos. Some participating teachers tape the videos which are broadcast on private channels by local educational television. But for most it is more convenient to receive copies of the videos on cassettes. There are also other resource materials provided in print and online such as copies of articles written about the theory and practice.

But all that material is not "the program." The heart of the program is in the learning communities of 25-30 teachers grouped by age level (elementary, middle school, and high school) with a peer facilitator who log into private online conferences to talk about the ideas and their experiences using and thinking about the materials. In geographic locations where it is possible, these learning communities get together during the year for face-to-face interaction. The key is that different parts of the program are delivered using different media. The online discussion provides a common room for the long term, peer-to-peer facilitated interaction which makes the program meaningful for participants.

3.6 Managing Culture

Heavy handed guidelines and rules about behaviour make for a boring experience, but it never hurts to state explicitly the kind of atmosphere you hope to create. Do you hope your virtual group will be supportive, deep, amusing, fast-moving, reflective, cutting-edge, information-intensive, risky, silly, focused, unfocused? What styles and behaviours would help or hinder the atmosphere you want?

Are the participants peer learners? Team members? Neighbours in a learning community? Is the moderator expected to provide expert knowledge? Support and encouragement? A guide to other resources? If you are not sure about these roles ahead of time, the group should discuss it. Different images of roles and relationships will provide cues to different ways of participating.

A community of distance learners is like any community in that its culture is a product of shared stories, shared rituals, and shared experiences. Designing opportunities for these aspects of a program is just as important as figuring out the order of topics to be covered.

The manager of a government agency training program for high potential managers from around the country wanted to establish a collaborative culture which she hoped would help the group form a community of practice. She established a joining ritual for the program where each entering participant created a special Web page with personal as well as career-related information and photographs of the participants in non-work settings. During the first week of the course, she paired up participants and replicated a familiar ice-breaking exercise of having

---

[5] Public Broadcasting System Mathline: http://www.pbs.org

them interview each other via e-mail and then introduce their partner to the rest of the group by writing up a response for their online bulletin board. Participants reported that they felt that this process really made a difference in how quickly they felt like members of the community - a very different feeling from simply being among those accessing a common body of information.

3.7   Managing Roles

There are many names for the facilitator role; teacher, instructor, manager, leader, facilitator, moderator. Learners are called student, participant, member. Obviously, the choice of term can connote a lot about roles and expectations and it is an important choice to make as part of your learning design.

In the old paradigm classroom, the roles were simple. The teacher taught and the students followed directions. In the new classroom, teacher facilitators need to help all the members of the learning community - including students and other adults who may be involved - identify roles. Virtual learning communities need to define some additional roles related to their communication strategy. They may need technical support, knowledge archivists, and specialists in using different media. For all roles, virtual learning communities need to spend more time being explicit about mutual expectations (for example, how quickly they can expect responses to their online postings) for participants because the patterns of behaviour and dynamics of interaction are unfamiliar and it is easy to fall into misunderstandings and become frustrated with each other.

Distance learning provides some new ways to use people in the role of "expert" resources. Participants in the advanced management program at George Mason University invited a well-known author to join them on-line to discuss and answer questions about his forthcoming book. He did not want to travel in order to appear in a three-hour class so he suggested that they meet online. They were able to interact with him over time rather than for a single-shot guest lecture and so could explore his ideas in greater depth. One of the "unintended" benefits of this was that students for whom English was not their first language felt better able to think and write in contrast to face-to-face when the conversation goes too fast.

Other members of the community can also serve in the role of teachers in a distance learning program. Bank Street College of Education created a program focused on supporting girls so that they would continue studying science in high school. Research had shown that girls did just as well as boys in science classes in the early high school grades, but they tended to drop out before the advanced courses. This was a big problem because these courses are often prerequisites for certain college majors and are factored into college admissions. Bank Street College created a distance learning program to link students with women mentors who have successfully entered careers in science and technology.

The program created small on-line groups made up of the student, her teacher, her parents, and a mentor. The student was also able to communicate one-on-one with her mentor. Students reported that they really appreciated the support of being able to ask their mentors questions about how to handle situations. For example, one student complained that the boys in her lab group made put-down type remarks to her which made her feel like quitting the course. Her mentor shared how she had had similar experiences but encouraged the student to continue with the course anyway. By expanding the notion of who could play a teaching role, the College was able to bring new resources into the program.

Distance learning also supports peer-to-peer learning by providing ways for learners to become facilitators for other learners. Creative Writers on the Net[6] is an advanced placement English program for high school students in Kalamazoo, Michigan. The essence of the course is to learn how to give and receive constructive feedback about all different kinds of writing. One of the advantages of the distance learning model is the ease with which it is possible to post and interact with multiple drafts of writing. Although there is a team of teachers with responsibility for the course, much of the learning happens as a result of students' interaction with each other. Posting writing online make it easy to read each others' work.

Union Institute is an accredited degree-granting program which is designed to support individual learning plans. Learners design programs with advisors which include combinations of traditional coursework, courses delivered at a distance, and individual study. One of the key components of this program is the requirement of Peer Days. Learners find a small group of fellow learners who share a need to explore a particular subject and pull together some kind of learning event (a guest speaker, group reading and discussion of a book, a workshop) collaboratively. Many of these Peer Days are held at a distance using online technologies which make it possible for geographically isolated learners to engage with each other. The students themselves thus take responsibility for managing a significant part of their own learning program.

3.8   Managing Time

In face-to-face and synchronous environments the challenge for the facilitator is to manage the respective air time for different class members so the extroverts do not dominate. The same issue arises in asynchronous learning where very active participants can create information overload for others. In an asynchronous environment some group members will check in four times a day and others will check in once a week. If you have several members who sign on very frequently they can make it difficult for the rest to engage with the virtual group because it feels to them like the conversation has run away form them. The *rolling present* refers to differences in participants' perception of what is current. People experience everything that has been entered since the last time they checked in as

---

[6] Creative Writers on the Net: http://www.tmn.com/efa

current. You need manage the pace of the group and create norms for how much time will be included in the rolling present of the community as a whole.

The fact that participants can access a distance learning *any time* can be a great advantage. However, the lack of familiar time-frames such as a class which meets on a certain day every week can make it hard for participants to manage the experience. One way facilitators can help participants is to create opportunities for explicit conversation about strategies for managing their time. For example, one moderator of an asynchronous course suggested to participants that they schedule a specific time to access the course, put it in their calendar just like any meeting rather than leaving it to chance (in which case it often got squeezed out by other priorities).

Facilitators can also help by providing time-based guideposts to help give a learning group the feeling of making progress and moving forward. For example, in a distance version of Stanford University's Creativity in Business[7] course for delivery in-house to corporate groups the course begins with a ½ day off-site meeting followed by ten weeks of exercises, journal-keeping, and reflection. It involves materials which are provided via CD-ROM which participants access via their corporate intranet and asynchronous Web-conferencing led by the course facilitator. Although the participants can engage in course activities at any time, the facilitator provides the group with a pulse created by weekly "Live With" reflections where participants share their experience applying each course module to their daily experience. Participants know on which day the new conference item will be posted online indicating time to shift from the focus on one module to the next. In this way, even though learners are participating at their own time and pace, the group has a whole shares a sense of progressing through the course together.

3.9   Managing Awareness

Both facilitators and learners need to be aware of how they are doing. Distance learning students need some different kinds of feedback to help them calibrate their participation with expectations. Teacher facilitators need to provide a lot more "work in progress" feedback than feedback on a final product because so much of this new type of project is process-oriented. Since using technology as a primary means to communicate will be new to most participants they need to spend more time than usual talking about the quality of their communication. The teacher can provide some feedback but it is even better if the teacher can help participants develop a norm of providing feedback to each other about communication style, quantity, frequency, clarity, etc. Teachers can help team participants access more of their own feelings and reactions to messages in different media. This kind of savvy about new media is an important new skill.

In a face-to-face class, teachers watch body language and facial expression and many other signals to develop a sense of what is going on. Participants in a virtual

---

[7] Insight Out Collaborations Creativity in Business Course: http://www.insightout.com

learning community convey this same information in different ways. And, much of what students will be doing will be done on their own - out of sight of the teacher. Some teachers are experimenting with using the Internet as a place to store electronic portfolios of student work so that it can be accessed at any time.

Facilitation is paying attention to what is happening in your group as distinct from what you wanted or expected would happen. It is not unlike facilitating any group; if participants are not participating as much as you had hoped, do not admonish them. Instead, notice what kinds of issues they are engaged in and find ways to weave those issues into your group activity. You must detect where members are now and work with that energy to move in the direction you need to go.

3.10   Managing Collaboration

While most people agree that collaborative learning is desirable and important, it has been difficult logistically in the past. Unless students are full time in a residential setting, it is unrealistic to expect them to be able to find the time and space to work together. Distance learning provides an opportunity to support collaborative learning in ways we have not been able to do before. But just putting participants together in a some kind of common electronic space will not turn them into a collaborative group automatically. The key is to design a framework for group work which requires the team to grapple with roles, protocols for working interdependently and mutual accountability.

For example in the George Mason University Program on Social and Organisational Learning (PSOL)[8] participants in a graduate level course on The Virtual Organisation used a wide variety of media including asynchronous Web-conferences, telephone conferences, shared white board, and e-mail to support collaborative learning. The class was divided into teams tasked with mastering sets of specific learning objectives and finding ways to transfer that learning to the class as a whole.

The distance learning cohorts within the California Institute of Integral Studies are required to present a Group Demonstration of Mastery to faculty and peers as a significant part of their doctoral program. This requires the cohort to select and commit to a common theme for learning over the course of a year or more and to integrate their distributed efforts into a shared whole.

It can be very difficult and time-consuming to self-organise into teams or small groups in an asynchronous environment. In face-to-face situations, people can quickly form small groups by making eye contact and moving physically near each other. Therefore, it is usually more effective to use synchronous media for initial group formation or for the instructor/facilitator to create teams to get a group

---

[8]   George Mason University Program on Social and Organizational Learning: http://mason.gmu.edu/~jforeman/vorg.syllabus.html

started. You can achieve the goal of self-selection of topics by letting groups define their mission or letting people switch groups after a while.

3.11   Managing Faculty Development

How can we help faculty make the shifts in thinking required to be effective in distance learning courses? What is the best way to learn to manage these new aspects of the learning process? The most effective strategy is to provide access to experienced faculty who can serve as coaches. Team teaching with a more experienced teacher is also a good approach.

The PBS Mathline program required more than 100 new facilitators to manage the virtual learning communities. It was not possible to bring all those people in for face-to-face training. Since audio tapes are cheap and easy to distribute, tapes were made of a panel of experienced facilitators and sent to the new group. Four to five experienced practitioners called in on a call-me audio call which was taped. In order to make the conversation feel spontaneous it was not scripted. However, it was planned and moderated. Three to four key theme questions were chosen ahead of time along with who would be first to respond to each question. After that it was a free flowing discussion. All the facilitators on the tape were also online so the new group of facilitators were able to ask them questions after listening to the taped discussion.

3.12   New Centres of Learning

"The organisations that will truly excel in the future will be the organisations that discover how to tap people's commitment and capacity to learn at all levels in an organisation," Peter Senge, *The Fifth Discipline*[3]

Increasingly, learning managers will be found outside traditional educational institutions. The theory of organisational learning has captured the imagination of many organisations. Most have found it challenging to figure out how to connect the theory with day-to-day practice. Distance learning approaches can play a significant role in turning organisational learning from theory to reality. But in a lot of companies, the first uses of distance learning technologies have been limited to creating packaged multi-media training courses either to individuals or to groups gathered to receive some kind of predominantly one-way broadcast of information. This does not do much to support organisational learning.

To harvest the knowledge and experience of people and make it available to the organisation as a whole, distance learning technologies need to be managed differently to support dialogue rather than just databases.

In the information age, education and training in organisations consisted of large amounts of explicit knowledge available to them through huge archival databases.

Quantifiable facts, formulas, and procedures were, and still are, available to anyone in these organisations. In contrast, today's knowledge or learning organisations create environments where experiential knowledge is learned through dialogue and interaction day-to-day. Communication technologies are needed which support this interaction. Previously tacit knowledge based on extremely valuable experience now supplements the quantifiable data.

The environment should stimulate and nurture the complex network of interpersonal relationships and interactions which are part of an effective management communications and decision-making process. People must be allowed to make choices about who they need to communicate and learn with without regard to traditional organisational boundaries, distance and time. In other words, they need to manage their own learning, to form new groups and teams as requirements develop and change.

The new framework for managing distance learning should be about managing the learning process rather than managing courses. The kinds of questions we need to be asking ourselves are not about how to plug one kind of technology into another or how faculty can be more effective on video. The more important questions are about how to use technology to leverage resources and group dynamics in new ways to make fundamental changes in every part of the learning process.

References

1. Bates, A.W. Tony (1995) *Technology, Open Learning and Distance Education*. Routledge.

2. Berreman, I. (1997) An Improvisational Model for Groupware Technologies. *Sloan Management Review*, Orlikowski, W. and Hofman, D., Winter 1997.

3. Senge, P.M. (1990) *The Fifth Discipline: The Art and Practice of the Learning Organization*, Currency/Doubleday, August 1.

4. Bentley, Trevor (1994) *Facilitation: Providing Opportunities for Learning*. McGraw-Hill.

5. Amy, E. and Kimball, L. (1997) Zen and the Art of Facilitating Virtual Teams. *Conference Proceedings, Organization Development Network Annual Conference*, Organization Development Network, 76 South Orange Avenue, Suite 101, South Orange, NJ 07079-1923.

6. Amy, E., Kimball, L., Silber, T. and Weinstein, N. *Boundaryless Facilitation* (in press).

7. Farry, Scott B. (1994) From Managing to Empowering: An Action Guide to Developing Winning Facilitation Skills. *Quality Resources*.

8. Kimball, L. (1995) Ten Ways to Make Online Learning Groups Work. *Educational Leadership*. Association for Supervision and Curriculum Development, Alexandria, VA, October.

9.   Oravec, Jo Ann (1996) *Virtual Individuals, Virtual Groups: Human Dimensions of Groupware and Computer Networking.* Cambridge University Press.

10. Porter, Lynnette R.(1997) *Virtual Classroom: Distance Learning with the Internet. John Wiley.*

11. Schrage, Michael. (1996) *No More Teams!: Mastering the Dynamics of Creative Collaboration.* Doubleday.

12. Schwartz, Roger M. (1994) *The Skilled Facilitator: Practical Wisdom for Developing Effective Group,.* Jossey-Bass.

Chapter 4

Collaborative Interactions in Support of Learning: Models, Metaphors and Management

*Kent Norman**

New digital educational environments invite almost unlimited possibilities for interactive learning and collaboration in the digital university. However, to support quality education, learning activities need to be guided by principled models of interaction, guidelines for the design of user interfaces, and policies for the management of interaction and collaboration. In this chapter a model of interaction among instructors, students, and educational material will be introduced to help define the types of collaborative interactions among instructors, among students, between instructors and students, and with materials. To further define learning activities, the structure of the human/computer interface will be discussed in terms of interface metaphors and a prototype system that provides tools for accessing materials, submitting assignments, asking questions and providing feedback, engaging in dialogue, and working on team projects. These metaphors and resulting systems add necessary structure, meaning, and limits to learning activities. Finally, both instructors and students need to manage interaction by scheduling, organising, and focusing activities. Policies may be implemented in the system to provide scheduled roll out of materials and assignments, automatic filing and storage of materials, and deadlines and constraints on submissions. Illustrations and applications will be drawn from seven years of experience in the Teaching Theatres at the University of Maryland and other collaborative projects.

* Department of Psychology, University of Maryland, College Park, MD 20742-4411, U.S.A. Email: Kent_Norman@mail.lap.umd.edu

4.1   Introduction

New digital educational environments, however construed on networks and computers, offer a full range of computer and communication facilities. In principle, everything that we might want to do in education can be done in the emerging digital educational environments. These environments supported by local area networks and the Internet provide new channels for collaborative models of learning, training, teaching, and ultimately the authoring of science and knowledge. Multimedia browsing and authoring, desktop video conferencing, and specialised animations, simulations, and games provide new media for learning.

As the infrastructure for this environment unfolds, the question is how to use it in new and effective ways to support not only current models of education but new methods of student-student, student-educator, and educator-educator collaboration in the educational process. New levels of interactivity, communication, and collaboration are now possible. However, the unlimited range of possibilities poses a design problem. The design and implementation of the interface to host these new activities is critical. The creation of this environment and the tools to support it involve at least three disciplines: (a) human/computer interaction for the design and evaluation of the interface, (b) cognitive psychology for theories of learning, knowledge comprehension, and collaborative thinking and problem solving, and (c) education for the models of pedagogy, curriculum development, and evaluation of learning effectiveness.

In this chapter a model for the interaction among students, instructors, and educational materials will be presented. A new model for spatially directed / spatially privileged collaboration will be used in conjunction with new techniques for visualising and constructing shared collaborative spaces. Research and teaching experience collected over the last seven years in the AT&T and IBM Teaching Theatres at the University of Maryland as well as other projects will be used to formulate new directions for software development for collaboration.

4.2   A Model of the Interaction Space

Collaboration requires media, methods, and members. Substantial bodies of literature already exist pertaining to Computer Supported Collaborative Work (CSCW) [1] and computer-based instruction (CBI) [2]. On the other hand, research is only beginning within the overlap of learning technology and collaborative tools. In this section a foundation for collaborative learning technology will be laid by discussing (a) the infrastructure of electronic classrooms, (b) the development of software methods of allowing collaboration to happen electronically, and (c) collaborative efforts across disciplines and distance.

4.2.1   Teaching Theatres Become Stages for Collaboration

In 1991 the AT&T Teaching Theatre opened at the University of Maryland. The room was equipped with 20 workstations for the students (for up to two students per workstation) and two for the instructor as shown in Figure 4.1.

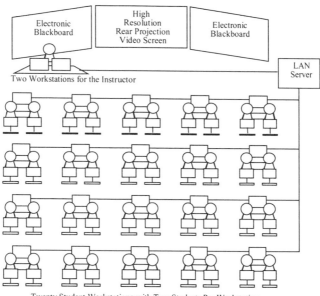

Twenty Student Workstations with Two Students Per Workstation

Figure 4.1. The electronic classroom.

The computers were networked to allow for communication and collaboration among the students and the faculty. Two large 4x6 foot displays were used for group viewing of material and a video switcher for exchanging screens. In 1994 a similar classroom was opened called the IBM-TQM Teaching Theatre. This last Fall another classroom was opened. These classrooms have been the result of efforts on the part of a Steering Committee composed of faculty members and administrators and the Teaching Technology staff in the Computer Science Centre[9].

Much has been learned about (a) what technology works and what does not work in the classrooms, (b) how to configure and manage the servers and networks, and (c) how to support and maintain the system reliably. But more importantly, much has been learned much about how the technology can be used for collaborative

---

[9] http://www.inform.umd.edu/TeachTech/

learning. Over the years a number of faculties at the university have taught a wide variety of courses to a large number of students. The trend has been for lectures to evolve from presentations to explorations, from passive learning to active engagement, and from the "sage on the stage" to the "guide on the side." Shneiderman *et al* [3] notes, "We originally called our electronic classrooms Teaching Theatres, but as faculty experimented with new teaching styles the Steering Committee shifted to the term Learning Theatres to convey an increased emphasis on student-centred learning styles."

During these years of operation a large number of collaborative learning exercises and approaches have been proposed. Collaborative activities ranged in size from small group projects to whole class and even groups of classes and in scope from short in class sessions (e.g., brain storming and idea formation) to whole semester projects (e.g., create a WWW site for a community organisation or develop a computer program). Many of these have been summarised in journal articles and technical reports [3, 4, 5]. Additional background and theory on the electronic classroom can be found in Chapters 4 and 5 of *The Switched On Classroom*[10] [6].

4.2.2   Collaborative Spaces

Collaboration in education, however, is broader than the stereotypic illustrations generally sited as examples. Collaboration is an inherent part of education, from teachers co-labouring with students in one-on-one tutoring to learning communities such as the one-room school house and from teachers collaborating in the preparation of materials to students collaborating in studying and even in attempts to cheat.

To help comprehend the range of collaboration in learning activities a model of interaction will be used. In 1990, Norman proposed a model of interactions to help define the interaction spaces [7]. At its most trivialised level, education can be viewed as the flow of information from one generation, however construed, to the next. Although education is a much richer event embodying not only the hopes and purposes of humanity but our very destiny as well, the technological schematic need only consider the flow of information from one point to another. Figure 4.2 gives a schematic diagram of some of these sets and some of the interactions that may occur.

---

[10] http://www.lap.umd.edu/ SOC/

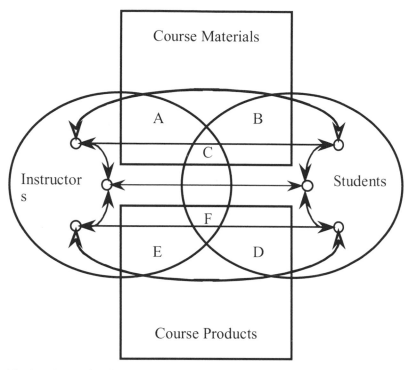

Figure 4.2. A schematic of the sets of agents and objects in the instructional process.

To this schematic we add the content of the information and the interaction of human agents about this information. The collaborative classroom and the underlying educational environment supporting it is a multifaceted electronic space involving complex interactions among two sets of agents (instructors and students) and two sets of objects (course materials and course products). The interactions among these sets form a complex network of relationships. On the left side of Figure 4.2, the double arrows indicate that instructors interact among themselves. In the hard copy classroom, this is by way of formal printed media such as books and journals and by way of informal methods such as conversation and the exchange of notes and ideas. On the right side of the figure, the double arrows indicate that students also interact among themselves. In the traditional classroom, student interaction is generally limited to informal methods of communication such as in-class discussion and out-of-class study groups.

The instructional process basically involves interaction across sets of agents. Instructors convey information to the students and students convey information back often in the form of questions, answers, and reports. In general, however, interactions are conveyed by means of the two sets of objects, the course materials and the course products. Course materials are previously existing texts, lesson plans, and compendia of materials such as references, collections, and databases. Course products are the result of educational activities and include such things as test results, class dialogue, original works produced by the students, and evaluative feedback. In general, the source of the information is from the set of course materials; it is conveyed by means of the instructor to the students or by students directly interacting with the information; and finally, results in the observable products of education which, hopefully, are diagnostic of lasting changes in the students themselves.

Switching to the electronic media, the course materials and course products are contained in hypermedia databases and interaction with these databases is by way of the human/computer interface. The interface is represented in Figure 4.2 as the intersection of areas covered by the domains. These are the six intersecting areas. The Instructor-Material Area A pertains to the instructor's access to course material outside of their direct interaction with students. Course preparation would be a major activity in this area. Similarly, the Student-Material Area B pertains to student access to course material outside of direct interaction with the instructors. This would include the activities of independent reading and studying. The Instructor-Material-Student Area C is a three-way interface of the instructors and the students together interacting with the course material. This area basically represents the activities of delivering lectures and classroom interaction with course material. The Student-Product Area D pertains to student authoring of papers, completion of assignments, and taking of exams. Since students may also be grouped, this area may also contain collaborative work. The Instructor-Product Area E pertains to instructor access to course products for evaluation and grading. Finally, and central to collaboration and mentoring, the Instructor-Products-Students Area F is a three-way interface of instructors and students with the products. Instructors and students may work together on collaborative class projects.

With this as a schematic one may then translate each space to a file server or device storing the course materials and course products. Each interaction among agents can be translated to some tool for transmitting information such as email, Listservs, file transfer protocol (ftp), multi-party chat channels, or "browsers" on the World Wide Web. The question then is how to design the educational space so that it is integrated, understandable, and usable by students, instructors, and administrators. The abstract information space must be instantiated, given substance, and made meaningful.

To further conceptualise the collaborative aspects of this interaction a spatially directed / spatially privileged model of collaboration is proposed in Figure 4.3 as a frame for organising past efforts and for identifying new innovations and requirements for collaborative tools. Collaboration is spatially directed in the sense that it can be lateral (with peers at the same level, e.g., students), hierarchical (between members of different levels of the same hierarchy, e.g., student and instructor), diagonal (between members of different levels of different hierarchies, e.g., a student in one class with an instructor in another), nested (with members in the same class or discipline), or crossed (with members of different classes or disciplines).

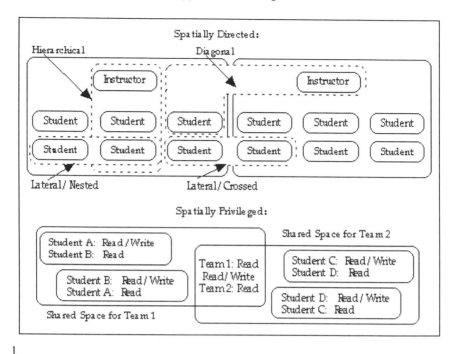

1

Figure 4.3. A spatially directed / spatially privileged model of collaboration.

Collaboration is spatially privileged in that team members have different privileges to read/write to shared areas. Each student has his or her own personal space in addition to a space that they can write to and others can read from. In Figure 4.3 for example, Student B can read part of Student A's space but cannot write to it. Outside of their personal spaces is a shared area that all students on that team can read and write to. Part of that area is a common space between teams and in that space part of Team 1's area can be read by Team 2 and part of Team 2's area can be read by Team 1 and part can be both read and written to by both teams. This structure of privileges allows members within teams to work individually, share products for review, and combine group work for the final report. It also allows groups to share work and ideas and to collaborate at a higher level.

4.3   Metaphors and the HyperCourseware Prototype

How we use things depends on how we think they work. In the case of new technologies that we are not initially familiar with, we often use metaphors and graphics to make them look like things that we are already familiar with. A multiple choice exam on computer uses the same structure of a stem and foils and can appear on the screen to look just as it might on paper. Only minor modifications are necessary so that a mouse click replaces a pencil check mark to indicate the selected alternative and changing your mind does not require an eraser.

In the new digital educational environment the interactions in Figure 4.2 and the relational structures in Figure 4.3 are channeled through software tools. Many tools have been developed specifically for this purpose and other general tools have been used in creative ways to provide for interaction and collaboration through email, Listservs, and Internet relay chat as well as complete courseware shells on the World Wide Web. In this section one prototype called HyperCourseware will be used to illustrate the use of metaphors and the need for an integrated digital environment in education.

One of the greatest needs in collaborative learning in digital environments has been an integrated software package which seamlessly ties all aspects of the learning, teaching, and collaborative processes together. The problem in education has not been the existence of software but the fact that most programs have been either (a) small-scale, one-off, subject-specific, platform-dependent programs written by educators or (b) general-purpose programs for business applications retro-adapted for educational use. To bridge the gap, Norman [7] proposed an digital educational environment which has now become known as "HyperCourseware." It is based on the idea of collaborative hypermedia, a system that allows multiple users to explore the same materials and communicate with each other while making use of dynamic metaphors in education.

4.3.1   HyperCourseware Prototype

The conceptual interactions and spaces shown in Figures 4.2 and 4.3 have been instantiated in an easy to use interface in HyperCourseware. The objective embraced by HyperCourseware has been quite broad: to provide an integrated and seamless hypermedia infrastructure to support the full range of classroom activities [8, 5]. Over seven years of development, HyperCourseware has become quite extensive. A sample of screens can be viewed at the HyperCourseware WWW site[11]. To illustrate a part of the interface, Figure 4.4 shows the Home Screen and a number of the current modules available around its perimeter.

At the global level, HyperCourseware is organised around educational tools, materials, and objectives rather than around semantic or domain specific knowledge. It is only at the local or content level in the materials that knowledge structure becomes important and is incorporated into the materials by the instructor or instructional designer. Consequently, HyperCourseware was written to host any subject and to support many learning activities common across many different types of courses. These activities range from record keeping and on-line testing to hypermedia presentations and from individual exploration to group collaboration and team projects [9].

---

[11] http://www.hypercourseware.com/

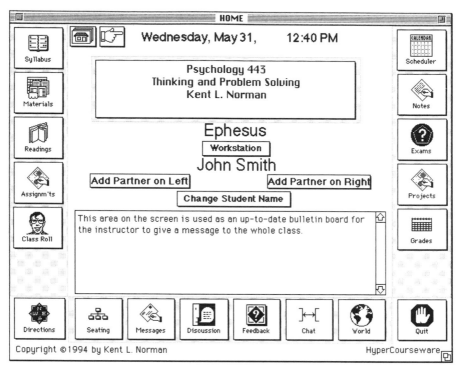

Figure 4.4. The "Home" screen of HyperCourseware which displays a number of linked modules making up the current educational environment.

HyperCourseware uses the conventional objects of classroom instruction and implements them in electronic form in the electronic classroom. Objects such as the course syllabus, the lesson plan, the lecture notes, the class roll, etc. are instantiated in graphic form in a hypermedia database. Furthermore, in HyperCourseware the database is used to provide the same sort of natural links between objects as one would expect in the educational materials themselves. For example, the syllabus is a natural navigational mechanism to jump to lectures, readings, and assignments; the class roll is a natural navigational jump to information about students and grades; and the grade list is a natural navigational jump to exams and assignments.

In addition to the multimedia course materials, the real advantage of the digital environment supported by HyperCourseware has been the wide range of collaborative tools. Each tool can be used in different ways depending on project goals and objectives:

Dialogue as Collaboration: A number of collaborative exercises in the electronic classroom have used different forms of multi-party chat sessions. These have been used for brainstorming, focused discussion, and group planning. Tools for organising, monitoring, and analysing chat sessions have been partially developed.

Additional tools that allow for visualisation of threads, clustering of ideas, and better integration with other tasks are needed.

Collection and Dissemination of Ideas: Initial collaboration begins with the generation and polling of ideas, materials, or parts. Several tools have been used for facilitating discussion by having the students start with an initial contribution. These contributions are aggregated and then disseminated to the group for inspection. Once the group has seen everyone's contribution, it can go to the next level of discussion. Other applications have involved collecting parts of a larger project from either individuals or from subgroups. For example, subgroups might contribute parts (e.g., subroutines for a program, sections of an article, or designs of rooms in a building). The parts are collected, aggregated, and disseminated. The group evaluates whether the aggregation works and/or what needs to be changed.

Project Spaces: Structured project spaces have been used for team collaboration. A structured project space is a template that allows different members of the team to contribute to their prescribed parts while also allowing all members to view and comment on any part of the project. Parts of the project space are write-protected so that only certain members may change the information. This approach helps to manage the accountability of individual members of the team rather than only being able to assess the overall project.

Ordered File Exchange: Collaboration is often serial. One person creates the first part, the next member adds the second part, and so on. Routing handlers are used to direct materials from one student to another. In one application, the first student wrote an article which was then passed on to four other students who read the article and critiqued it. The critiques were then passed back to the first student. Similar procedures can be programmed for other routing of materials in learning environments.

4.3.2   Interface Design for Collaboration

The challenge to the software designer is to develop interfaces for these tools that are easy to use and assist both the students and the instructors in using the collaborative tools in a productive and efficient manner. A number of books and articles deal with the problem of interface design [10, 11, 12]. These outline the methods of interaction, the principles of screen layout, the importance of consistency, the need of clear directions, and the need for the interface to match user expectation.

In the area of interfaces for collaboration there are some additional concerns that need to be mentioned. First, navigation is a pervasion problem in all software, however, in collaborative tools it is sometimes critical. Clear navigational tools are needed to find where to go for a particular collaborative session. There are many times when all of the students need to be at the same point in the system to perform an exercise. A homing function that jumps all of the systems to an instructor defined location is one solution for group navigation.

Second, clear displays are needed to inform the student of important parameters of the interaction and controls to set those parameters. For example, student identity or anonymity in collaboration is an importance factor. The screen should clearly indicate whether the contribution is anonymous or what identification is associated with the transmission. Figure 4.5 shows such controls on a chat tool in HyperCourseware.

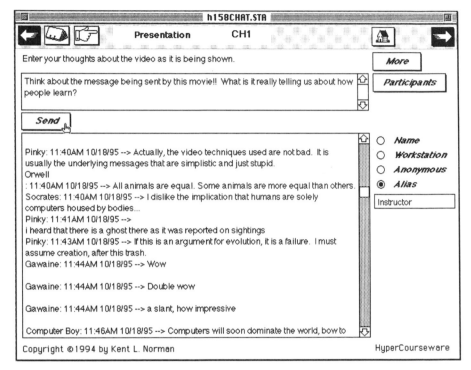

Figure 4.5. A chat channel screen in HyperCourseware.

Finally, the interface needs to provide information and feedback on how collaborative information is shared among the students, who can see and modify information, and how group consensus is achieved for the final product.

4.4   Policies for Managing Learning Activities

The tools for collaborative learning activities are only effective if they are put to good use. Just setting up a Listserv for a class does not ensure that it will have any educational use or redeeming value. It must be put to the right use and monitored to ensure that it is properly used. In this section we will look at some of these uses and ways of monitoring and managing the collaboration to ensure that learning objectives are being met.

As indicated in Figure 4.1 there are many areas for collaboration in education in addition to the stereotypic "group project". A sampling of collaboration is listed below:

Collective Note Taking: Students vary in their ability and readiness to take notes in class or to write notes on readings. Collective note taking distributes the responsibility for digesting the information across a group and provides a collective set of perspectives that can be discussed and edited to provide a set of study notes and will be more complete and balanced than individual notes. Collaborative word processing tools can be used to collect individual notes, sort by time and topic, and allow for editing by the students and the instructor.

Study Groups: Students study together by discussing topics, explaining concepts to one another, working problems together, and quizzing one another. Dialogue tools can be used for discussion and explanation. Shared work spaces can be used for problems and illustrations. Quizzing can be done using chat tools. However, for each of these activities, the current generic tools need to be refined to facilitate the specific activities.

Collective Information Search: The skills of information search and retreival are becoming more and more important in education. Collaborative information search on the part of the students helps them to share ideas, techniques, and resources. Students may search individually at first or they may divide the task among themselves and then combine the results at the end. They may share needs so that if one hits upon a source of interest to another that student can be informed of the lead. Again generic search tools and communication tools need to be designed to make these tasks easy and efficient.

Group Projects: The intent of the group project is to allow students to work together on a project that involves more work than any one individual could perform during the course of the semester. It involves the collective skills of dividing the project into subtasks, assigning subtasks to group members, overseeing the progress of the work, and finally bringing the parts together for completion. Rarely, however, are students given instruction on project management let alone tools for scheduling and monitoring the overall project. They are left to struggle with failure, missed deadlines, and inequities. It is here that easy-to-use tools for group project management are desperately needed in education.

Collaborative Exams: In many courses after we expound on the virtues of collaboration and cooperative learning activities, we then give them a traditional competitive final exam. However, tools exist and can be further developed to create exams that assess the collaborative abilities of individuals while testing the collective knowledge of the group. These exams monitor contributions to group answers to essay questions and the division of labour in answering objective questions.

The many collaborative activities of the students can cause problems of monitoring and control. Listservs and chat sessions can go off onto extreme tangents, useless volumes of banter and filler, and sometimes destructive directions and flaming.

Group projects can become resentful one person efforts or total stalemates. Initial rules with continuous monitoring and control can alleviate these problems.

Setting Rules of Interaction: Unrestrained discussion can quickly go awry. In general it is best to avoid anonymity and aliases in on-line discussion. Furthermore, it is useful to set rules for entries and to assign grades based on compliance with those rules. For example, in a focused discussion on the pros and cons of some issue, one might require each student to make three reasoned entries, the first being an opening position, the second being a criticism of the opposition, and the third being a defence of the original opinion or a repositioning of opinion.

Roll Out Subtasks Over Time: Another method of controlling collaborative activities is to reveal and assign parts of a larger task over time. For example, the first step might be to assign a brain storming task to the group, then an evaluation of possible alternatives, then a decision of the preferred alternative, and so on until the final report is turned in. Scheduling helps to structure the task, reduce procrastination, keep milestones on a timely basis, and even out distribution of work. The down side is that this entails additional work on the part of the instructor. However, this may be handled automatically with assignment tools as in HyperCourseware that distribute materials at predetermined times.

Rotating Exposure to Information: Collaboration can also be controlled by rotating the exposure of materials among the members of a group in a set order. In a three person group for example, initial input from Student A could be handed to Student B, B's initial input to C, and C's to A. After each has reviewed the initial input and modified it, it would be handed to the third student. A round robin approach ensures that all students are active in the collaborative process and routing tools help to structure and subdivide the process.

Continuous Monitoring of Group Interactions: It is assumed in the new electronic educational environment that many if not all collaborative interactions leave records in a database. Thus over the course of a project, one can look at the number of transactions and contributions by each member of a group. At the end of the semester the instructor can assign grades not only on the final product but also on the level and type of interactions by the students. Furthermore, during the semester, the instructor can monitor the progress of the groups and spot problem groups and problem members and plan interventions to correct the problems. Needless to say, tools are needed so that the instructor can see at a glance the progress of each group and the patterns of collaboration. Figure 4.6 shows a mock-up of one possible system in which the instructor can select teams, members, and tasks for observation. Graphs at the bottom show effort over time as vertical bars and effort by members as horizontal bars. Graphs among the members show the structure of the group as hierarchical, egalitarian or independent.

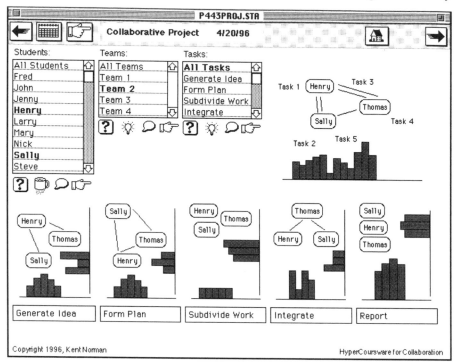

Figure 4.6. A visualisation of collaborative activities.

4.5   Conclusion

A key to effective learning has always been collaboration in one form or another between the instructor, the students, and the material. However, the question through the ages has been whether or not the key has been turned to unlock the power of collaboration to engage the interest of students, meaningfully relate to the information, and learn to work together. In the past it has been the exceptional teacher who has drawn the students into engaging dialogue and constructive projects or the adventurous student who has explored and interacted with others. Today the new media of instructional technology in an digital educational environment presents new tools to suggest, enhance, and facilitate collaboration that has not been possible in the past. While many possibilities exist, this chapter emphasises the importance of interface design and new tools for managing collaborative activities so that educational objectives will be met in the process.

References

1. Baecker, R.(1993) *Readings in groupware and computer-supported cooperative work: Assisting human-human collaboration,* San Francisco, CA: Morgan Kaufmann.

2. Chambers, J. A. and Sprecher, J. W. (1983) *Computer assisted instruction: Its use in the classroom.* Englewood Cliffs, NJ: Prentice-Hall.

3. Shneiderman, B., Alavi, M., Norman, K. and Borkowski, E. (1995) Windows of opportunities in electronic classrooms, *Communications of the ACM, 38,* 19-24.

4. Alavi, M. (1994) Computer mediated collaborative learning: An empirical evaluation. *MIS Quarterly, 18,* 159-173.

5. Norman, K. L. and Carter, L. (1994) An evaluation of the electronic classroom: The AT&T Teaching Theater at the University of Maryland. *Interpersonal Computing and Technology: An Electronic Journal of the 21st Century, 2,* 22-39.

    (http://www.helsinki.fi/science/optek/1994/n1/norman.txt).

6. Norman, K. L. (1997) *Teaching in the switched-on classroom: An introduction to electronic education and HyperCourseware.* (http://www.lap.umd.edu/SOC/).

7. Norman, K. L. (1990) The electronic teaching theater: Interactive hypermedia and mental models of the classroom. *Current Psychology Research and Reviews* (Special Issue: Hypermedia and artificial intelligence). *9,* 141-161.

8. Norman, K. L. (1994) HyperCourseware for assisting teachers in the interactive electronic classroom. *Proceedings of STATE 94: Fifth Annual Conference of the Society for Technology and Teacher Education,* Washington, DC, 473-477.

9. Sebrechts, M. M., Silverman, B. G., Boehm-Davis, D. A. and Norman, K. L. (1995) Establishing an electronic collaborative learning environment in a university consortium: The CIRCLE project. *Computers in Education. 25,* 215-225.

10. Norman, K. L. (1991) *The psychology of menu selection: Designing cognitive control at the human/computer interface.* Norwood, NJ: Ablex Publishing Corporation.

11. Norman, K. L. (1994) Navigating the educational space with HyperCourseware. *Hypermedia., 6,* 35-60.

12. Shneiderman, B. (1997) *Designing the user interface: Strategies for effective human-computer interaction (3rd ed).* New York: Addison-Wesley.

Chapter 5

Towards the Virtual Class: On-line Hypermedia in Higher Education

*Philip Uys**

The use of educational new media and in particular on-line hypermedia in higher educational institutes is analysed and discussed. This discussion takes place within the framework of the current transition in higher educational institutes from traditional learning to virtual class learning.

The virtual class is an electronic meeting place of students and lecturers for the purpose of learning and teaching - an educational experience of real people in a virtual dimension. In the virtual class the activities of the traditional educational institute are performed mostly without the movement of physical objects (e.g. getting students and lecturers into a physical venue). Emerging as a strong rationale for using distributed on-line education is that it can greatly enhance the quality of learning.

5.1   Introduction

In this chapter the use of educational new media and in particular on-line hypermedia in higher educational institutes is analysed and discussed. This discussion takes place within the framework of the current transition in higher educational institutes from traditional learning to virtual class learning (also called "telelearning"[1] and "distributed on-line education"[2]).

On-line hypermedia and the advent of Intranets extensively increased the ease and feasibility of offering the same educational facilities to local students and distance students. This convergence of what traditionally has been called "distance

* Wellington Polytechnic, Private Box 756, Wellington, New Zealand,
Email: philip.uys@wnp.ac.nz

education" and "on-campus education" means that on-line learning and teaching materials are available to both local and distance students using the same interface (i.e. a Web browser). Hence the term "distributed on-line education", coined by the author, which will be used throughout this chapter to denote learning in the virtual class.

"Hypermedia" is defined as multi-media (which includes text, movement, sound, pictures, colour) with hyper-links, which seamlessly transports the reader to other hypermedia materials.

The virtual class is seen as an electronic meeting place of students and lecturers for the purpose of learning and teaching - an educational experience of real people in a virtual dimension. In the virtual class the activities of the traditional educational institute are performed mostly without the movement of physical objects (e.g. getting students and lecturers into a physical venue); this includes the challenge of providing social interaction and a "campus experience" to on-line students.

The virtual class can take many forms, it might be for example on-line education using the Internet or an Intranet, or meeting in virtual reality as telepresences, or combining these methods with traditional educational modes. Moving towards the virtual class for some higher educational institutes might mean moving all education from traditional education to virtual class methods, or it might mean incorporating the virtual class as one of the key educational strategies.

The reasons why higher educational institutes are considering moving towards the virtual class include the need for lifelong learning. Education is becoming more of a lifelong endeavour than a few year's stint after school because most careers require continued training to keep up with the growing body of relevant knowledge and also because of the tendency of people to develop more than one career during their working life. Distributed on-line education is attractive to those already in the work force because of its open and flexible nature.

Distributed on-line education is seen by some as the only way to efficiently address the huge increase in learning needs and numbers. For instance in South Africa the term "Massification of Education" is used, and in the Western States of the USA higher educational institutes are planning to cater for the learning needs of the "Second tidal wave" i.e. the babies of the baby boomers' children which in the USA is expected to dramatically increase the student population in the next ten years. The Western States, as well as a large number of educational institutes in South Africa, see the only solution as open and distance learning with specific reference to distributed on-line education.

Emerging as a strong rationale for using distributed on-line education is that it can greatly enhance the quality of learning. It can lessen two huge problems in traditional distance education i.e. decrease in personal motivation and a sense of isolation. Both asynchronous (e-mail, message boards) and real-time on-line communication facilities (voice, video, Internet Relay Chat and shared whiteboards over the Net) can be used very effectively in this area. It also bridges the boundaries and limitations of time and space, and provides for a variety of learning styles as well as for different navigational preferences. Students can take more control of their learning and can develop "life" skills like time management and research skills, by students having to set there own study plans, find additional Web resources, having to evaluate its validity and then drawing sound conclusions.

This discussion also refers to the progress that the Wellington Polytechnic [3] has been making towards the virtual class since September 1995.

This chapter addresses:

- Some intrinsic qualities of the Internet and Intranets and the implications for education

- Some key management issues in higher education in progressing toward the virtual class

- Supporting on-line education with hypermedia courseware

- Issues in the development of on-line hypermedia courseware.

5.2   Some Intrinsic Qualities of the Internet and Intranets and the Implications for Education

The Internet is the external vehicle for deploying on-line hypermedia in education, while an Intranet is the internal vehicle. Some qualities of the Internet do not transfer to an Intranet, and will be indicated below. The qualities of the Internet and Intranets discussed below both created and sustain on-line education and the use of hypermedia therein. The educational implications of these qualities are listed in three areas: quality learning, effective teaching and sound management.

5.2.1   It is a Global Phenomenon

The Net links hundreds of countries around the globe. Any on-line hypermedia course materials on the Net is immediately available to any student, locally or internationally with access to the Net.

An Intranet by definition, however, is an internal platform.

Quality Learning: Both real-time and asynchronous international student interaction is facilitated. Information sources that may be scattered across the globe can be made immediately available to the students via hyperlinks, as if they are local resources which are part of the course.

Effective Teaching: Whatever is produced locally is also available internationally. Research resources that may be scattered across the globe are available to lecturers.

Sound Management: National and international marketing possibilities of local education becomes feasible. It is a vehicle for the internationalisation of education.

Global partnerships are facilitated and necessitated through the ease of entrance to on-line education.

5.2.2   Ease of Publishing and Maintenance

Web (World Wide Web) browsers used on the Net as well as on an Intranet, translate documents which are in HTML (hypertext mark up language) which is very simple and easy to learn. (There are also other languages which can be used like Java, which are more like a programming language and not as easy to use). Various software packages now have the facilities to convert documents into HTML.

On the Net, all that is additionally required to publish is often only an Internet account! This is because Internet Service Providers (ISPs) generally also include hosting space for Web pages as part of their package for account holders.

Quality Learning: Up-to-date materials can be accessed, since it is easy for lecturers to keep course materials up to date (only one source in a easily published language). Cyber students do not only have to be "consumers" of the information, but can be providers / publishers as well.

Effective Teaching: Keeping material up-to-date is easy (only one source in an easily published language). There are very few technicalities to learn to start developing on-line course materials.

Sound Management: It levels the playing field between large or great institutes and others that are not - all (with Internet access) can participate in on-line education. Extremely low cost of publishing compared to paper-based / CD-ROM materials.

5.2.3   Consistency of Interface

With Intranets becoming more popular, the Web browser interface is the same for both internal and external documents; this interface is also consistent across computer platforms (eg MAC / PC).

Quality Learning: Students doing internal / external studies have a consistency of interface. Students can use their preferred computer platform to access course materials and course related on-line facilities.

Effective Teaching: Lecturers can use the same course materials for on-campus and extra-mural students because of the consistency of interface. Intranet and Internet information can be linked in a seamless and integrated way. Lecturers can use their preferred computer brand / type to produce course materials and select on-line course-related facilities and materials.

Sound Management: Lower cost of making information available internally and externally since duplication of information is not necessary; Intranet and Internet information can be linked in a seamless way.

The convergence of traditional on-campus education and distance education means that instead of spending on capital projects to increase the number or size of lecturing theatres, on-campus students can access on-line hypermedia courseware instead of attending lectures; this can naturally also be done in combination with tutorials (whether on-line or face-to-face).

5.2.4   Natural Interface

In using the following elements of hypermedia i.e. text, movement, sound, pictures and colour, in both asynchronous and real-time modes, an interface closer to face-to-face, natural communication than that which is possible with paper-based materials, is offered to students and lecturers. Real-time communication facilities such as voice, video, shared whiteboard and Internet Relay Chat (IRC) contribute substantially to more natural on-line communication.

Quality Learning: Better learning by supporting the narrative with various hypermedia elements; the student also uses more faculties to interact with the educational materials.

Effective Teaching: Can emphasise and present course materials in a more effective way by employing combinations of hypermedia elements.

Sound Management: Can emphasise and present promotional material on an educational institute in a more natural and effective way.

5.2.5   Seamless Access

Hypermedia pages are linked together via hyperlinks in a seamless way; transfer is passed from one page to another in a way which makes it hardly noticeable. This is true for both pages within the same environment as well as pages in other environments (whether local or global).

Quality Learning: Other resources around the globe on the Web can be easily accessed instead of just local materials.

Effective Teaching: Other resources around the globe on the Web can be easily linked to and in such a way be incorporated in the course readings / materials.

Sound Management: Own institute's educational resources are hugely enlarged and enhanced by what is already available on the Net.

5.2.6   Highly Interactive

Facilities like pop-up comments, e-mail, on-line forms, message boards, news groups and on-line real-time communication facilities create the potential for high inter-activity using on-line hypermedia.

Quality Learning: High level of involvement with the course materials through personal questions and responses.

The social need of students to communicate with other students and the lecturer is provided for in a variety of ways; on-line real-time meetings, which includes video conferencing on the net, create a near "face-to-face" experience

Effective Teaching: Supports individual students better through personalised feedback. Accountability and motivation of students can be enhanced through periodic on-line real-time meetings or asynchronous communications.

Sound Management: Reputation for high quality and personalised student support.

5.2.7   Unbound in Space/Time

On-line information is available (pending network operation) every day, around the clock, around the world (on-line information on Intranets however is only available internally).

Quality Learning: On-line courses can be done in a truly flexible way at times and locality convenient to the student.

Effective Teaching: Through asynchronous communication facilities like e-mail, message boards and news groups, lecturers can communicate effectively with students, fellow researchers and others bridging both distance and time barriers.

Sound Management: Student enrolment can be much larger than with conventional teaching.

Administration, including enrolment, payment of fees etc. can be performed across distance and time barriers through asynchronous communication facilities like e-mail, message boards and news groups.

5.2.8   Distributed, Non-hierarchical [4]

The Net's and an Intranet's technical organisation is based on a distributed network model where control and processing is distributed among the nodes i.e. the participants.

Quality Learning: Independent student learning (or otherwise described as "individual autonomy" and seen as an acceptable educational goal by many educationalists [5]) and learning by discovery is facilitated in a natural way.

The constructivist learning approach, where students can construct their own knowledge, is facilitated in a natural way.

An on-line course supports a range of navigational paths from totally random navigation to a strict linear approach.

Effective Teaching: The lecturer can be more of a facilitator through independent student learning, learning by discovery and the constructivist learning approach.

A range of navigational paths can be provided / engineered for students.

Sound Management: Ease, effectiveness and low cost of distribution of on-line materials since students access materials themselves; minimum postage and preparation, minimum time of distribution.

5.2.9 Is in Line with the Emergence of the Information Society

In developed countries there is a transition from an industrialised society, where physical production technologies strongly influenced the forms of service and way of living, to an Information Society where information technology plays a key role in the forms of service and way of living, and where information becomes a key building stone.

Quality Learning: Distributed on-line education (or tele-learning) will increasingly become a very natural way of learning, just like tele-banking, tele-shopping etc. have become natural ways of performing these activities.

Effective Teaching: Distributed on-line teaching (or tele-teaching) will increasingly become a very natural way of teaching.

Sound Management: Educational institutes engaging in distributed on-line education will gain a positive reputation as participants in this transition to an Information Society.

5.3 Some Key Management Issues in Higher Education in Progressing Toward the Virtual Class

Four key management issues are discussed here: convergence of traditional on-campus and distance education, an approach for organisational change, ensuring adequate motivation for virtual class facilitators and dealing with an increasing proximity between industry and education.

5.3.1   Convergence

With the advent of Intranets, the ease and feasibility of offering the same facilities to local students that are being offered to distance students have increased extensively. With the same interface (i.e. a Web browser), on-line education and teaching materials are available to both local and distance students.

Traditionally, centres for distance education were often the minority who understood and used information technology in education out of necessity because of its ease of distribution, ease of maintenance and later because of its potential for increasing the quality of learning and teaching. At the same time their colleagues carried on with face-to-face education with workload formulas based on contact hours and lecturing in bigger and bigger lecture halls.

On the other hand, some educational institutes have the majority of their on-line materials solely for the use of local students.

Scenarios like these indicate that the possibility and reality of convergence of both local and distance education modes is a paradigm shift which is currently being made by only a minority of higher educational institutes.

How can this convergence look in operation? Teaching and learning materials are available and used by academic staff as well as local and distance students in a creative way. Local students may have all their lecture notes on-line as well-designed hypermedia courseware which include on-line communication facilities, different navigation paths, catering for different learning styles, access and pointers to other Web resources and exercises. The local students may also have face-to-face tutorials to work through exercises and sit tests and exams in a physical building. Distance students may also have all their lecture notes on-line as well-designed hypermedia courseware, have on-line real-time tutorials, attend workshops on the physical campus, but do their assignments on-line. However the synergy of this convergence is that local and distance students can meet on-line as well as physically, evaluate each other's on-line published materials, do group assignments together, form informal study groups etc!

Instead of trying to meet traditional workload formulas and extend often ineffective class room and distance education techniques, this convergence rather looks at creating the best possible learning scenarios for both local and distance students in a more flexible way. Hence the term: "distributed on-line education".

Managing this convergence is a key aspect in the transition towards the virtual class.

5.3.2   An Approach for Organisational Change

The concept of the virtual class is new to most higher educational institutes and introduces organisational change; this was also the case at Wellington Polytechnic where an On-line Campus [3] has been created while traditional educational strategies have also been continued.

The On-line Campus is part of the vision to combine hypermedia on the World Wide Web as an on-line education medium, with other educational strategies to provide education to both overseas, national and local students in an open and flexible manner.

The main aims of the project are to increase:

- the quality of learning

- educational opportunities

- profit

- student numbers and

- staff productivity.

A key factor in the success of the on-line campus project at Wellington Polytechnic was that the vision of on-line delivery was a shared one between the President and the Project Manager. This assisted tremendously in introducing this new concept.

For acceptance of the "virtual class" concept , it has been important to create a general awareness following both a top-down and bottom-up approach. After the President accepted the proposal and appointed the Project Manager, the Project Manager then asked staff who had shown some personal interest in on-line education, to join the project in the required roles. The President agreed to launch the concept at a breakfast for the Directorate (top management) - with other specially invited staff - and the project team. The project manager also provided input on a monthly basis at the Senior Management's meetings. A number of general sessions were held for other staff. Each deliverable has also been publicly launched.

The concept of a pilot project to develop the Wellington Polytechnic Homepage [6] was used so that the team could learn the Web technology and gain an understanding of the resource requirements.

The pilot project concept was again used when the first on-line course, 'Teaching Techniques for Adult Learning'[3], was developed. This free sampler provides interested parties with a taste of what on-line courses at Wellington Polytechnic can be like (different delivery approaches however are followed in other on-line courses.

Overall, the seven stages of Lewin and Schein's model for organisational change [7] were followed. These stages are listed as well as how it was applied in this project:

1   *Scouting*: Identify potential areas or systems that may need change: educational planning, development and delivery.

2   *Entry*: Stating the problems and the goals: included and described in the
        initial proposal document.

3   *Diagnosis*: Gathering data and determining resources required: described
        in the initial proposal document and further developed during the pilot
        project and the development of the Sampler course.

4   *Planning*: Examining alternatives and making decisions: some early
        decisions were contained in the initial proposal document, for example that
        the Web is to be used as key delivery medium; others were made by using
        the prototype and sampler concepts where a large degree of exploration,
        discovery and experimentation was allowed for in all areas : educational,
        technical and design.

5   *Action*: Implementing the decisions: decisions were followed through in a
        consistent manner.

6   *Evaluation*: Determining whether the changes satisfied the initial
        objectives and solved the problems identified: this process has been
        carried out continuously in weekly and later fortnightly project meetings,
        informal and open discussions, feedback by students who were asked to
        "test-drive" the courses and by enrolled students. Valuable feedback from
        trusted colleagues at other higher educational institutes was also obtained.
        It is essential that continual student feedback is sought and also that
        ongoing technical evaluation occurs to ensure that the most appropriate
        technologies are being used in an effective way.

7   *Termination*: Transferring the ownership of the new / changed system to
        the users and ensuring efficient operation: if the content providers are
        intimately involved from start to implementation, this transition should
        take place in a fluent and satisfactory way.

The above model seems to work well if the seven stages are not seen as
consecutive, but as dynamic dimensions of a process. Flexibility and giving a high
priority to people-issues proved to be essential ingredients in the success of
introducing this change in Wellington Polytechnic.

5.3.3   Ensuring Adequate Motivation for Virtual Class Facilitators

It is essential that reward systems are tied to the strategic objectives and directions
of an institute. If an institute desires to move towards the virtual class, its reward
systems should encourage those involved to become more effective and committed
to it.

In general it can be said that academics do not like changes to their jobs and how
they work. In the virtual class environment a large number of changes are required,
for example moving from text based to digital media, being more of a facilitator
(following a developmental rather than a dissemination approach [8]) than a

lecturer, spending more time on on-line communication than face-to-face communication etc.

Workload requirements need to be revised to incorporate these on-line activities as well as the involvement in developing on-line hypermedia courseware.

Intellectual Property Rights should be debated and negotiated, especially in a virtual class environment where a large proportion of the courseware is published on an international medium from where materials can be easily copied.

5.3.4 Dealing with an Increasing Proximity between Industry and Education

Corporate universities are emerging which do not have the same academic philosophies or handicaps as traditional higher educational institutes (eg Microsoft, Andersons and Macdonald's are active in this area). These proprietary institutions often focus on what makes money, for example courses like MBA, ESL, certificating teachers following an industrial model of education: through an intermediate process, inputs deliver outputs which can be marketed and sold.

Education and entertainment is getting closer too! Hollywood Studios are also getting involved in partnerships (there are currently projects with Warner Bros to identify how each student learn and what they need to learn, and then to match them up with specific computer mediated learning systems). Currently in the UK the BBC, Open University (UK) and the British film industry are exploring joint projects in education.

Will we soon see "The Ultimate Consortium" delivering the same quality of education, at the same cost or less, but more entertaining and taken shorter for degreeing students? A consortium consisting of a huge financial sponsor, a computer giant (eg MS) and a prominent company in the film industry drawing on the "best professors" available for the content and educational process? Will free academic discourse, critique and research be valued, encouraged and supported when the bottom-line is moving to achieve a target profit margin?

Higher educational institutes will need to rethink missions, objectives and strategies to turn threats into opportunities in this volatile and dynamic environment!

5.4 Supporting On-line Education with Hypermedia Courseware

Key design principles of on-line education using hypermedia courseware which emerged from our experience are simplicity, clarity, practical needs of on-line students and full learning support.

An On-line Campus has been created to contain the on-line hypermedia courses as well as all the elements to support our on-line students. Supporting on-line students includes constructing appropriate:

- communication structures among students as well as between students and lecturers

- enrolment for the on-line courses

- down loading mechanisms for the courses

- navigational paths and other facilities for different learning styles

- help information

- providing an ability to publish directly on the Web from within the On-line Campus.

5.4.1   Communication Structures

One of the problems with traditional distance education courses is the isolation that these students often experience. They often do not know who their fellow students, previous students or even their lecturers are!

We have employed a number of mechanisms in our attempt to solve this problem.

One mechanism is the use of an "Ideas Exchange" [9] which is referenced via a hyperlink at the bottom of every page in the courses. Here students can place public messages for other students on a dedicated message board - with or without an e-mail address (some courses uses hypermail threaded message boards while others use open message boards). They can also place public messages for the lecturer on a dedicated message board - with or without indicating their e-mail address, as well as send private messages to the lecturer via e-mail.

Once larger groups ("pockets") of students in certain locations are established, it is envisaged that either lecturers and support staff will visit on-line students (both overseas and New Zealand) or agreements with local higher educational institutes will be made to:

- conduct student group work

- present key lectures and

- address learning problems.

In some courses, students will be invited/expected to attend some on-campus workshops.

Some of our on-line courses are using real-time on-line communication facilities like Internet Relay Chat (IRC), voice, video-conferencing and shared whiteboard facilities over the Web. These facilities provide social interaction in a more natural way, and also build some accountability into these courses.

5.4.2 Enrolment for the On-line Courses

Wellington Polytechnic expects students to sign an enrolment form which is legally binding. With the problems surrounding electronic signatures, an on-line application form is available within the On-line Campus which arrives as electronic mail at the delegated staff members' e-mail address. An enrolment form is then generated and mailed to the prospective student. Payment can be done via bank transfer or other general international measures for fund transfers.

However, if the registration form is hosted on a secure server, credit card transactions will be possible. Other forms of "virtual" money can also be investigated to increase the ease whereby payment is made.

5.4.3 Downloading Mechanisms for the Courses

On-line courses can be done in a variety of modes, for example off-line, on-line or a combination thereof. The approach of the hydi Educational New Media Centre [2] is to use a combined approach.

Each on-line course (the text and all graphical elements) is compressed into a single file (in a format appropriate for both PC and Macintosh computers) that can be down-loaded by students onto their hard drives by simply taking the hyperlink and indicating where the file must be placed on their own computer. This is done to save students Internet access costs and time as well as the frustration of waiting for materials to be down-loaded item per item.

In conjunction with this, a "Revisions page" exists on the Web where all changes are listed since the making of the last compressed file. This page assists students to download these amended areas.

Students get on-line to use Internet-related activities in the courses such as investigating other sites from the "Library" section as well as the asynchronous and real-time communication facilities.

5.4.4 Navigational Paths and Other Facilities for Different Learning Styles

Hypermedia assists the instructional designer in catering for different learning styles and ways of navigating a course. Mediated individualised instruction is a sound educational goal and supported by educationalists like Romiszowski [10]. Two basic navigational preferences are being addressed in the Wellington Polytechnic's on-line courses: sequential and random navigation.

The Web and Intranets cater very naturally through hyperlinks for the random learner. No strict sequence is built into the courses, although some suggestions of a sequential progression are made. The learner can thus take any route through the content and activities; the only fixed requirement is that the assessments need to be completed before credit can be obtained!

For the sequential learner, special measures are taken in our on-line courses. A clickable navigational "course map", which is a graphical presentation of the proposed sequence of the main sections in a course, is presented at the start of the course. One of the standard hyperlinks at the bottom of each page within a course is a link to this "map" to help students orientate themselves whenever required.

From the page that contains the "course map", students can also access an "Index" page which contains an extensive list of most of the hyperlinks within the course. The inherent capability of Web browsers to change the colour of all followed links is used on this "Index" page, so that a student can access this page and see exactly which parts of the course have been visited and which parts not.

Other facilities in the On-line Campus which are included to support specific learning styles can be described in terms of a conventional classification of learning styles namely that of being a pragmatist, activist, reflector and theorist. (It is recognised that every student has a blend of these - and other - learning styles and approaches).

Pragmatist: learning best by understanding / seeing and actively engaging in a practical application of the content - a "Gymnasium" section is a standard hyperlink at the bottom of each Web page within courses where students are provided with exercises of both a practical and theoretical nature.

Activist: learning best when the content contains a large number of activities and concrete experiences, is exciting and when there are a variety of "discoveries" - the "Gymnasium" section also assists this learning style. The Web also naturally lends itself to "discoveries" through hyperlinks - within the course or to external sources. Students can experience excitement in their learning through:

- random navigation

- high level of inter-activity through e-mail, message boards, on-line feedback on assignments

- the use of multimedia i.e. graphics, colours, sounds and movement.

Reflector: learning best by reflective observation - a "Reflection" section is a standard hyperlink at the bottom of each Web page within courses where students are provided with "thinking" exercises - often more advanced questions or points to ponder on. The "Gymnasium" section also assists this learning style. Since a large proportion of on-line communication in hypermedia courses on the Web is asynchronous, the student has the opportunity to reflect before responding to students, lecturers, the content or to assessments.

Theorist: learning best abstract conceptualisation i.e. by understanding the principles of theory - a large proportion of some courses are the narrative elements (i.e. the instructional pages which consist largely of direct information-giving).

5.4.5 Help Information

It is important that comprehensive on-line assistance is provided within hypermedia on-line courses so that it is readily available for on-line students, and also because these courses often use a variety of information technology. In the Wellington Polytechnic On-line Campus, a "Help" section is included to assist students in a variety of areas.

Technical issues covered include more information on down-loading the compressed course file, setting up the Web browser to send e-mail, down-loading applicable plug-ins for the Web browser and the minimum computer configuration required.

General aspects explained are how to enrol for on-line courses, how to communicate on-line with lecturers and other students, how to navigate through the course and how on-line note-taking may be conducted.

5.4.6 Providing an Ability for Students to Publish Directly on the Web or Intranet

An on-line hypermedia course has the potential for students to publish directly on the Web or Intranet. A message board in some of our distributed on-line courses is available for students to publish completed work on the Web. This feature enables students to have their work critiqued by fellow students, to personally experience Web publishing, to have a stronger sense of identification with the course materials and the relevant higher educational institute, and also creates a valuable resource for other current and future students.

5.5 Issues in the Development of On-line Hypermedia Courseware

Two key issues in the development of a on-line hypermedia courseware are discussed.

5.5.1 Systems Development Methodology

It is important to select the appropriate systems development methodology. Among others, two base information systems development methodologies are the traditional (waterfall) model and the prototype (spiral) model.

In the traditional (waterfall) model each of the six phases i.e. implementation, analysis, design, implementation (which includes construction and testing), maintenance and review, are done consecutively - this approach is followed when there is a high degree of certainty about inputs and outcomes.

In the prototype (spiral) model, each of the six phases are basically executed per module / prototype.

The Web technology allows a large degree of intrinsic flexibility due to the course materials being in a "living" format which is in contrast to paper-based, video or CD-ROM materials. Web pages can be changed continuously and furthermore only one source copy needs to be updated.

The spiral systems development methodology was used to develop the courseware in the early stages of the project due to the high degree of uncertainty and because of the flexible nature of the technology. Prototypes were developed which were greatly improved on or totally discarded as the content providers, the graphic designers and the computer specialist grew in their knowledge and experience.

The courseware development now occurs using a combination of the traditional approach and the prototype approach. The investigation is done for the system (i.e. a course or group of courses) and the other phases are carried out per module / prototype.

Whatever systems development methodology is selected, it is important to utilise the inherent flexibility of on-line hypermedia.

5.5.2   Project Team Composition

The following roles have emerged at the Wellington Polytechnic for effective research and development of on-line hypermedia courseware:

- *sponsor* supports the progress of the project

- *project manager* manages the project

- *content provider* provides and ensures the quality of the content (rotating role for each course)

- *creative director / graphic designer* responsible for all visual aspects including creating graphical elements

- *computer specialist* advises and supports on software, hardware and network matters

- *educational director* ensures sound educational processes

- *on-line media developers* integrate the text and graphical elements into on-line hypermedia formats e.g. HTML.

Depending on the size of the project, more than one person can be employed in most of the roles. One of the interesting aspects in such a multi-disciplinary project team is to achieve a balance in educational purposes, graphic design and the capabilities of information technology.

One reason for the success of this project at Wellington Polytechnic is that then people involved are flexible as well as motivated by a personal interest in on-line hypermedia delivery.

Key characteristics of team members have proved to be flexibility, openness to each other and expertise in the area of responsibility.

5.6   Summary

The Internet and Intranet technology has wide implications for higher education and the way that higher educational institutes are managed on strategic, tactical and operational levels.

Distributed on-line education can effectively address the needs of both extra-mural and on-campus students. New approaches, not possible with paper-based educational materials, should be researched further and employed where appropriate.

Asynchronous as well as real-time communication facilities should be used in tandem to support communication over time and space, to address social interaction needs of students and to increase accountability in distributed on-line education.

When distributed on-line education is designed and used effectively, it:

- increases personal motivation and breaks isolation of students

- bridges the boundaries and limitations of time and space

- provides for a variety of learning styles

- provides various navigational paths

- allows students to take more control of their learning

- assists students in learning important supporting skills like time management and how to conduct research.

A paradigm shift needs to take place in higher educational institutes to be able to effectively utilise the new educational media and to design new management and delivery processes.

The rapid growth, wide application, open architecture and natural interfaces of the Internet and Intranets, have left me with no doubt that these phenomena will have a profound effect on the way we educate in the emerging Information Society.

"In a time of drastic change it is the learners who survive; the "learned" find themselves fully equipped to live in a world that no longer exists"   Eric Hoffer

References

1.   Tiffin J and Rajasingham L. (1995) *In Search Of The Virtual Class*. Routledge, London.

2.   The hydi Educational New Media Centre. http://www.wnp.ac.nz/hydi

3.   The Wellington Polytechnic On-line Campus. http://www.wnp.ac.nz/onlinec/virtcamp

4.   Web Development: Web Characteristics. http://www.december.com/web/develop/character.html

5.   Boud D. (1988) *Developing Student Autonomy in Learning.* 2nd Ed. Kogan Page, London.

6.   Wellington Polytechnic Homepage: http://www.wnp.ac.nz

7.   Stair R.M. (1992) *Principles Of Information Systems - A Managerial Approach.* Boyd & Fraser, Boston, MA. p.396.

8.   Hodgson, Munn and Snell (1987*) Beyond Distance Teaching - Towards Open Learning*, Open University Press.

9.   Ideas Exchange. http://www.wnp.ac.nz/onlinec/introcer/alpha/ideasexc.htm

10.   Romiszowski AJ. (1984) *Producing Instructional Systems*. Kogan Page, London.

Chapter 6

Creating a Community of Learning Using Web-based Tools

*Sylvia Wilbur**

Our work aims to extend the concept of computer-supported collaboration in the classroom to include asynchronous activities that take place outside the face-to-face setting. The need for support of collaboration outside the classroom is particularly relevant to Masters-level courses, where students are expected to engage more actively in learning activities by presenting papers, contributing handouts, and engaging in team practices. This chapter discusses a Web-based initiative to develop interactive support for a *community of collaborating learners*.

An approach was taken based on design principles from Computer Supported Cooperative Work (CSCW) research. These principles state that critical dimensions of successful support for collaboration are: effectiveness, engagement, and flexibility. It is essential also that the system be easily modifiable, and can evolve in line with the changing needs of the teaching environment. A system designed on these principles has been implemented and is being successfully used in the context of a Masters course.

6.1   Introduction

Collaborative Learning systems are now an important application domain of Computer Supported Cooperative Work (CSCW). The focus so far has been mainly on distance learning tools, and the development of the 'virtual campus' approach based on media-conferencing, multimedia courseware, and messaging systems [1, 2]. Distance learning enables more students to attend courses without

* Department of Computer Science, Queen Mary and Westfield College, Mile End Road, London, EC1 4NS. Email: sylvia@dcs.qmw.ac.uk

having to be physically present in a classroom, and to study at a time of the students' own choosing by accessing course material on the Web or other servers. For face-to-face teaching, traditional lecture theatres may be enhanced for collaborative learning by the installation of networked workstations and multimedia software tools. These "electronic classrooms" enable two or three students to work together on problem-solving tasks instead of listening passively to the lecturer [3,4]. Computer-support for exploration of Newtonian physics teaching is described in [5], and group programming by children using AlgoBlock is the subject of [6].

Electronic classrooms encourage the development of new styles of teaching and collaborative learning, but only within the face-to-face setting. Our work extends the concept of collaborative learning to include asynchronous activities that occur between classes. The process of learning is not confined to the lecture theatre; the keen student will both prepare for and follow-up on material presented in scheduled classes. Collaboration in these spheres can provide added benefit to both students and teachers when sources of new information are shared and useful tools collaboratively explored. The need for support of collaboration outside the classroom is particularly relevant to Masters courses, where students are expected to engage more actively in course activities, in order to develop the skills appropriate to this level of university education, i.e. skills in investigation, critical analysis, and presentation.

Masters classes in Computer Science at Queen Mary and Westfield College are typically organised as seminars rather than lectures, and students take turns in presenting course topics to their peers. In this way, students effectively collaborate in the teaching process, and learn from each other. Presentations are based on papers and books recommended by a teacher. Students may also be encouraged to contribute information on new sources of material for the course, and to research topics of interest.

There are, however, two difficulties with this approach to Masters teaching. The first challenge lies in making effective use of the various media for sharing and updating source material and administrative information, i.e. paper, Web pages, and email. Problems here include the lack of integration, consistency and coherent structure for information spread across these various media. The second challenge is to engage the students actively in the various pedagogic processes, and in learning as a collaborative activity. The transition to this new paradigm seems to be difficult for some students, accustomed to a more passive, individual style of learning. The key to the solution to this problem lies in promoting the feeling of belonging to the group, and in promoting awareness of how everyone is contributing.

The approach we have developed aims to increase student motivation and make learning more effective, by promoting a new computer-supported paradigm for learning. This paradigm seeks to replace the traditional divide between teachers and students by a *community of collaborating learners*. For each course of study, its community of learners jointly explore, present, and share material and tools.

And by seeking out new sources of information, each learner augments the group's knowledge of the area.

The Web-based tools we have built to support this new approach draws extensively on ideas and principles from Computer Supported Cooperative Work (CSCW). This chapter describes how the application of CSCW principles to the specific requirements of a Masters course has enabled us to develop a low-cost course environment that is popular with our students and effective for its purpose.

6.2 Application of CSCW Principles to a Masters Course

The motivation for developing a collaborative environment for Masters courses has already been outlined: mainly, the requirement to motivate students to participate more actively in their Masters courses, plus the need to maintain a central source of up-to-date base of specialist knowledge. By developing a shared computer-based environment for the course, accessible over a network, we aim to meet these requirements more effectively than is possible with current media. We begin by providing more detail on the problems experienced with current media.

6.2.1 The Problem Space

Collaboration by the students in the teaching process - i.e. by making presentations - is a central feature of our Masters courses. The process of commitment to making a presentation was carried out in various ways: in conversation with the teacher, by email, or by annotating a printed list of papers. An integrated record of which students had made presentations, and which papers remained to be allocated a speaker, was difficult to maintain in this situation. Each presenter is expected to prepare overhead transparencies, and to make copies available to the audience. In the past, paper copies were provided, and sometimes were not available until sometime after the class. Other activities involving student/teacher interaction include coursework specification, hand-in, and return after assessment. In the past, paper has been the main medium for coursework submission, except in the case of programming exercises.

In addition to the need to support teacher/student collaboration more effectively, we have the requirement to handle course information and source material in a more coherent way. For general course information, Web pages are used, but these have not always been regularly updated due to a lack of tools to do this rapidly. Important changes that do not get recorded on the appropriate Web pages can cause confusion among students. Course material is drawn from books and published papers, which are handed out at the start of the course. Other sources of information, such as URLs, are provided at appropriate times. Email and mailing lists are used for communication between classes.

In summary, then, the information needed to deliver and organise the course has been spread across a variety of media in a rather disorganised way, making the delivery of the course less effective than we would wish. Also, students are sometimes reluctant to contribute presentations and participate actively in course activities. Finally, Masters students are frequently accommodated off-campus and may work part-time, making it difficult to share information that is only available on site.

6.2.2   Solutions Based on CSCW Principles and the Web

We proposed a solution to the problems outlined above, based on a CSCW approach. CSCW research states that collaboration only really works when the people involved have fully grasped the group concept, and can appreciate its benefits. A group has been defined as 'a relatively closed and fixed ensemble of people sharing the same goal and engaged in direct communication' [7]. A major aim of the CSCW approach is therefore to promote a feeling of 'belonging' to the group and identification with its goals.

A theory of coordination of groupwork states that the achievement of *goals* relies on the cooperation of the *actors* responsible for carrying out the necessary *activities* of the group [8]. Adopting this approach, Figure 6.1. maps the abstractions of *goals, actors, and activities* to a Masters course.

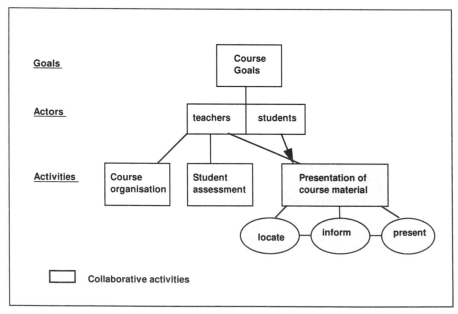

Figure 6.1. Collaborative aspects of Masters course provision.

Some activities, such as the setting of examinations and coursework assessment, must remain the sole preserve of those officially designated the role of course (i.e. teachers). Students, however, can increasingly contribute to the gathering and presentation of course material, drawing on the huge sources of information provided on the World Wide Web.

Concerning group awareness, the work of Buxton and Sellen [9] and Ensor [10] shows that the impression of being part of a group can be created at the user interface to a CSCW system by:

- identifying the members of the group, and their roles

- showing how each member is contributing to group activities

- providing easy access to channels for interpersonal communication

- providing awareness information, i.e. of who else is around to talk to in the virtual environment.

A group collaborating on a long-term basis acquires documents and tools needed for their shared tasks. They may also need to maintain records of meetings, decisions made, and workplans. An electronic environment can provide a long-term group with a persistent, shared virtual place, accessible over a network, where the files, documents, applications, and toolkits needed for the group's tasks can be stored. The requirements for such a persistent place, or 'virtual meeting room' have been realised in systems such as Rapport [10] and DIVA [11]. For a Masters course, a persistent virtual environment can provide a single place where all information relating to the organisation of the course can be stored and maintained in a consistent way. Students and teachers meet face-to-face for weekly seminars, but can visit the virtual environment for information-sharing and asynchronous collaboration at other times. This approach offers a solution to the problems of handling course information, described earlier.

Finally, issues about privacy and ownership of information in the environment are important, and appropriate access controls must be provided.

6.3   Dimensions of Course Support

Identification of critical aspects of computer-support provides a set of useful dimensions for guiding design and evaluation. The dimensions of interest are:

Effectiveness: The questions here are, *does the virtual room effectively support the various asynchronous activities of the group, and provide easy access to information on course material and organisation?* An important issue here is whether use of electronic media is an improvement on previous paper-based methods. Ease of access should include access from home and the workplace (for part-time students) via modem connections. Ease of navigation, and user interface design are also important. Effectiveness should be evaluated from the point of view of both teachers and students.

Extensibility and flexibility: *To what extent can the system be easily changed and extended? Also, can the system be adapted to meet the needs of other courses?* All courses tend to change year-by-year, to reflect advances in the area, or the perspective of a new teacher. Computer-based support should enable these changes to be incorporated as easily as possible. Similarly, the structure of the system should be flexible enough to suit a range of courses.

Engagement: *How motivated are students to contribute to course activities?* Useful measures here include: how much additional source material is added by students; how often do they visit the environment, and for what purpose? Comparison should be made with other courses using traditional media such as paper and email.

The extent and quality of engagement with a virtual teaching environment reflects the level of participation by teachers as well as by students. Teachers provide the core curriculum, the course structure, and a list of required reading on each topic. Without this information, students are unable, for example, to volunteer ('sign-up') to make a presentation to the class on a topic of their choice. Information concerning new sources of course material is contributed by both teachers and students.

6.4   Design Issues

In line with our previous discussion, the design goals for building a collaborative environment for the course were:

- to promote the group concept among teachers and students

- to provide a persistent 'place' for information-sharing and coordination of activities

- to support specific tasks involving asynchronous collaboration.

The nature of the support provided is explained below.

6.4.1   Support for the Group Concept

This involves creating awareness at the user interface of who is in the group, what their role is, and what they have contributed. Ideally, images, photographs, or icons representing members can be used, although this raises problems when the group is rather large. Links to personal information help people to feel acquainted with each other, and our design includes a registration facility for members to provide their names and links to personal Web pages. New students register with a course, and can see a list of all other registered students and their email addresses.

6.4.2 Properties of a Virtual Course Environment

The environment should provide a shared place for storing and accessing group documents for the duration of the course, that is, a place accessible over a network where students and teachers can at any time browse, deposit and update information relating to the course . Some of this data relates to course organisation, including curriculum details, specifications of items of work students are required to complete, and examination details. Students can view this information, but only the teacher can update it. For each topic covered by the course, relevant source material must be listed (textbook references, journal papers, Web pages, etc.). Teachers provide references to essential source material, but students are encouraged to amplify this with information on additional sources they have discovered. Access to notes/transparencies accompanying each weekly presentation should also be available. All of these documents should be easily accessible at the user interface, with appropriate access controls. Some additional status information is also required by the teacher; for example, how many papers still lack presenters.

Other desirable properties of the environment are that it should be private to the group that owns it, if this is required. Easy access to channels for interpersonal communication is also desirable, for example, over video-conferencing or email. Unplanned encounters in a virtual environment can also be supported by the system noticing when two users have entered the shared workspace simultaneously. Each user can be notified of the other's presence, and given the opportunity to communicate over audio and video (A/V) channels. Real-time A/V facilities are, however, hard to provide in a Local Area Network environment where bandwidth is limited.

6.4.3 Support for Asynchronous Collaborative Tasks

The following tasks are currently supported by the system we have built for a Masters course, based on Web pages and forms. A user (teacher or student) performing one or more of these tasks is contributing asynchronously to the course, in their capacity as a member of the community of learners.

1 Tasks associated with presentations of course material to a class by a student:

- provide list of papers to be read by all students in preparation for seminars, each paper to be presented by one student [teacher]

- select a paper and sign-up to present it (with 'undo' facility) [student]

- attach file (containing the transparencies/notes for the seminar) at the appropriate point in the list of papers [student].

The teacher or student who performed each sub-task owns the relevant information, and only he/she can modify it. For example, if a student signs-up for a paper, it should not be possible for another student to alter this. Similarly, electronic copies of transparencies or notes can be modified only by the author.

2   Information-sharing, i.e. source material for course topics, in various media [contributed by both teachers and students]:

*   adding references for papers, CD-ROMs, Web pages, etc. to lists

*   deleting out-of-date information

*   accessing information on source material for specific topics.

3   Tasks related to course organisation and student assessment:

*   provide curriculum, course structure, requirements, etc. [course organiser]

*   provide specifications of required work [course organiser]

*   submit required work for assessment [students]

*   receive, assess, and return students' work [course organiser].

Clearly, the various kinds of data exchanged in the execution of these tasks must be protected from unauthorised access.

Another important design issue is ease of navigation among the various kinds of information available, and among activities. The browsing facilities provided by tools such as Netscape for accessing the Web are, of course, ideally suited to this purpose. Finally, although the design metaphor for our system fits well with the 'virtual room' approach adopted by projects such as Rapport [10, 13], we have not attempted as yet to design an interface to the Web based on the appearance of a physical room.

6.5   Implementation

It was decided to build a pilot implementation of a system to support Masters students taking a course in Multimedia Systems. A pilot implementation would enable us to carry out early evaluation of the approach, and select the most appropriate development environment. Two potential environments were initially identified: Lotus Notes R.4 and the World Wide Web. Both systems incorporate useful features for groupwork support. Lotus Notes supports views of shared, replicated databases, provides a built-in editor for document production, fine-grained access controls, and email facilities. The Notes R.4 development environment includes a new version of its scripting language enriched with Lotus Notes classes, a significant improvement on earlier versions. User interface development in R4 is also more flexible than before. However, despite these improvements, user interface design is still constrained by the views and menus approach for interaction with databases, and has no concept of non-linear structuring of information. The Web, on the other hand, supports the hypermedia approach, and developers can now choose from a wide variety of languages and development tools, including Perl, Neoscript and Java. Dynamic updating of information is, however, still a problem on the Web, although the use of forms provides a partial solution. Protection for Web-based information is typically based on capabilities, and is less flexible than the Notes mechanisms.

In order to compare the two environments, pilot systems were developed on both the Lotus Notes and Web platforms, using the design approach outlined above. Both versions were then informally evaluated by a small group of Masters students. The Notes application enabled access to databases, forms and documents to be controlled very flexibly, and had the advantage of an in-built editor; however, students found navigation between menus and views confusing, and commented negatively on the general layout of the user interface. The Web-based version was significantly more popular (although account must be taken of the fact that subjects were already familiar with navigating in a Web environment). From the application developer's point of view, Neoscript for the Web was judged easier to learn and more flexible to work with than the scripting environment for R4 Notes, even though she had been trained in Notes development and had previous experience. Neoscript is, however, an unsupported language, and several bugs in the system were discovered during implementation. A more detailed evaluation and comparison of the pilot implementations is published elsewhere [14].

On the basis of this evaluation, the Web-based application was selected for further refinement and development, and this process is now underway. The system is in regular use for the course, and feedback from the students will aid the development process.

Figure 6.2. shows the top-level page for Version 1 of the Web version of the application. This is the entry point to the environment, where course goals are described. In the left frame, links to people (i.e. the group members, comprising teachers and students) and to activities provide the other elements of a framework supporting the fundamental concepts of groupwork - goals, actors, and activities. Students register their names and passwords, and their names then appear in the list of people involved in the course. Clicking on 'Modules' takes the user to the page where course modules are described and the papers for presentation are listed. Located next to each paper, a *sign* button enables a student to sign-up for a paper. Immediately a paper has been signed-for, *sign* disappears and is replaced by buttons that allow the student to *attach* the notes he/she has prepared, or to *undo* the sign-up process.

The Activities link allows access to specifications of required work, and a mechanism for submitting completed items. Work is returned to each student in a similar way after assessment by the teacher. Finally, the link to additional material enables students and teachers to view the latest additions to lists of source material in various media, and to add or remove items.

6.6   Informal Evaluation

The initial evaluation of the pilot Web application was positive overall, but also identified various design deficiencies. Subjects were given tasks to carry out, and informal observation techniques and questionnaires were used to evaluate the user interface and the overall functionality of the system. Tasks included: signing for a paper and attaching presentation notes; coursework submission and return; viewing and adding source material. Further details of this evaluation are given in [14].

Some weaknesses in the system could be dealt with satisfactorily, for example, an 'undo' facility was needed for the activity of signing for a paper, and when information had been erroneously added in the wrong place. Other problems stemmed from acknowledged weaknesses of the Web system itself - for example, ease of updating information. Although forms can be designed to enable new data to be entered, the structure and length of the data is constrained by the design of the form, and error-handling can be poor. Also, feedback on the changes is not received immediately - users must reload the relevant page. Despite these slight drawbacks, subjects found the system easy to understand and navigate. The use of page frames enabled users to navigate the environment easily, and switch quickly between different activities.

This page:	**MSc in Advanced Methods In Computer Science**
<u>Aims of the course</u>	
	Multimedia Systems
Links	
	• **Aims of the course**
<u>Registration</u>	
	We aim to do the following:
<u>Essential Info</u>	
	- study, discuss and research into all aspects of multimedia systems
<u>People</u>	
<u>Modules</u>	**- explore the application and use of multimedia**
<u>Activities</u>	
	- develop knowledge of and skills in multimedia programming abstractions.
<u>Additional Material</u>	

Figure 6.2. Entry to the Web-based environment for a Masters course.

With reference to the dimensions of course support discussed in Section 6.3, the system appeared effective in meeting the requirements for the course. Course teachers have provided information on course material, and students have used the system to volunteer to make presentations and contribute their own material. New information - relevant publications, copies of presentation slides, useful URLs, etc. can easily be added, and the system indicates who contributed each new piece of information. The degree of engagement with the environment, and the effect of this on student motivation generally, must be gauged over time, but looks very positive so far. Extensibility will be tested at a later stage, when new features are incorporated, and the application is adapted for other courses.

Various technical problems were encountered, not least the well-known difficulties of entering persistent state information from a Web page and allowing students to add new pages into the overall structure. Version 2 of the system is now under development, based on a Tcl/tk interface.

6.7   Conclusions

The main goal of this work has been to support a new paradigm for Masters courses, based on a community of teachers and students collaborating on the various activities required by a course on Multimedia Systems. Achieving this goal meant that we had to motivate students to actively engage in the various course activities, rather than just passively attend classes. The approach we took was to adopt principles from CSCW research - providing support for group awareness, coordination of asynchronous activities, and a persistent shared study space that students could visit at any time. Facilities provided by the Web provided the basic platform for our implementation, and these were largely successful once the problem of creating persistent files during run-time was overcome. In general, the students seem to have enjoyed the experience, although no formal evaluation has been carried out so far.

For the future, we plan to extend the system by making it easier for students to add their own notes at appropriate points and by improving the structure of course information. Other features to track student participation and enable coursework handins will also be added. We will also investigate the usefulness of supporting 'chance encounters' in the environment. More extensive evaluations are also planned.

Acknowledgements

This work was carried out as part of the ACOL project, and the authors would like to thank their partners in the project (Steve Wilbur, Stephen Hailes, and Reza Hazemi) for their help and encouragement. Funding for the project was provided by UKERNA, and we were grateful for their support.

References

1. Hiltz S.R. (1994) *The Virtual Classroom - Learning without limits via computer networks.* Ablex Publishing. Norwood, NY.

2. Thomas P.J. and Tuckett J. (1996) Accessing the Digital Campus and the Digital Library. *Proceedings of 3D and Multimedia on the Internet, WWW and Networks.* Bradford.

3. Shneiderman B, Alavi M, Norman K, and Borkowski EY. (1995) Windows of Opportunity in Electronic Classrooms. *Communications of ACM,* 38, 11, 19-24.

4. Narayanan N.H., Hmelo C.E., Petrushin V. *et al.* (1995) Computational Support for Collaborative Learning through Generative Problem Solving. *Proceedings of CSCL 95 Computer Support for Collaborative Learning.* Indiana. USA. 247-253.

5. Cockburn A. and Greenberg S. (1995) TurboTurtle: A Collaborative Microworld for Exploring Newtonian Physics. *Proceedings of CSCL 95 Computer Support for Collaborative Learning.* Indiana. USA. 62-74.

6. Suzuki H. and Kato H. (1995) Interaction-Level Support for Collaborative Learning: AlgoBlock - An Open Programming Language. *Proceedings of CSCL 95 Computer Support for Collaborative Learning.* Indiana. USA. 349-355.

7. Bannon L.J. and Schmidt K. (1991) CSCW: Four Characters in Search of a Context. *Studies in Computer-Supported Cooperative Work,* Bowers and Benford (Eds). Elsevier Science Publishers.

8. Malone T.W. and Crowston K. (1991) What is coordination theory and how can it help design cooperative work systems? *Proceedings of CSCW 90,* Los Angeles. ACM Press.

9. Buxton B., Sellen A. and Sheasby M. (1997) User Interfaces to Multiparty Conferencing. *Video-Mediated Communication.* Finn K. Sellen A. and Wilbur S. (Eds). Lawrence Erlbaum Assoc. 385-400.

10. Ensor, J.R. (1997) Virtual Meeting Rooms. *Video-Mediated Communication.* (Eds). Finn K., Sellen A. and Wilbur S. Lawrence Erlbaum Associates. 415-435.

11. Sohlenkamp M.. and Chwelos G. (1994) Integrating Communication, Cooperation, and Awareness: The DIVA Virtual Office Environment. Proceedings of CSCW 94, Chapel Hill, North Carolina.

12. Norman D.A. and Spohrer J.C. (1996) Learner-Centred Education. *Communications of the ACM.* 39, 4 (April).

13. Seligmann, D.D., Mercuri, R.T., and Edmark P. (1995) Providing Assurances in a Multimedia Environment. *Proceedings of Human Factors in Computing Systems,* ACM SIGCHI '95, Denver Colorado. 250-256.

14. Hazemi R., Hailes S., Pitsika M., Wilbur S.R. and Wilbur S.B. (1997) *Final deliverable of the ACOL project.* University College London (December 1997)

Chapter 7

Using the WWW for Teaching and Learning: Raising Awareness within University College London

Kim Issroff* and Reza Hazemi **

The majority of the use of the World Wide Web within higher education is currently passive. The WWW is largely used as a medium for providing static information. Only a very limited number of institutions use the WWW for interactive learning and teaching. This chapter discusses the experiences of one institution in trying to encourage active use of the WWW for teaching and learning.

This chapter starts by reviewing current theory and practice regarding the use of the WWW in higher education. It then highlights aspects of teaching and learning which can be particularly well supported by Web-based learning environments. A case study describes the current situation at University College London (UCL) and documents a short project to encourage effective use of the WWW within UCL. The chapter concludes with a discussion of the issues and factors which influence active use of the WWW within higher education.

7.1   Introduction

The WWW has a great potential to be used as a teaching and learning medium. The Web can be used as a domain for teachers to provide information and for learners to access information. It can also be used as a medium for communication between

* Higher Education Research and Development Unit, University College London, Gower Street, London, WC1E 6BT, U.K. Email: K.Issroff@ucl.ac.uk
** (Department of Computer Science), University College London, Gower Street, London, WC1E 6BT, U.K. Email: R.Hazemi@cs.ucl.ac.uk

learners and teachers. This communication can be synchronous or asynchronous. The WWW can be used to support teaching and learning by encouraging people to be more active in their studying. It can also be used for distance learning by providing coursework and on-line communication facilities. It is thought that a broader range of students can be accommodated in Higher Education if the WWW is used to support their learning.

Assessment tasks can be handled using the WWW. The processing of multiple choice questions is fairly easy. However, these sorts of tasks can also be used for self-study and are not confined to assessment. Assessment of tasks requiring free text (for example, essays) is more problematic. At present, the lack of good pattern matching recognition software makes it virtually impossible to use the WWW for this type of assessment, and email is more appropriate for the submission of free text type questions. Other activities which could be performed using the Web and the Internet include discussion, debates, group projects, submitting course work, etc.

The WWW has the potential to change the nature of teaching and learning in Higher Education. Currently, the level of usage of the WWW for teaching and learning is in its early stages and it is the appropriate time to experiment, investigate and to set the standards. An appropriate strategy at this time is maybe to get acquainted with the resources, and to decide how to use them [1].

In this chapter the authors present a project which encouraged effective use of the WWW in University College London (UCL) for teaching and learning. The chapter describes a Web-based portfolio which was developed in order to show staff the range of activities that the WWW can support.

7.2   The Potential of the WWW in Higher Education

Groupware is an umbrella term for software which support collaboration, enabling people to work together on-line without space or time restriction. There are ever increasing groupware products in the market enabling this collaboration, including Lotus Notes, Microsoft Exchange, Collabra Share, etc.

Since its first appearance in late 80's, the WWW has become more and more widespread and is a very useful tool for information access and sharing. The recent popularity of the use and development of the Internet and WWW resources has created new opportunities for using the Web for teaching and learning. There are now numerous publications and tools for what is termed the Virtual Classroom [2] or Virtual University [3], and given the open nature, global scope and availability of the Internet and the Web, they are a potential platform to support teaching and learning.

What are the advantages of using the WWW in education? While it is obvious that the WWW provides access to vast amounts of information, the potential of the

WWW is more than just an alternative method for the delivery of existing course material. The WWW can support innovative forms of teaching and learning (although at present, it is not used in this way). We would firstly like to distinguish between active and passive use of the WWW. This is analogous to the distinction between active and passive learning. Active learning is an umbrella term, encompassing a plethora of concepts but is generally understood to include the student seeking a search for meaning and understanding; the student having responsibility for their learning; an emphasis on skills as well as knowledge and an approach to students' study which includes the wider career and social setting [4]. These can be linked to deep (active) and surface (passive) approaches to learning [5], however, in reality most students adopt these approaches at different times, depending on the demands of the course. This can also be thought of as taking a student-centred approach to the use of the WWW in teaching and learning.

Passive use of the WWW for teaching and learning occurs when students simply use the WWW to gain access to information. For example, if a lecturer puts their course notes on the WWW, the students will, in all likelihood, print them out, and take them home (and perhaps read them!). However, the WWW can be used for active learning, for example, by the use of discussion fora, where students actively post messages about a subject relevant to their course.[12]

However, there are significant difficulties to be overcome in order to ensure that we make effective use of the WWW for active learning. In order to do this, we need to ensure that we structure our Web-based materials and applications in such a way as to foster active learning. But this may not be sufficient. Our students' attitudes towards their learning may also prevent active use of the WWW for teaching and learning. Daniels [6] points out that learner-centred thinking can be at odds with what students want. He highlights the need to have students who are prepared to change from traditional teaching methods to the more student-centred use of technology for teaching. Forsyth [7] discusses the ways in which the use of the WWW in teaching and learning will change the role of the student. He characterises this as changing from "... primarily being a recipient to one of being participant. ... the learner becomes a searcher with a level of responsibility for their learning that is generally not available in face-to-face teaching" (page 32).

However, it is not just the role of the student which changes, the role of the teacher changes as well. Forsyth [7] points out that the teacher is no longer the person who has all knowledge, but becomes a monitor and mentor with a less instructional role.

Tools are being developed which will increase effective active use of WWW for asynchronous collaboration. These tools enable automatic processing of students' records and assessment which has the advantage of increasing awareness and collaboration between academics and students by enabling academics to keep track of student progress and by enabling students to monitor other students' progress as well as reducing the administration load on academics.

---

[12] We would argue that even when students have a series of linked pages about their course, which they navigate in order to learn, this is still passive use of the WWW, as students do not have to actively engage with the information.

A further advantage of using the WWW for teaching and learning is that its use is increasing rapidly, which means that many members of staff and students are able to use a browser and understand the basic concepts involved in using the WWW. Thus the need for training is diminished. Additionally, the WWW will be increasingly closely integrated with staff and students' existing computer-based working environments.

Exponential increase in use of PCs, modems and WWW browsers increases the accessibility to course material and tools. It also removes the location and time restrictions. Students are no longer bound to studying at certain times, they can access information and tools for their learning whenever they wish, from any location they want as long as they have access to a WWW browser.

Course notes and course materials are usually written in HTML (HyperText Markup Language). There are now editors that allow the user to create HTML documents without knowing any HTML (for example the built-in editor in Netscape). There are also tools which enable automatic conversion of electronic copy of material to HTML format. These enable lecturers to rapidly produce course information which is accessible to students.

7.3   Current Use of WWW

The vast majority of Higher Education institutions use the WWW for providing information such as: publicity, course notes, staff portfolios, an address book, etc. In another world the WWW is only used for dissemination of data.

What was once provided on paper and sent through postal mail can now be delivered through electronic mailing lists or the World Wide Web [3]. But this new medium does not take full advantage of the technology as an enabler of reengineering of the education process itself [8].

There is an ever increasing number of Web sites however which go beyond passive presentation of material. Some examples are described below. *The World Lecture Hall* (http://www.utexas.edu/world/lecture/index.html) contains several hundred links to courses created by faculty members worldwide who are using the WWW to deliver class materials. It contains course syllabi, assignments, lecture notes, exams, class calendars, multimedia textbooks, etc.

Peterson's   Education   Center   (http://www.petersons.com:8080/)   contains information on all the courses available at US colleges and universities.

The *City University of Hong Kong* (http://wwwtools.cityu.edu.hk/) gives links to a range of sites with WWW tools for teaching and provides an introduction to using the WWW for teaching.

The *Virtual-seminars for teaching and learning* (http://info.ox.ac.uk/jtap/) outlines a project called virtual seminars aimed at supplying a tool for distance learning as well as a role model for other academics to see how effective modern technology can be used in delivering remote educational resources.

Electronic Education Environment [3] provides the flexibility needed to match market demand with customised contents. When a student registers for a certain course, the system automatically matches the student with one or more instructors. The students pay for the resources they use.

Use of computer mediated communication for teaching and learning show that [2]:

- Mastery of course material is equal or superior to that in traditional classrooms

- Students report higher levels of subjective satisfaction compared with a traditional classroom on a number of dimensions, including access to their instructors, and overall quality of the educational experience

- Students perceive the experience as *group learning* rather than individual learning.

7.4 UCL's Use of the WWW for Teaching and Learning

UCL's current position is very similar to many other Higher Education institutions in that the majority of the use of the WWW is to provide static information. All departments (academic and support) who make use of the WWW use it for publicity and provide general information. On the teaching side, just under 50% provide course materials and syllabi, and less than 10% provide other information such as assessment information, timetables, links to other relevant pages etc.

Our review of UCL's WWW pages found three teaching applications which are currently used for active teaching and learning. These is a multiple choice questionnaire application (in Computer Science) used for students, submitting coursework, which is automatically marked and a copy of the mark is sent to the lecturer and the student; a quiz application (in Physiology) which is used for coursework; and a similar application (in Phonetics and Linguistics) which includes an interface for creating questions. Additionally, we found two projects which are developing Web-based coursework (English and Mathematics) but these are not currently used with students.

Additionally, feedback from staff development courses on using Information Technology in teaching and learning, had indicated that while many members of staff use the WWW for research, they have little conception of its potential for teaching and learning.

Given this situation, we decided to establish our project, Collaboration in Higher Education using Web (CHEW) to encourage active use of the WWW for teaching and learning in UCL. Although the project includes some development work, the overriding aim is to increase awareness of the ways in which the WWW can be used for teaching and learning.

7.5   Our Approach to Encouraging the Use of the WWW: CHEW

CHEW was a collaboration between the Department of Computer Science in UCL and Higher Education Development Unit which carries out research and development in learning and teaching in UCL. A portfolio of Web-based tools was developed and three workshops were held to demonstrate these tools and encourage the computer literate and non-literate to gain hands-on experience of using these tools for teaching. However, we initially needed to find out what sorts of applications and support our staff required. We therefore interviewed a range of staff and these interviews are discussed in Section 7.5.1. This is followed by a discussion of the approach that we took to introducing our staff to the range of activities using the WWW available to them for use in their teaching.

7.5.1   Interviewing the Staff

We identified several members of staff across a range of disciplines who either had expressed an interest in using the WWW for their teaching or who were thought to be knowledgeable about the WWW and the teaching activities within their departments.

We individually interviewed these members of staff, and asked them broad questions about how they currently use the WWW for teaching, how other people in their department use the WWW for teaching, what they would ideally like to use the WWW for, if they had seen anything they thought we should look at and whether or not they would be prepared to take part in an evaluation.

While some members of staff were already actively using the WWW for teaching, the majority of staff said that their departments were only using the WWW for providing passive information, much of this designed for publicity rather than for teaching. When asked about how they ideally would like to use the WWW in their teaching, many of them shrugged their shoulders and said that they were unclear of the potential of the WWW to support their teaching.

One member of staff was particularly imaginative in the ways in which he would ideally like an Web-based application to function. He taught on a Masters course which was distributed across several departments and colleges. The students had to complete a dissertation and he felt that the WWW could be used to enable staff to keep track of their students' progress and to encourage communication between students and between students and staff.

However, it was clear from our interviews that the vast majority of staff had no conception of how the WWW could be used in their teaching and we therefore decided to develop a Web-based portfolio of Web-based applications which have been used to introduce staff to the use of the WWW in their teaching.

7.5.2 Why a Portfolio Approach?

In order to encourage staff to use the WWW for teaching and learning, we needed to create a process of change. According to Lloyd [9] the first phase of this sort of change is a cognitive process, in that it involves awareness. This is followed by understanding, support, involvement and commitment (the latter being a social process). Thus under this model of change, we needed to raise awareness, and move towards understanding, with the hope that support, involvement and commitment would follow.

The decision to develop a portfolio rather than spend all our time on developing particular applications and helping staff to integrate them into their teaching, was driven by the information obtained from our interviews and discussions with members of staff. Developing a portfolio meant that we could include a large number of different types of Web-based applications that can be used in teaching and learning and these could easily be shown to members of staff. Additionally, it meant that staff could explore these applications in their own time, and from a variety of locations. This seemed to be the most cost-effective way of raising awareness.

7.5.3 Description of the Portfolio

Our aim was to increase awareness amongst staff, demonstrating how the WWW and the Internet can be used to suport teaching and learning activities on line. We wanted to create a reference point where staff could search the Net for further information, and share information.

Our portfolio contains five sections which are described in this section. As a source of dissemination of information we have also added links to example courses on the Web and created a discussion fora.

Monitoring students' progress
This application consists of forms which students fill in detailing their current progress on their projects. Once a student has filled in the form it is saved on the server and is used as a mode of interaction between the student, instructor and other students. Some parts of the form have restricted access for that particular student, the supervisor and the course tutor.

The application incorporates a discussion forum for each project and students use this forum for discussion about their dissertation. There is a list of all the dissertation titles and keywords, which can be searched.

The aims of this tool are:

- To allow academic staff to keep track of students' progress

- To help students and staff to be aware of the nature and extent of other student projects on the course

- To foster effective communication between students and staff

- To foster effective communication between students

- To give students access to other students who may be facing or have overcome the same difficulties

- To enable students to produce a portfolio of their progress and development during the course of their dissertation, which could be used for assessment purposes or for job applications

- To enable additional informal input from external experts

- To help students to reflect on their progress during their dissertations.

Authoring and using multiple choice questions on the WWW

This tool allows lecturers to create quizzes which students can access. The QUestion and Answer System for the Internet (QUASI) was developed by Kevin Boone in the Physiology Department. It incorporates confidence assessment and immediate feedback. The CGI scripts processes a question at a time and the file processing is done using the C programming language.

Multiple Choice Questions (MCQ) for assessed coursework on the WWW

This tool allows lecturers to create MCQ for coursework and is used by students to submit their coursework and get feedback on the answers and marks.

When a student starts a coursework, this tool selects a random set of questions from the pool of questions and presents it to the student. In other words each student is presented with a different set of questions. Developing a pool of questions is time-consuming but is one method of preventing cheating..

After students enter their names, a selection of question sets become available. Students select the question set they wish to practice or be tested on. When they start, they are presented with a page of questions concerning their chosen subject. Each question has four answers. Students see a row of four buttons for each answer. They select the appropriate button to indicate whether they think the answer is correct, partly correct or wrong. If they are not sure about an answer, they choose the "Don't know" button. The purpose is to assess each answer list for a question in these terms, rather than just picking one correct one. The score they can achieve for a test depends on how well they assess all the different options.

Once students have assessed all the options to all questions they click the "submit" button. Their responses are processed and results appear in a few seconds. If they score less than 2 marks for a question, they are given some advice which should help them to improve.

Students may choose to practice on a set of coursework questions, or attempt assessed coursework questions. The practice option allows them to get an idea of the kind of questions they will face when taking the assessed coursework, and look identical to the real coursework. The question sets are made up of ten variants of each question, which are selected at random and therefore students are unlikely to ever receive the same set of questions.

As a result of this project, a new tool is now being developed at UCL's Department of Computer Science called TACO (Teaching and Coursework On-line) which will enhance the functionality described above.

Collection of example courses on the WWW

One of our aims was to create a reference point which instructors could use as an initial step for surfing the net. As explained in Section 3, we looked at over 50 WWW pages provided by institutions worldwide. We have made a collection of these WWW sites available, with a brief explanation of each course and the interesting features and links to institutions. The idea was to enable staff to experience the range of teaching and learning activities which can be supported by the Web, and to provide example courses to be used as reference models.

Discussion fora

Although there is a huge potential for enhancing communication for teaching and learning using the WWW, this is barely used within institutions and UCL is no exception.

There are now tools widely available (e.g. Hypermail) which can be used for this purpose. Discussions with staff indicate that they do not know how to create discussion fora. We have created a discussion database for this project and provided pages which can guide staff through the steps that are needed to create a discussion fora on UCL's network.

7.6   Tools for Creating Courseware

There are now ever increasing number of products that could be used for the development of teaching and learning applications. When we were searching for a tool to develop our applications we looked at a number of these tools. The tools that we looked at include: WebCT (http://homebrew.cs.ubc.ca/webct), JTAP's

Virtual Seminars for Teaching (http://info.ox.ac.uk/ctitext/service), W3LP (http://www.comp.it.brighton.ac.uk/w3lessonware).

At the time of our survey, WebCT was the most developed application and supported a wide range of teaching and learning applications. We therefore decided to use it for our development tool. The main reason for selecting WebCT was because it can be used to create Web-based environments with little or no technical expertise, which is an important criteria because not all members of every faculty is computer-literate.

An article in PCWeek (http://www8.zdnet.com/pcweek/reviews/0818/18ibt.html) evaluated a number of tools and concluded that *Internet-based training tools run a close race*, (on a scale of 0-100 all scored between 82-98.).

7.7   The Workshops

Although theoretically staff could access the WWW page of the portfolio from their own office, we felt it was necessary to hold workshops, partly as an awareness-raising exercise, but also so that we could do some hand-holding for those who needed it. Our workshops were designed to introduce staff to use of the WWW for teaching and learning, to demonstrate the portfolio, to provide time for discussion of the portfolio and to give staff hands-on experience with the applications within the portfolio. This was followed by supporting and helping interested lecturers in creating their own Web-based course material.

In fact, we were overwhelmed with responses to our invitations to attend the workshops, and we had to put on an extra workshop. Over 50 people attended the workshops, and over 40 expressed an interest, but could not attend. In our experience, these numbers are very high in relation to other courses, and three months later, staff are still contacting us expressing interest in the project.

We evaluated the workshops and our approach by sending an email questionnaire to all the participants. The results of the questionnaire is summarised in Table 7.1.

One of the problems in large institutions such as UCL is lack of funding. This problem coupled with the fast speed of change in computing technology results in a very slow upgrade of very large number of PCs. The main reason for people saying that they were not likely to use the student management tools was because they can not access it from the UCL computer clusters which use Windows 3.1. (Our tool is based on Java technology which is not supported by Windows 3.1).

In reply to the question of what support they need, respondents wanted hands-on help and advice with setting up tools. They also want to be kept informed of new techniques and developments.

The range of staff knowledge and experience with Web-based tools made things difficult within the workshops. The level of knowledge ranged from people who had never seen a Web browser to those who provide all their course material on the

Web and in future, we need to pay close attention to the ways in which we support the different skill levels.

We think our approach of holding workshops was very useful because it created awareness to all groups of users about using the Web for teaching and learning.

Question	Very interesting/ likely %	Interesting/ likely %	Not interesting/ likely %
How useful did you find the workshop?	40	53	7
How useful did you find the student management tool?	27	60	13
How likely are you to use the student management tool?		20	80
How interesting did you find the MCQ tool?	53	40	7
How likely are you to use the MCQ tool?	13	20	67
How interesting did you find the quiz tool?	53	40	7
How likely are you to use the quiz tool?	13	27	60
How interesting did you find the collection of the example courses?	27	40	13
How likely are you to use the collection of example courses?	7	20	73
How likely are you to use discussion fora in your teaching?		47	53
How likely are you to use the discussion forum on using the Web in teaching and learning		47	53

Table 7.1. Summary of responses to the questionnaire.

7.8   Conclusions

This chapter has described the CHEW project and the way in which it tried to raise awareness amongst academic staff at UCL. The project was successful in that it has raised awareness amongst staff and there is now a portfolio of materials for teaching for staff use. The TACO (Teaching and Coursework On-line) application has been developed and is being piloted in a range of departments. However, we do not know how many members of staff will actually use the information and developments from the project in their teaching.

Through the course of the project, we identified several difficulties with the use of the WWW in teaching and learning within UCL. One major difficulty, as with all teaching innovations, is staff time. Our academics do not have time to develop their own applications and we therefore need to provide tools which enable them to use the WWW for teaching and learning while not requiring long hours of development time.

The second difficulty was determining the appropriate development environment. UCL's clusters still uses Windows 3.1 and we are therefore limited to non Java-based technology.

A related problem is that of access, ensuring that our students could access the Web-based courseware. Although theoretically one advantage of using the Web for teaching and learning is that students can access the coursework at any time from any place, we have severe access difficulties and a lack of student computers (largely owing to the cost of space in central London). Our research shows that about 40% of students have access to computers at home, but very few of these students have a modem, which prevents them from using Web-based systems.

CHEW raised awareness of the potential of the Web for teaching and learning at UCL. However, we still have significant hurdles to overcome if we are to ensure effective and appropriate use of the Web for teaching and learning at UCL.

Institutions should provide awareness programs and support facilities in order to educate members of all departments about the potential of World Wide Web. Using Web-based technology will revolutionise teaching and learning methods within universities and the institutions providing support and education for these tools will lead the revolution.

References

1. Sangster, A. (1995) World Wide Web- what can it do for education, *Active Learning*. CTISS Publications, 2, 3-8.

2. Hiltz, S.R. and Wellman, B. (1997) Asyncronous Learning Networks as a Virtual Classroom. *Communications of the ACM*, 40, 9, 44-49.

3. Chellappa, R., Barua, A. and Whinston, A.B. (1997) An Electronic Infrastructure for a Virtual University. *Communications of ACM*, 40, 9, 56-58.

4. Denicolo, P., Entwistle, N. and Hounsell, D. (1992) What is active Learning? *CVCP Universities Staff Development and Training Unit*.

5. Marton, F. and Saljo, R. (1976) On Qualitative differences in learning 1 - outcome and process. *British Hournal of Educational Psychology*, 46, 4-11.

6. Daniel, J. (1996) Mega-Universities and Knowledge Media: Technology, Strategies for Higher Education. Kogan Page.

7. Forsyth, I. (1996) Teaching and Learning Materials and the WWW. Kogan Page.

8. Hamalainen, M.., Whinston, A. and Vishick, S. (1996) Electronic markets of learning: education brokerages on the Internet. *Communications of ACM*, 39, 6, 51-58.

9. Lloyd, P. (1996) Enhancing Communication - Communication Strategy and Change. *Napier Univeristy Strategic Change Initiative Conference*, Edinburgh.

Chapter 8

An Asynchronous Collaborative Learning System on the Web

*Claude Viéville**

This chapter gives the functional specification of a communication system accessible by a Web browser. The main advantage of this system is the encouragement of a collaborative way of learning using asynchronous communication channels. A conversation always occurs in the context of a task where each user plays a particular role. The conversation is strongly structured by the system itself, which helps the users to coordinate their actions when playing their respective roles within a task. The system is built around the notion of active form, which is the way that the user communicates with the system.

8.1   Introduction

This chapter presents the functional specification of an asynchronous collaborative learning system which aims to support a distance education process on the Web. What attracts an educational institute in using the Internet is a large communication network to exchange information in two ways: the on-line browser and the courseware package distribution. So the challenge we have to face is to transform information exchanges into learning activities. For this reason, we are interested in second-generation servers which respond better to educational needs: better interactivity between video-clips, text, images, and so on; enabling re-use of all the aids we have developed in a fully integrated manner; and inclusion of graphics and formulae (which is essential for many curricula). Embedded courseware corresponds with the multiplicity of training pathways for individualised training

---
* Laboratoire Trigone, Universite des sciences et technologies de Lille 1, Batiment B6 - Cite scientifique, 59655 Villeneuve d'Ascq CEDEX - France.
Email: Claude.Vieville@univ-lille1.fr

and the ease of navigation required. As a minimum requirement, the system needs communication facilities to enhance real collaboration between users and tutors.

In the EONT project[13], in which we are participating, we are verifying these hypotheses. We must offer, free of charge, on-line courseware that could be re-used by other institutes, but we must also offer integrated services to our own audience. Moreover, our practice is based on a mix of the constructivist and cooperative theories of learning, but the courseware must support other pedagogical theories and practices in order to be transferable. Therefore, to develop our system we distinguish three spaces in which the activities of learners take place: information space, action space and communication space. The communication space depends on the institute, and organises the interactivity between the different spaces to correspond to a pedagogical practice. After a short introduction to the application field, the chapter presents the functional specification of the system we are currently designing. A participative approach with a user group has been organised and usability metrics of the system are also presented.

8.2   The Educational Context

The CUEEP (Centre Universite-Economie d'Education Permanente) is an institute of the University of Sciences and Technologies of Lille in northern France. It is concerned with several activities: further education for adults; research into educational engineering (open learning and new communication technologies); and transfer within the context of new technologies in education.

Since the late 70's, we have introduced new learning technologies and important work has been done in designing and experimenting with courseware in traditional situations and in distance education. In addition, there has been research and development of new tools with the help of European programs such as DELTA where a system of cooperative learning (the Co-Learn project) has been designed and experimented with.

Since the late 80's, we have set up an open and distance learning system mixing several modes of training (group, individualised, distance, self-training in resource centres). At the moment, people who are registered in distance education are principally those who take a specific examination for adults equivalent to the baccalaureate. They learn from multimedia course material (written paper, audio-tape, video-tape, courseware) and they are in contact with a tutor by phone, fax and Minitel.

Some experiments using the Co-Learn cooperative system have been undertaken during the past two years. Now we are aiming to integrate this communication system into our distance education organisation.

---

[13] An experiment in Open Distance Learning using New Technologies - part of the Socrates programme of the European Commission.

To continue our work of research into the use of communication tools in distance education, we are conducting a project to deliver a course on the Web, based on collaborative learning. This project is mainly supported by the European Commission, through the Telematics for Education programme. In this framework, we are setting up a delivery platform for the Microelectronics training through Europe (MODEM project).

8.3   The User's Domain

In this section, the user's domain is clarified and the role of each *actor* in this area is given as precisely as possible to avoid confusion. From the user's point of view, the prototype that is specified in this document is an asynchronous communication system that favours the cooperation among people belonging to the same "social organisation". More precisely, in this document, the organisation is a training institution that proposes this communication system in the framework of its distance education service. We focus only on the delivery side of the training institute - the course material production as well as the administrative side are outside the scope of this study. Two roles have been defined to provide an interface with both of these activities. People in this organisation have different roles, such as:

- *teacher*: he/she is responsible for all the courses of a given domain proposed by the organisation to the trainee. He/she is the interface with the course material production teams

- *tutor*: his/her function is to give daily help to a well-defined set of learners. He/she works under the direction of a teacher

- *trainer*: he/she leads a course, also under the guidance of a teacher

- *counsellor*: a counsellor builds individual or group learning paths in negotiation with the learners themselves or human resource managers of the customer companies

- *course manager*: he/she is responsible for providing the requirements of tutors, teachers and learners in order to support the training services. This person interfaces with the administrative side of the training organisation

- *learner*: he/she is trained by the institution. A learner may work for another "client organisation", but when he/she uses the services provided by the training institute they belong to the same "social organisation"

- *human resource manager*: while working for an external organisation, his/her function is to negotiate learning paths with a counsellor

Figure 8.1 represents the conceptual graph defining relations between roles and several basic objects of a training organisation. The number of roles portrayed inside a training organisation has been selectively limited as we are only interested in the "delivery side" of the process. Roles such as editors, course material designers, researchers, administrative staff, and many others are not taken into account in the specification of this communication system.

The system needs to be flexible enough to support various pedagogical scenarios. This means that it has to support several communication modes and it also needs to be *adaptable*, both during the installation phase and even during the operational process. Flexibility of the communication modes between users is one of the major challenges for this type of system.

This section has described the context in which the communication system will be used. The following gives a description of the services that the system will provide to its users.

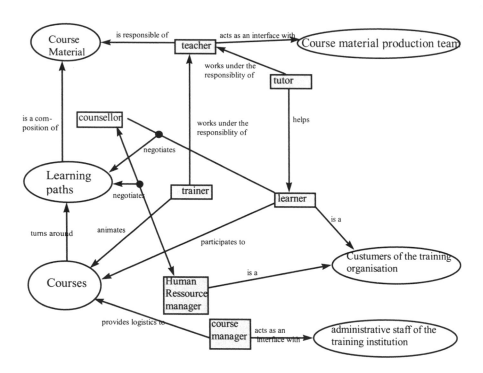

Figure 8.1. Conceptual graph linking objects of the user's domain.

8.4   Overview of the Services

This asynchronous communication system will provide a set of services from the same family as those already provided by electronic mail (email), electronic forums (forum), Bulletin Board Systems (BBS) and the News. Its ambition is to give users real help with their *tasks* by avoiding several well-known drawbacks of current systems [1] and to propose a structuring of the conversation so that it is very efficient to communicate and collaborate via such a system [2]. The measurement of the efficiency of this system could be made upon the following:

• time-saved during the coordination phase of a collaborative process [3]

• time-saved when reading each other's contributions

• enhancement of the quality of arguments produced during a debate [4]

• closer involvement of users in the collaborative processes.

The Co-Learn project is an important input to the specification of such a system. In [5], the interest of developing Collaborative Learning activities has been explained. It is outside the scope of this document to argue in favour of educational processes that are based on collaboration between learners and tutors.

In [6] it is also written as a result of the Co-Learn project, that:

"it might have been preferable to put emphasis on the Asynchronous Communication mode as the basic substrate for communication between learners and tutors... In this way the Asynchronous Communication Mode would provide the glue which would hold a course together, inter-linking the real-time sessions, and providing a forum for continuing discussion and collaboration after each of these sessions."

The reader who is interested in this discussion will find pertinent papers on this subject in the reference section [7, 8, 9]. Jonassen, in [10], gives an excellent overview of the possibilities of Computer Mediated Communication (CMC) in educational process.

8.4.1   Basic Services

The ACLS offers a set of basic services enhanced by a subset of complementary services which are needed to manage, adapt and integrate the system using existing communication tools to meet users' needs [11, 12, 13].

Globally, the basic services provided by this asynchronous communication system are:

• informal exchanges

• question-answer exchanges

• date negotiation [14]

• pro-con argument production

• action negotiation [15]

• opinion collection.

Each of these services could involve people regardless of the context of a collaborative task, or be used in the framework of a task process involving the group. In this latter case the exchange is automatically classed as public, unless specifically defined as private. The task in which the communicators are involved in is very fundamental as it will define the context in which the exchange has occurred [16]. In this ACLS, electronic mail is not distinguished from electronic forums or news systems as a means of communicating between people. The ACLS provides an integrated view of exchanges whatever channel is used (i.e. email, forums, news, BBS etc.) [17].

This basic service will allow the members to select, fill in, edit, and submit a form that will complete an exchange. Exchanges are linked to each other by a temporal relation. The creation of a new exchange is a particular case of the creation of a contribution that becomes the root of the exchange.

The ACLS also proposes other services complementary to its basic services. These will be described in the following section.

8.4.2   Complementary Services

To encourage cooperation ACLS will provide a service that gives information on its *users*. The communication needed by users during the task process will be supported inside a *group activity*. The group activity is the context in which the *exchanges* of a communication occur. One and only one organisational group is attached to a group activity. The exchanges of a communication are structured sets of contributions. Each exchange is regulated by a set of global rules pre-defined at the installation of the ACLS. This set of rules depends on the way people of the organisation work together [2]. Obviously, default rules are proposed during the installation phase. To participate in a group activity a user needs to be added; he then becomes a *member* of the group activity.

It is also possible to create subgroups task by task in which all the members play an identical role with regards to the aim of the task. For example, if a collaborative writing task is started, subgroups of *authors*, *editors*, *reviewers* are created by the initiator of the task. Belonging to a subgroup will give different rights to the objects in the ACLS.

A search service is available for all the users who want to find any objects in the ACLS. Users, group activities, sub-groups, forms, exchanges and tasks are searched and displayed to the user of the search service. To start a search operation, the user must fill in fields of a search form. The user has to define in the form which criteria the search should use. It is possible to search on the attributes and/or the contents of any types of objects of the ACLS.

Authorised users will use the administration service to create/modify attributes; delete/archive/open/close user and group activities. This administration is done by filling in an administrative form.

Users are added and removed from group activities by using the registration service. A subset of authorised users with appropriate rights will have access to this service. Registration is performed by filling out a registration form. Only when a group activity has appropriate parameters may a user register himself for that activity.

A notification service allows members, who have subscribed, to be notified when something is appended to the group activity. Filling in a notification form is the proposed way to subscribe to the notification service. The notification service allows to the user to receive (or avoid reception of) the events generated inside the ACLS. The kinds of events are:

- "group activity" list has changed

- list of users of the ACLS has changed

- status of a group activity has changed

- list of tasks for a particular group activity has changed

- list of exchanges for particular tasks has changed

- list of forms for a particular exchange has changed

- a deadline relative to a task is going to arrive

- a deadline relative to a task has been detected

- a particular user activity has been detected

- a particular group or subgroup activity has been detected.

The events are sent to the notification recipient which could be an electronic mail address, a news group, or another task of any other group activity.

8.5 Specification of the User Interface

8.5.1 Basic Principles

The principle of the user-system dialogue relies on the submission of *active forms* [18]. This dialogue implements a schema of information interchange between the user and the system similar to that which already exists on the Web with the HTML form. Within these forms, there are three main objects manipulated by the user inside the ACLS. Another particular object is also manipulated, documents; however, these are outside the scope of this study. The ACLS forms are too generic to be considered as an object; they are containers for the main objects presented in this section. The semantics which define articulation between these main objects are summarised in Figure 8.2.

Task: to perform a task the organisational group can decompose it into several sub-tasks. The aim of a task is achieved by performing actions externally to the system. A task can be personal or collaborative. A task organiser manages the list of tasks by communicating with the mediation agent (mediator). Each group activity has its task organiser.

Exchanges and contribution forms: the contribution form (contribution for short) is the basic element by which users communicate, coordinate and work together. A contribution is a semi-structured message [19]. It is a container for output and entry fields (list of items, dates, links etc.) and user actions (initiation and commitment of tasks, exchange, validation of forms. etc.). The exchange is the container that structures a set of contributions that appear as a tree-like structure. A mediator manages one and only one exchange; all contribution forms are communicated to the mediator. The mediation agent composes the contribution form according to its status and the role of the communication agent. A contribution is posted with a privacy level.

Group/user: according to his/her role in the organisation or inside a task, a user can belong to one or several group activities and several sub-groups. A group activity is an organisational group visible, for example, by administrative staff; it is known by the organisation. In contrast a sub-group is not known or seen by the organisation. A sub-group is created according to the needs of the different tasks. A member of a subgroup plays a functional role towards achieving the task and consequently receives suitable rights to carry out the work for which he/she is responsible. Each user owns one communication agent (communicator for short) which is representative of all the rights, duties and involvement of that user based on their relationship to a group activity [20, 21]. The communication agent in turn communicates with the mediation agents to post forms.

Documents: Documents are external to the ACLS, but can be attached to main objects of the ACLS. The following rules allow inheritance of attachment through interconnected objects of the ACLS:

- attached documents of a task are also accessible within child tasks

- attached documents of an exchange are also linked within child exchanges and in all the contributions of these exchanges

- attached documents of a group activity are linked to all the tasks and exchanges and contributions

- attached documents of a subgroup are attached to the relative tasks for which this subgroup has been created.

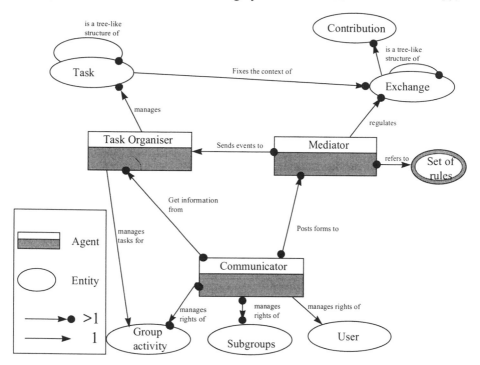

Figure 8.2. Semantic network of basic objects of the ACLS.

8.5.2 Agents of the ACLS

In addition to the main objects, there are also agents which "help" the users in their work:

The notification agent (notifier): This entity is responsible for distributing the events that occur in the ACLS to the subscribers who are users of the system. By default the notifier sends mail to signal each event. A notification agent is attached to a social organisation.

Communication agent: It is attached to one user. This agent knows the group activity and the sub-groups each user belongs to; using this knowledge it is able to give rights on objects of the ACLS.

The mediation agent (mediator): Organises contributions and, in conjunction with the communication agent, proposes to the user a well chosen class of forms to fill in. It also receives forms posted by the communication agent and sends back the form as it will be recorded by the ACLS if the user validates it.

Task organiser: The task organiser manages the users "to-do list". This to-do list is built from **events** sent by the mediation agent. The task organiser is associated with one and only one organisational group.

List of events:

Here is the list of events that occur inside the ACLS:

- the list of group activities is modified

- the list of tasks of a group activity is modified

- the list of tasks that a user must do is modified

- the list of exchanges within a group activity is modified

- the list of contributions of a group activity is modified

- the status of a task is modified

- the status of an exchange is modified

- a user contributes to a group activity

- a user begins consulting the group activity

- a user ends consulting the group activity.

Each event contains a detailed report with all the required information in order to define what is happening in the ACLS.

8.5.3   Consistency of the Interface

For each object, the following attributes require particular attention to be paid to their representation:

Contextualisation:

- the context link between two objects. This signifies that the content of an object is a part of the context of another one. For example, if a contribution form has been submitted by a member to progress a task, this contribution has a context link with the task:

- the document link with an object of the ACLS.

Status:

- the status of a task (planned, running, finished, suspended, aborted)

- the status of an exchange (running, finished, suspended, aborted)

- the recorded status of a contribution.

Collaboration awareness:

- the owner of the object and highlighting the user when an object belongs to him

- the privacy attribute of a contribution or of fields of contributions which will signal that a contribution (or a part of it) is private or public

- the collaborative attribute of a task which allows the user to see at a glance if the task is individual or collective

- the role played by a user in a task. This is found by examining whether the user belongs to the sub-groups of the task.

Structure of the conversation:

- the types of exchanges

- the types of contribution.

8.6 Specification of the Usability Metrics

8.6.1 Introduction

The classification of the targets for the usability of the ACLS relies on the book of G. Lindgaard [22]. This books classifies usability tests in four dimensions:

- effectiveness

- flexibility

- learnability

- attitude.

At the current stage of the study it is not possible to fix the target results of the usability tests because we lack feedback from user groups. Nevertheless, we are able to define what the metrics of the usability tests will be. The targets will be fixed, not by this study, but by a future study made by the user group exploiting this data in a participative methodology of design.

The user group must now propose a realistic scenario as representative as possible of the ways in which this system will be used. Given the scenario, significant tasks are selected. These tasks will characterise the usage of the ACLS in the framework of the distance education.

Two different situations would certainly be distinguished:

Learner-tutor asynchronous communication: a situation in which a learner works alone on an individualised learning path. In this case, the tutor needs to guide and check student progress. Three different tasks representative of the help the ACLS could provide are defined:

- A: to define and explain the aims of the student's work

- B: to negotiate the different steps and deadlines with each student

- C: to follow through student's work and progress.

Group coordination of work: The ACLS will be used to support the setting-up of a collective project for the whole group and each sub-group carrying out the work. The group size will be limited to 20-25 students and each subgroup will not exceed 4 or 5 persons. Five tasks are identified:

- D: to define and explain the aims and constraints of the project

- E: to negotiate a breakdown of activities within a project: tasks identification

- F: to negotiate responsibilities and deadlines for each task with subgroups

- G: to follow through all the tasks of the project

- H: to decide that the aim of a task is reached.

8.6.2   Effectiveness

In [22], the effectiveness is defined as:

"the requested range of tasks, completed at the specified level of performance within a certain time ... by some required percentage of the specified target range of users ... within some required proportion of the range of usage environments"

The effectiveness will be measured during trials where the users will do one of the tasks A to H described in previous section:

- measure the number of times a dialogue is aborted

- measure the number of loops to submit a form with success

- compute the average time before or after which the users initiate a task B or F when the tasks C or G are going beyond the deadline

- analyse the results of tasks C and G and compute the percentage which cope with aims defined in tasks A or D proving that the high level of clarification and presentation of information made during the discussion in these tasks (A or D)

- compute the percentage of users who agree on the breakdown of tasks resulting from task E

- compute the time taken by a group to present and to agree on a written text reflecting their opinion about the work done in tasks G. This value will reflect the efficiency of task H

- measure the delay taken by the negotiation tasks like tasks B, E and F in relation to their respective deadlines.

8.6.3 Flexibility

In [22], the flexibility is measured "with flexibility allowing adaptation to some specified percentage variation in tasks and/or environments beyond those first specified".

The flexibility is measured by collecting the following information:

- the number of times each type of form is used in the ACLS

- the number of "new patterns of communication" the ACLS has completely supported (by judicious combination of proposed patterns)

- the count of the number of negative answers to help requested by users to get advice about the type of exchange to initiate, to set up a new pattern of communication.

8.6.4 Learnability

In [22], the learnability is quantified:

"within a certain specified time, relative to the beginning of user training ... based upon some specified amount of training and user support ... within some specified relearning time each time for intermittent users"

The learnability of the ACLS will be measured for each of the following criteria:

- the number of times the users access the help pages

- the number of times a user accesses the same help page

- the time taken by each user to use a type of form for the first time

- the number of times an inadequate type of form is used.

Each of these measurements is a set of values representing the value week by week in the first month of use, and month by month in the following months in order to show if the users learn more and more about the usage of the ACLS.

8.6.5 Attitude

In [22], the attitude is measured:

"within acceptable levels of human cost in term of tiredness, discomfort, frustration and personal effort ... so that satisfaction causes continued and enhanced usage of the system".

The attitude will be measured by questionnaires filled in at the end of the trials by the users. The set of questions relative to the evaluation of the ACLS should be able to confirm or disprove that:

- users have the feeling that the ACLS respects privacy of communication

- users have confidence in the reliability of the ACLS

- users are sure that the ACLS give the correct status of each other's work

- users have the feeling that they control the communication and that the ACLS is an assistant which helps them to be efficient.

8.7   Conclusion

Particular attention will be paid to the methodology of design in order to work with the user group. The system will be designed incrementally, meaning that the system must be usable by the members of the user group rapidly and with only a few functions, so that they can send feedback to the designers. This participative approach will certainly produce a system with a high level of usability.

References

1.   Terry D. (1991) 7 steps to a better mail system. *Message Handling Systems and Application Layer Communication Protocols*, P. Schicker and E. Stefferud (Eds.), Elsevier Science Publishers B.V. (North-Holland), 23-33.

2.   Vieville C. (1995) Structuring conversation in asynchronous communication systems to support collaborative learning at a distance. *Proceedings of ED-MEDIA 95*, Graz, Austria, 816-817.

3.   Bussler C. and Joblonski S. (1994) Implementing Agent Coordination for Workflow Management Systems Using Active Database Systems. *IEEE software* ,1994, 4, 53-59.

4.   Desaranno S. and Put F. (1994) Co-ordinating group communication. *Computer networks and ISDN Systems*, Elsevier Science B.V., S129-S138.

5.   Derycke A. *et al.* (1992) Representation models for collaborative educational situations and collaborative learning activities, *Deliverable 4 of Co-Learn D2005*, DG XIII of European Commissions.

6.   Kaye A. (1995) Final evaluation report, synthesis of Co-Learn trials and experimentation. *Deliverable 33 of Co-Learn d2005*, DG XIII of European Commissions.

7.   Harasim L. (1993) Collaborating in cyberspace: using computer conferences as a group Environment. *Interactive Learning Environment*, 3, 2, 119-130.

8.   Henri F. and Rigault C. (1994) Collaborative distance learning and computer conferencing. *Advanced Educational Technology: Research Issues and Future Potential*, T.Liao (Ed.) NATO, ASI series, Springer-Verlag, 45-76

9. Kirsche T., Lenz R., Ruf T. Wedekind H. (1994) Co-operative problem solving using database conversations. *ICDE'94, International Conference on Data Engineering, 10,* 1994, 134-143.

10. Jonassen D. (1996) *Computers in the classroom; mindtools for critical thinking.* Prentice Hall.

11. Palme J. (1992) Computer conferencing functions and standards. *Collaborative learning through computer conferencing,* Kaye A.R., 225-245.

12. Palme J. (1993) Standards for asynchronous group communication. *Computer Communication,* 16, 9, 532-538.

13. Turoff M. (1991) Computer-mediated communication requirements for group support. *Journal of Organizational Computing,* 1991, 1, 85-113

14. Woitass M. (1990) Coordination of intelligent office agents applied to meeting scheduling. *Multi-User Interfaces and Applications,* S. Gibbs and A.A. Verrijn-Stuart (Eds.), Elsevier Science Publishers B.V., North-Holland, 371-387.

15. Rogers I. (1995) The Use of an automatic "TO Do " list to guide structured interaction. *Proceedings of CHI 95,* Denver, Colorado, USA, 232-233.

16. Ellis C. and Wainer J. (1994) Goal-based models of collaboration. *Collaborative Computing,* S. Benford (Ed.), Chapman & Hall, 61-86.

17. Benford S., Turroff M. and Palme J. (1992) An ISO standard to support asynchronous group communication. *Computer Standards & Interfaces* Elsevier Science Publishers B.V. (North-Holland) 1992, 14, 363-373.

18. Hammainen H. (1991) Form and room: metaphors for groupware. *Proceedings of COSC,* ACM conference, 51-58.

19. Malone T. (1987) Semi-structured messages are surprisingly useful for Computer-Supported Collaboration. *ACM trans. On Office Information Systems,* 1987, 5, 115-131.

20. Danielsen T., Folkow T. and Richardsen. P. W. (1987) Relation and inheritance in group communication. message handling systems. *Message Handling Systems,* Speth, R. (Ed.), Elsevier Science Publishers B.V. (North-Holland), 239-252.

21. Hoogstoël F. (1995) Une approche organisationnelle du travail coopératif assisté par ordinateur. Application au projet Co-Learn, thése de Doctorat en Informatique à l'université des Sciences et Technologies de Lille.

22. Lindgaard G. (1994) *Usability testing and system evaluation; a guide for designing useful computer systems.* Chapman and Hall.

23. Smith C. (1994) Co-Learn usability audit, Deliverable 29a of Co-Learn project D2005, DG XIII of European Commissions.

Chapter 9

Modifying Multi-user Discussion Systems to Support Text-based Virtual Learning Environments on the Web – the coMentor Experience

Graham R. Gibbs[*]

MUDs and MOOs (Multi-User Domains and MUDs Object Oriented) are multi-user programs which support both synchronous and asynchronous discussion over the Internet. They support a rich, text-based virtual environment developed using a built-in object-oriented programming language. They have been used in various educational contexts such as creative writing, language learning, virtual campuses and to support research communities. Experience suggests they are good at encouraging cooperative and creative learning.

However, they are text-based, use a command-line interface and are isolated from other Internet services, like the WWW. Several projects are trying to link MOOs with the WWW. One such is coMentor, which supports a variety of facilities through a WWW interface to a MOO. These facilities include private group-work areas, role-playing, annotation and threaded discussion, concept mapping and synchronous chat in all parts of the system, yet users only need standard Java-aware WWW browsers. Early evaluation of the system is discussed.

[*]Department of Behavioural Sciences, University of Huddersfield, Queensgate, Huddersfield. HD1 3DH, UK
Email: G.R.Gibbs@hud.ac.uk

9.1 Introduction

There is a good deal of research about collaboration in learning in traditional settings which has demonstrated its utility. Some show that the benefits arise from the motivation and encouragement that collaboration can create. For instance, Madden and Slavin [1] and Slavin [2] suggested that students in collaborating classes felt that their peers wanted them to learn. However, more centrally, there is evidence of improved learning through collaboration. Dansereau [3] had students cooperate by taking turns as recaller and listener. They read a section of text, and then the recaller summarized the information while the listener corrected any errors, filled in any omitted material, and thought of ways both students could remember the main ideas. Learners working together on structured cooperative tasks learned technical material or procedures far better than those working alone. The utility of elaborating explanations to peers was confirmed by Webb [4] who showed that students who gained the most from collaborative learning were those who provided elaborated explanations to others. There is some evidence that peer learners have to take appropriate roles, for instance the one with more to say taking the role of task-doer while others might become observers, monitoring the situation [5]. This does not necessarily mean that only the more active collaborators will gain, even the observers may learn from the exchanges. As McEndree and Mayes argue, students can learn much from observing the dialogues of other learners. This they refer to as 'vicarious learning' and it often consists of learning from the (observed) mistakes in the dialogues and discussions of others [6].

The development of a range of computer-based communications technologies has provided new opportunities for designing systems to support collaborative learning. Other chapters in this volume focus on a range of asynchronous approaches to supporting computer based collaboration. This chapter will focus on another approach which offers both synchronous and asynchronous support to networked learners in a text-based virtual environment – the Multi-User Domain or MUD.

9.2 MUDs and MOOs

9.2.1 Definition

The MUD or MOO (MUD, Object Oriented) derives from the interactive, role-playing, multi-user dungeon games:

> "MUDs ... are programs that accept network connections from multiple simultaneous users and provide access to a shared database of 'rooms', 'exits', and other objects. Users browse and manipulate the database from 'inside' the rooms, seeing only those objects that are in the same room and moving between rooms mostly via the exits that connect them. MUDs are thus a kind of virtual reality, an electronically-represented 'place' that users can visit." [7]

MUDs, however, differ from most other virtual reality systems in significant ways:

- MUDs generally do not employ graphics or special position-sensing hardware to immerse the user in a sensually-vivid virtual environment. Instead they generally rely on plain, unformatted text to communicate with the users. For this reason, MUDs are frequently referred to as text-based virtual realities.

- MUDs are extensible from within. MUD users can add new rooms and other objects to the database and give those objects unique virtual behaviour, using an embedded programming language. The adding of new objects is done interactively.

- MUDs generally have many users connected at the same time. All of those users are browsing and manipulating the same database and can encounter both the other users and their newly-created objects. MUD users can also communicate with each other directly, in real-time, usually by typing messages that are seen by all other users in the same room.

The original MUDs were adventure games based on role playing books, and text-based computer games. The first MUD was started in spring 1979 by Richard Bartle and Roy Trubshaw, then students at the University of Essex [8]. In the late 1980s, many users lost interest in the gaming and fantasy aspects and just used the MUD for discussion. A new variety of 'social MUDs' were established and by the end of 1993 there were over 400 MUDs operating.

The creation, through a text-based interface of an imaginative world is fundamental to many MUDs. Users often refer to the distinction between life in the MUD and life outside the MUD, referred to as RL — real life. Text descriptions of rooms, places, people and objects are used to give a sense of place and reality along with a general atmosphere to MUDs and MOOs. For example, Figure 9.1 shows the introductory 'page' to the VUW MOO at the University of Waterloo, Canada, which sets the tone for an academic campus.

One of the most commented-on aspects of MUD and MOOs is that users can adopt different characters or personas from those they have in real life. A new user can create a description of themselves along with a gender (which may be male, female or neutral) and their identity may even be plural (as in a flock of seagulls) [9, 10]. This description guides their own behaviour and especially how others behave towards them, since initially the description is the only information other users have about the player.

9.2.2 Educational MUDs and MOOs

The potential of MUDs in education had been recognized in a variety of ways [11]. Not surprisingly, one use of them is to support creative writing, building upon the creative, and imaginative dimensions of MUDs. However, in general, it has been the support for rooms and chat that has most attracted educationalists. The technology offers new opportunities for conducting classes and seminars. Long distance learning is one obvious example, but, with the hypertextual qualities of text-based virtual realities, opportunities abound for unusual student projects which engage imaginative and structured thinking in written texts. In higher education, the uses of MUDs and MOOs have divided into four main areas:

- Writing

- Language learning

- General Campus

- Research community support.

```
<*>The University Of Waterloo - Virtual Campus Information Kiosk<*>

~~~~~~~~~~~~~~~~~~~~~~~~~~~~~~~~~~~~~~~~~~~~~~~~~~~~~~~~~~~~~~~~~~~~~~~

You are standing on the outskirts of campus. A welcoming white booth
rests on a low grass hill. Below it, there's a comfortable red plank
bench. You can find out lots of things about the Virtual Campus here.
Just type 'enter' to go into the Information Kiosk. North leads you
onto campus, south leads to Off-Campus and student housing.

It's quite chilly. The setting sun is obscured by low-hanging clouds.
There is a light breeze wafting in.

---Contents: Objects and People---
You see VUW INFORMATION KIOSK here.

---Available Exits---
<north> to Ring Road -- Southern Intersection
<south> to University Ave -- South of Kiosk
<west> to A grassy hill
<enter> to Inside VUW Information Kiosk
```

Figure 9.1. Introduction 'Page' for VUW MOO.

9.2.3   Writing MUDs and MOOs

The 'Composition in Cyberspace' course ran in part in a MUD and attempted to achieve a kind of engaged writing [12]. It involved pairing composition classes at different US universities, and used both an asynchronous email journal and synchronous class meetings on Diversity University MOO to connect the two classes and to create a public forum for the students' writing. Students submitted examples of their writing and others were able to read them, comment on them and learn from them. As Harris notes:

"students wrote much more carefully... They learned to express their ideas clearly and convincingly – and they wanted to do so, because they knew how easy it would be for others to challenge unsupported claims. They were thus more effective, engaged writers, not only in the 'informal' or 'fun' settings of MOOs and email lists, but also in the work they submitted to their instructor" [12].

9.2.4 Language MUDs and MOOs

There are quite a number of language MUDs and MOOs. (See appendix 9.A for a list). A typical example is MundoHispano, a Spanish language MOO being developed by Lonnie Turbee with the support of the department of Languages, Literature and Linguistics and ERIC's AskERIC project, both at Syracuse University, USA. It constitutes a community of native speakers of Spanish from around the world along with teachers and learners of Spanish, and computer programmers.

A key advantage which organisers and users of language MUDs and MOOs claim is that students get the chance to 'chat' (albeit, written chat) with native language users. Although the language experience may be far from the structured programme of the language class, the experience of native speakers' conversation constitutes a kind of ultimate authenticity in the electronic exchanges.

9.2.5 Campus and General MUDs and MOOs

One of the largest and best known general campus MOOs is Diversity University. Designed as a virtual campus the program provides facilities for large numbers of students, teachers, and administrators worldwide to use its classes, literature, and consulting services. Other examples include the Virtual Online University at the University of Athena, USA, which has submitted a formal application for accreditation as a university, and VUW (the Virtual campus at the University of Waterloo). VUW was developed in 1995 for use with an entirely on-line Technical Writing undergraduate course.

9.2.6 Research Community MOOs

These MOOs support academic research activities rather in the way that conventional conferences and workshops do. Examples include BioMOO and MediaMOO. At MediaMOO media researchers from around the world discuss current projects, teachers meet weekly to discuss ways of using computers to teach writing and there is a large group of rhetoric and composition subscribers who meet weekly in the (virtual) Netoric Cafe to discuss a wide range of issues, particularly integrating technology and writing. Two important points about MUDs and MOOs are illustrated by these activities. First, MediaMOO is acting as support for the same kind of informal meetings, discussions, and chats that are often some of the most stimulating parts of traditional face-to-face academic conferences and workshops and through this it fosters a sense of belonging to a community. Second, although it is possible to 'drop in' at any time, most users and operators of MUDs and MOOs find it necessary to schedule meetings and events, just as in 'RL'.

9.2.7 Pedagogy in MUDs and MOOs

Several advantages for the use of MUDs and MOOs in education are claimed. Most can be linked to the kind of imaginative virtual reality created by users and the object and room descriptions found in MUDs. Moock suggests that the natural conversational and community features of a MOO encourage users to converse and conduct themselves in ways that are close to those of "real life" meetings and conversations. In this way, remote learners, and even those from different cultures, can experience not just the language and discourse of those in the MOO but also some of the social and communal features of people meeting together [13].

Many MUDs and MOOs also seem to foster strong senses of mutual help and peer support. This has been noted by Bruckman in her account of learning to program in a MOO, where, in the absence of good manuals and off-line support, the learner was helped by other participants in the MOO who gave freely of their time [14].

However, there are also some problems associated with the use of MUDs in teaching. As Germundson points out, one can arise simply from the popularity of the medium.

"For instance, if 30 people show up, how do you decide who talks when and for how long. Talks can often be multi-threaded meaning that everyone is typing and reading text at the same time, it can become quite confusing" [15].

Another problem that comes with success is that of overload of students or teachers.

"With larger groups of students, the email journal can produce significant work for the students and for the faculty members. If a collective group of 40 students write two or three email messages a week, instructors and students end up reading 80 to 120 messages each week. Although some of us are used to that volume of mail, many students are not (and many faculty members are on a number of Internet discussion lists already), and so the journal can become tiresome if not over-burdening" [12].

But probably the most serious problem, at least from the point of view of the learners, is the need to master the technology of MUDs and MOOs. The programs are still on the whole operated via text commands in a Telnet session. They have none of the ease of use of modern graphical user interfaces and none of the visual richness students have become accustomed to on the World Wide Web. Some students simply do not like computer-mediated communication. As Turbee points out,

"teachers need to provide plenty of in-class 'debriefing' time during which complaints and problems can be aired... Co-learners are often the best resource for solutions to problems encountered in MOO experiences, but it is a good teacher who must have the insight to set up these sessions and facilitate peer support" [16].

9.2.8 Technical Issues: MOO and the Web

Not only are most MUD's interfaces non-graphical, but perhaps even more importantly now, with the rapid growth of the WWW, MUDs and MOOs are isolated from other services and information available on the Internet. It is not surprising, then, that there have been several attempts to combine MUDs or MOOs with the WWW. The major problem faced by those attempting this is that the two systems employ incompatible forms of communication. The HTTP protocol used by the WWW is stateless. Once a page has been sent to a browser in response to a user's request, the link between server and client is severed. In contrast, MUDs and MOOs maintain a constantly open channel of communication between the server and the client. It is this that enables users to receive messages sent by others as soon as they are posted.

The solutions which have been developed at the server end fall into two categories, those that modify the MOO (or sometimes the MUD) so that it acts as if it were a HTTP server, responding to user requests not with text, but with HTML. Commonly this is done by quite complex programming of the MOO so that it generates HTML 'on the fly'. This is the solution chosen by ChibaMOO. The MOO programming language is used to develop a set of 'WOO' protocols so that the MOO can serve WWW pages. It is still necessary to use a Telnet client to run the MOO and chat.

The alternative is to create some intermediary program, often a set of Perl scripts running on the server alongside the MOO and an HTTP server, which handle communication between MOO and Web server. For example, CardiffMOO's gateway to the Web is provided by the COMMA HTTP Server. When the HTTP server is accessed, a Perl script is executed which makes a normal Telnet connection to the MOO. The script issues a request for information which is handled by code in the MOO database. The program interacts with the database and returns HTML text to the calling script. The script then removes any unwanted information from this response and passes the results back to the browser.

On the client side, several different solutions are possible. A common one is to have the Web browser (Navigator, Internet Explorer etc.) running alongside the normal Telnet client in a multi-tasking operating system. Users get visual information about the MOO and its rooms on the Web browser, and may even navigate around it using buttons on the Web page, but still use the Telnet program for chat communications. In some cases added functionality can be provided by the use of special client programs. One example of this approach is the Monash EdMOO. This has a Web-enhanced server, which will work with Telnet and Web browser, but there is a special client application, Drover, which provides some of the features of a graphical user interface and adds multimedia capabilities to the MOO. With Drover users can display graphics, sounds, movies and even VRML scenes.

An alternative is to make use of frames and forms on the Web page to eliminate the need for a separate Telnet application. Forms can be used to send text communications, but receiving a constant stream of text back requires an inelegant use of the browser, whereby it is fooled into thinking that the current page is still being loaded – throughout the whole of the session. This approach is taken by APECKS/WOOM. This system, developed by Jeni Tennison at the University of Nottingham, uses a modified MOO database to generate HTML 'on the fly', but supports both frame and form communication in the browser and separate, standard Telnet communication.

The introduction of Internet-aware languages such as Java has made other, neater solutions possible. The Telnet application can be implemented as a Java applet which can be embedded in the Web page, or Java can be used to substitute both the form for sending messages and the frame used to display text sent to the browser by the server. For example, as well as allowing standard Telnet access running alongside a Web browser, Diversity University supports the use of frames and an embedded Java applet, Cup-O-MUD, which gives Telnet client facilities inside a HTML frame. The operators of EdMOO are also following this route by developing an embedded Java applet with all the functionality of the separate program, Drover.

All these systems are still in development, but it seems likely that the future of MUDs and MOOs will be some kind of MOO/WWW combination, possibly with VRML features. However, the advantages and imaginative potential of text-based VR should not be underestimated. It can provide users with near complete anonymity, needs minimal equipment at the client end and makes full use of the imaginative abilities of subscribers. Some users even report that they have the sensation of having 'heard' speech, whilst chatting in a MUD.

9.3   coMentor

9.3.1   Introduction to coMentor

The coMentor project is an attempt to address the computer aided learning (CAL) needs of the social sciences. The potential for CAL in the social sciences like sociology, politics and social policy is large. In 1993 there were over 6,500 academics in social science departments in higher education in the UK. The figure is now probably nearer 8,000, and the staff student ratio is about 1:14. However, teachers in these disciplines have been relatively slow to adopt CAL. An important reason for this is the difficulty of applying CAL to subject matter that is mainly textual, discursive or disputational; in other words to those disciplines and topic areas, such as those found in much of the social sciences, where the subject matter is predominantly theoretical or non-empirical and essentially contested. Many computer-based approaches, such as modelling and visualization are inappropriate because they generally assume an empirical subject matter and/or a universally agreed paradigm. In contrast, in disputational topics there is no real empirical content and debate is the essence. Typical examples are philosophy, methodology and social theory.

The use of MUDs or MOOs to support such teaching and learning therefore seems to hold much promise. However, as noted above, most MUDs and MOOs use relatively complex interfaces and are cut off from the main WWW resources on the Internet. Social science students are among the least enthusiastic about computers and departments commonly do not have good access to high-end equipment. The coMentor project is attempting to address these issues in using a MOO modified to operate through standard WWW browsers to support teaching and learning in philosophy and social theory. To this end coMentor supports the following facilities:

- Graphics, icons, visual tools, identification of users

- Users may adopt persona for different philosophical positions (e.g. sceptic, rationalist) along with the necessary support materials students need to remain 'in character'

- Debate – encourages chat and discussion

- Rooms – or at least virtual spaces where groups can meet in relative privacy

- Objects – to include documents, notes, URLs, FAQs They can be left by teachers, mentors or learners. Unlike most MOOs these will not be programmable by users

- Both synchronous and asynchronous communications

- Annotation of texts produced by others

- Learning tools, e.g. structured argumentation tools.

The technical solution the project has adopted is based on the APECKS/WOOM system discussed above. We have modified the MOO database further to remove separate Telnet access, so all access is now via a WWW browser. In addition we are developing Java applets, Perl scripts and Java applications to extend the functions of the browsers and to support MOO to HTTP communications on the server. All development reflects the design principle that students should be able to use standard browsers such as Netscape Navigator and Microsoft Internet Explorer without any separate, extra software. At the server end we are using LambdaMOO running on a UNIX workstation. This is a MOO developed at the Xerox Palo Alto Research Centre and there are versions for PowerMac, several kinds of UNIX and soon Win95/NT. A linked HTTP server delivers images and Java applets, to give full graphical and interactive functionality. There is also a small Java application running on the server which supports some aspects of MOO-HTTP communications.

9.3.2   coMentor Design Philosophy

Development of the system involves the rapid production of prototypes with feedback generated by a form of user-centred evaluation based on the Supportive

Evaluation Methodology developed by Robinson and Fitter [17]. Early formative evaluation using observation of current teaching sessions, group interviews and a Web-based questionnaire with undergraduate and postgraduate students suggested that needs fall into four main areas:

Group and Seminar Work. Students wanted to choose who is in their group and to be in different groups for different topics whilst maintaining access to work done by other groups. They wanted greater linkage between the lecture topics and associated groupwork or seminars. Although they wanted to be able to ask some questions anonymously, they did want rewards for contributing to group work.

Each Other's Work. Again, students wanted access to each other's work and they wanted access recorded to reward good work and prevent problems of plagiarism. They also wanted input from tutors on work in progress and feedback on presentations from tutors and fellow students.

Resources. Students requested three main types of resource: course support, such as a FAQ of queries to lecturers, lecture notes and supplementary material, framework-giving summaries, and key articles; a pre-course pack, including such things as an introduction and contextualisation of philosophy and its relation to other social science subjects, a guide to writing theoretical and philosophical essays, and examples of past essays and exam answers; and, lastly, outside resources, such as discussions and seminars with or between external experts, and audio-visual material such as talks, interviews, and documentaries.

Access. Most Master's students were part-time and only came into the university one day a week. Many said they did not use the university computer laboratory and so would be unlikely to use coMentor unless they could use it from home or work. Many Master's students also wished for more communication with fellow students in between their seminar days.

To meet these needs, the facilities in coMentor are situated within a common environment, which allows learners to chat and send messages whilst working together in a particular area. These facilities currently include:

- Allowing many learners to connect simultaneously to a server (essentially already provided by the MOO) and allowing identification of learners (both personal and ideological) through graphical representations. In coMentor users will have the option of choosing identities which have relevance to social theory or philosophy and will be expected to "stay in role" whilst on the MOO. Thus a user could adopt the identity of a rationalist, and would be expected to take that viewpoint and defend it in debates.

- A spatial organization of contents so that learners interact in "places" or can "visit" depositories of information on previous discussions. Virtual groupwork is supported by providing the facility for students and teachers to establish groups and virtual places where they can meet and discuss. Such "places" include groups for specific purposes, for instance to prepare a paper, or thematic groups such as one focused on Popper's view of science.

- A "library" of reference materials. This will include selected texts from student discussion, specially constructed FAQs and other materials (e.g. good texts to read) deposited by students and teachers. This includes examples of previous year's essays and exam questions and answers. The issues of plagiarism, consent and copyright this raises are, in part, addressed by the provision for audit trailing and user tracking. We also hope to have guest contributions from well known academics in the area and sponsored areas for book and journal publishers of relevance to the subject matter.

- Asynchronous communication tools such as email (i.e. the ability to leave messages on the system), newsgroups, tutorial rooms, "whiteboards" (especially via the ability to comment on or annotate displayed text). In this way students can comment on contributions made by others and annotate reference materials available in coMentor.

Facilities under development include:

- Tools to promote the active investigation and structuring of information on the system. These will include searching tools, structured argumentation tools or concept mapping tools [18, 19]. The idea here is to help students understand the underlying logic of the arguments and discussions they are having.

- Supporting student access to information and debates and student mentoring raises similar issues to the management of organizational memory in CSCW systems. Some ideas from this field, such as inquiry escalation [20] will be adapted to the learning environment.

- A means of housekeeping and quality control, so that students get feedback on the quality and usefulness of contributions and so that they have some confidence in the accuracy of what they are reading.

- Mechanisms for audit trailing and user tracking. In part these will allow some control over issues of plagiarism, but principally they will enable the assessment of peer tutoring or mentoring contributions.

- Tools for both the teacher administration of the system and computer system operator maintenance.

These developments constitute coMentor as a learning tool [21, 22]. By using the facilities of the WWW to provide much content, and student and teacher discussion to provide the rest, the MOO itself and the software additions we are making to it are almost free of content. coMentor can thus be seen as a CAL package which assists learning but which itself has little knowledge content. The function of the tool is not to get the student to learn by acquiring surface knowledge from manifest information in the software, but to get the student to master new concepts by manipulating the program in ways made possible by the latent concepts on which its design is based. A key advantage of this approach is that the software is not made specific to one teaching context or to one educational institution or department. Although for the purposes of development and evaluation, coMentor is supporting the teaching and learning of philosophy and social theory, the design of the system is such that with relative ease, and with some knowledge of HTML, the system could be adapted to support learning in other knowledge domains.

9.4   Extending the Geographic Metaphor of Rooms

coMentor draws on and enhances the familiar MOO use of rooms. However, we have avoided simply reproducing the geographic character of rooms and places associated with a real university. Many current educational MUDs, especially the campus MUDs do this. For instance, schMOOze is a MOO-based system to support the teaching of English as a second language or as a foreign language (ESL/EFL). Figure 9.2 shows the text-based campus map users are presented with.

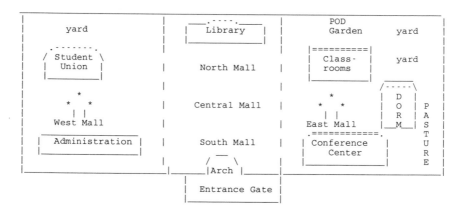

Figure 9.2. Text-based map of schMOOze.

As some have noted [23], this can easily undermine many of the advantages and opportunities for collaborative learning a MOO can offer. Of course there is much utility in the current metaphor of rooms in a teaching context. It makes implicit references to a periphery, a context, which helps create a set of expectations in the users of the system. This is what has been referred to as 'genre' by Brown and Duguid [24]. We believe that this can be extended without undermining the usefulness of the room metaphor to give users a much richer set of expectations about the nature of what will take place in the MUD. Creating virtual lecture theatres and seminar rooms may have the advantage of familiarity, but just as in real life they are not always the best forums for promoting dialogue and discussion, so in the MOO they may not be the best metaphor for promoting learning. We believe that *what* is taking place and its ground rules may be significantly influenced by *where* it is taking place. To this end we are exploring ways of visualizing the places where debate and discussion take place in ways that give strong messages about the kind of activities and behaviour expected there. The underlying motive is to help make it clearer to students the nature of the discussion they are taking part in and hence promote a more active style of learning. Figure 9.3 shows some of the possible metaphors for learning places and the expectations they should promote in learners. They suggest other ways of structuring debates and discussions in coMentor and suggest other objects that might be useful (e.g. manifestos for philosophical positions, agony aunts for those with philosophical/theoretical problems) and other forms of ground rules for discussions and debates.

Metaphor	*related concepts, issues*
Seminars	focus on "leaders", topics
Debates	taking sides, argument, evidence, propositions
Meetings	Diaries, slots, members, work, tasks, minutes
Chats	informal, my friends, unfocused
Visits	arrangements, guides, occasional
Journeys	trips, going somewhere, fellow travellers, companions, landscape
Groups	members, set (learning) tasks, group processes.
Clubs	interests, hobbies, membership, newsletters, meetings
Elections	votes, winners, soundbites, manifestos
Battle/fight	sides, weapons, winners/losers, reinforcements/support
Advice desk	Expert support, focused on my problems
Agony Aunt	Sympathetic, personalised
Play	make-believe, acting out, preparation/learning
Sport	practice, competition, skill, trainers.

Figure 9.3. Alternative metaphors and users' expectations.

9.5 Further Developments

Major in-class evaluation of coMentor will be taking place during the 1997-98 academic year. Figure 9.4 shows coMentor being used to support philosophy students. Following feedback from this we shall be examining the technological and educational feasibility of further visualization development. One possibility is the development of a virtual reality (VR) interface for coMentor, based on VRML2. Despite the potential, there are several issues that need addressing before a virtual reality system for supporting discussion and debate is developed. First, it is not clear the extent to which the visual aspects of VR (and, at the moment, its slow response over remote networks) might interfere with the basic educational functions of supporting collaborative working and learning through debate. For example, the forms of visualization which VRML allows may be distracting and/or limit the kinds of metaphorical elements discussed in the preceding section. Moreover, text-based discussion and VR do not mix easily. This can be seen in existing VR systems where typed chat is restricted to small talk bubbles that are acceptable for informal chatting but are inappropriate for the more extended discussions which coMentor is designed to support.

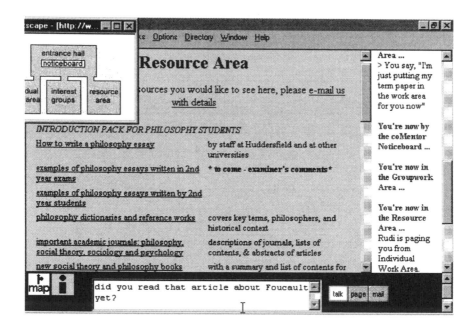

Figure 9.4. The coMentor resource area.

The second possible visual development of coMentor is the use of desktop video (or possibly just audio) as an alternative input and output medium. Use of video as input overcomes any resistance there might be to using typed input. However, the barriers to using video as a medium of debate and discussion in the social sciences are great. For the foreseeable future at least, few social science departments have the kinds of capital budget than can support the equipment needed, and beyond that there are problems of how video messages can be edited, archived and searched.

Although all our development so far has centred on extending existing MOO servers, there is now another alternative which could involve completely re-implementing the MOO and its database. That alternative is WWW push technology. More accurately called intelligent pull, this approach is being promoted by some of the major companies in the WWW field. Already, for example, Netscape, through the use of its Netcaster system can support on-line interactive games and chat rooms. If this becomes an 'industry standard' then, in line with our design philosophy of keeping things very simple for the user at the browser end, it may be worth re-implementing coMentor as a Netcaster 'channel'.

Acknowledgement

The coMentor project is supported by the JISC Technology Application Programme, Project JTAP 2/75.

References

1. Madden, N. E. and Slavin, R. E. (1983) Cooperative learning and social acceptance of mainstreamed academically handicapped students. *Journal of special education*, 1983, 17, 171-182.

2. Slavin, R. E. (1990) *Cooperative Learning: Theory, Research and Practice*. Prentice Hall, London.

3. Dansereau, D. F. (1988) *Learning and Study Strategies: Issues in Assessment, Instruction, and Evaluation*. Academic Press, New York.

4. Webb, N. (1985) *Learning to cooperate, cooperating to learn*. Plenum Publishing. New York.

5. Dillenbourg, P., Baker, M., Blaye, A. and O'Malley, C. (1994) The Evolution of Research on Collaborative Learning. http://tecfa.unige.ch/tecfa/research/lhm/ESF-Chap5.text

6. McKendree, Jean and Mayes, J T. (1997) The Vicarious Learner: investigating the benefits of observing peer dialogues. *CAL '97*, Easter 1997, University of Exeter.

7. Curtis, Pavel and Nichols, David A. (1996) MUDs Grow Up. Social Virtual Reality in the Real World, Xerox PARC, Palo Alto, CA. ftp://ftp.lambda.moo.mud.org/pub/MOO/papers/MUDsGrowUp.txt

8. Bartle, Richard. (1990) Early MUD history. http://www.apocalypse.org/pub/u/lpb/muddex/bartle.txt

9. Bruckman, Amy. (1993) Gender Swapping on the Internet. *The Internet Society*, San Fransisco, CA, August 1993 ftp://ftp.media.mit.edu/pub/asb/papers/gender-swapping.txt

10. Reid, Elizabeth. (1995) Virtual Worlds: Culture and Imagination. *CyberSociety: Computer Mediated Communication and Community*, Jones, Steven G. (Ed.), Sage, London, 164-183.

11. Haynes, Cynthia and Holmevik, Jan Rune (Eds.) (1997*) High Wired: On the Design, Use, and Theory of Educational MOOs*. The University of Michigan Press, Michigan.

12. Harris, Leslie. (1998) Composition in Cyberspace: A Model for Collaborative Teaching and Learning. Susquehanna University, n.d.
    http://www.cyberstation.net/~idd/v2/lharrisj.htm

13. Moock, Colin. (1996) Communication in the Virtual Classroom.
    http://colinmoock.iceinc.com/nostalgia/virtual_classroom.html

14. Bruckman, Amy (1994) Programming for Fun: MUDs as a Context for Collaborative Learning. *National Educational Computing Conference*. Boston, MA, June 1994.
    ftp://ftp.media.mit.edu/pub/asb/papers/necc94.txt

15. Germundson, Noel (1994) The Social and Educational Aspects of MUDs. *Carleton University Working Papers in Communication Technology and Culture*,
    http://www.oise.on.ca/~jnolan/muds/about_muds/mud.paper

16. Turbee, Lonnie (1996) MOOing in a foreign language: how, why, and who? *Information Technology Education Connection's International Virtual Conference/Exhibition on Schooling and the Information Superhighway*, June 3-9, Centre for Teacher Librarianship, Charles Sturt University,http://web.syr.edu/~lmturbee/itechtm.html

17. Robinson, D. and Fitter, M. (1992) Supportive evaluation methodology: a method to facilitate system development. *Behaviour and Information Technology*.11, 3, 151-159.

18. Kommers, P., Jonasson, D. and Mayes, J.T. (Eds.) (1992) Cognitive Tools for Learning. Springer-Verlag, Berlin.

19. Gibbs, Graham R. (1997) SocInfo Guide to IT Resources in Sociology, Politics and Social Policy. SocInfo CTI Centre, Stirling.

20. Ackerman, Mark S. and McDonald, David W. (1996) Answer Garden 2: Merging Organizational Memory with Collaborative Help. *Proceedings of the ACM Conference on Computer Supported Cooperative Work (CSCW '96)*, November 1996, 97-105. [Also at http://www.ics.uci.edu/~ackerman/docs/cscw96.ag2/cscw96.ag2.html].

21. Gibbs, Graham R and Robinson, D. (1998) CAL as learning tool: lessons from educational theory. *Using Technology Effectively in the Social Sciences*, Henry, M. (Ed.) Taylor and Francis, London.

22. Chute, D. L. (1995) Things I wish they had told me: developing and using technologies for psychology. *Psychology Software News*. 6, 1, 4-9.

23. Fanderclai, Tari L. (1995) MUDs in education: new environments, new pedagogies. *Computer-Mediated Communication Magazine*, 2, 1, (January 1, 1995) page 8 http://www.december.com/cmc/mag/1995/jan/fanderclai.html.

24. Brown, John Seely and Duguid, Paul. (1996) Keeping it simple. *Bringing Design to Software*, Winograd, T. (Ed.), Addison-Wesley and ACM Press, New York, 129-145.

Appendix 9.A   A Selected List of Educational MOOs/MUDs

Most of these MUDs and MOOs allow guest access.

APECKS/MOOtiny   http://spsyc.nott.ac.uk:8888/
Uses WOOM, a WWW access to the MOO

AskEricMOO   io.syr.edu 1234
http://io.syr.edu:8080/

AstroVR   No guest access
Astronomy MOO. A WWW/MOO system. Needs AstroVR
client, X-Window display and microphone.
http://astrovr.ipac.caltech.edu:8888/IntroductionToAstroVR

BayMOO   baymoo.org:8888
http://baymoo.sfsu.edu:4242/

BioMOO   bioinformatics.weizmann.ac.il 8888
A professional community of Biology researchers.
http://bioinformatics.weizmann.ac.il/Gustavo
WWW interface http://bioinfo.weizmann.ac.il:8888

BushMOO   bushnet.qld.edu.au 7777
http://www.bushnet.qld.edu.au/~jay/bushmoo/graphics.html

CardiffMOO   http://www.cm.cf.ac.uk/htbin/Andrew
Web access usually available between 19:00 hours and 06:00   W/moo_browser?look+79
hours GMT.

CHIME
http://www.psychology.nottingham.ac.uk/aigr/papers/CHIME/
CHIMEabstract.html

ColdStorm   turkle.musenet.org 3993
http://turkle.musenet.org:3994/

CollegeTown   galaxy.bvu.edu 7777
Supports small seminars, workshops, and collaborative
research groups for all ages.
http://www.bvu.edu/ctown/

coMentor   http://comentor.hud.ac.uk:7000
http://www.hud.ac.uk/comentor

Daedalus MOO   moo.daedalus.com 7777
Users are generally collaborating on writing projects
http://www.daedalus.com/mooinfo.html

DaMOO   DaMOO.csun.edu 7777
Learning Resource Center at California State University,
Northridge
http://DaMOO.csun.edu:8888/

Dhalgren   dhalgren.english.washington.edu 7777
An electronic community devoted to the exploration and
criticism of virtual reality and postmodern science fiction

Diversity University (DU)   moo.du.org:8888
http://www.du.org

E_MOO   tecfa.unige.ch 4242
http://tecfa.unige.ch:4243/

El MOOndo   gsep.pepperdine.edu 7777
http://moon.pepperdine.edu/~lpolin/MOOStuff.html

ExploreNet
A MUD-like system. Support role-playing games and
cooperative learning
http://www.cs.ucf.edu/~ExploreNet/index.html

FrenchMOO   moo.daedalus.com 8888
LanguageMOO

hiperMoo   moo.hipernet.ufsc.br 5000
Portuguese/Brazilian MOO. http://www.hipernet.ufsc.br

Internet Public Library MOO   moo.ipl.org 8888
http://www.ipl.org/moo/

JHM   jhm.ccs.neu.edu 1709
A MOO/WWW system. http://jhm.moo.mud.org:7043/

LambdaMOO   lambda.moo.mud.org 8888

Le MOOfrançais   logos.daedalus.com 8888
French langauge MOO

LinguaMOO   lingua.utdallas.edu 8888
Community for teachers and students in the Rhetoric and
Writing program at The University of Texas at Dallas
http://lingua.utdallas.edu:7000

LittleItaly   little.usr.dsi.unimi.it 4444
Mainly for foreign students of Italian
http://kame.usr.dsi.unimi.it:4444/   or, kame.usr.dsi.unimi.it 4444

Mars   math.washington.edu 777

Private education/research MOO; guest access not yet allowed

http://math.washington.edu:7776/

MediaMOO   mediamoo.cc.gatech.edu 8888

http://www.cc.gatech.edu/fac/Amy.Bruckman/MediaMOO/

MiamiMOO   moo.cas.muohio.edu 7777

(at Miami University, Ohio) http://moo.muohio.edu/

MirrorMOO   mirror.moo.mud.org 8889

http://mirror.moo.mud.org:8080/

MOOfrançais   moo.syr.edu 7777

LanguageMOO. http://moo.syr.edu/~fmoo/

MOOsaico   moo.di.uminho.pt 7777

Portuguese language MOO.

http://mes01.di.uminho.pt/RVirtual/AMB_VIRT/amb_virt.en.
html

MOOville   moo.ucet.ufl.edu 7777

postscript version of the MOOville manual at

http://www.ucet.ufl.edu/writing/MOO

MorgenGrauen Lpmud   mg.mud.de

German LanguageMUD. http://mud.uni-muenster.de/

MTMOO   maryann.hu.mtu.edu 8888

MundoHispano   europa.syr.edu 8888

LanguageMOO http://web.syr.edu/~lmturbee/mundo.html   moo.syr.edu 8888

MuseNet, the Multi-User Science Education Network   michael.ai.mit.edu

http://www.musenet.org/

Painted Porch Maud   maud.cariboo.bc.ca 4000

(Multiple Academic User Domain)

http://www.assiniboinec.mb.ca/www/isiit/maud.htm

PennMOO   moo.sas.upenn.edu 7777

Latin LanguageMOO http://ccat.sas.upenn.edu/MOO

http://www.english.upenn.edu/PennMOO

PMC-MOO   hero.village.virginia.edu 7777

The on-line magazine, Postmodern Culture, set up this MOO

for researchers in cooperation with The Institute for Advanced

Technology in the Humanities.

http://jefferson.village.virginia.edu/pmc/pmc-moo.html

Regina MOO   du.unibase.com 8888

A k-12 MOO

RiverMOO   kelp.honors.indiana.edu 8888

http://river.honors.indiana.edu:8889/

SchMOOze University   schmooze.hunter.cuny.edu 8888
ESL/EFL MOO. http://schmooze.hunter.cuny.edu:8888/

SenseMedia Snow   sapporo.sensemedia.net 9030
Uses the WOO transaction protocol
http://sensemedia.net/snow

SkooMOO   newsserver.iti.gov.sg 5577
An educational MOO meant for 7-18 year-olds, the first to be
set up in Singapore, and one of the first Asian MOOs
http://www.sol.com.sg/virtual/moo.html

SvenskMud   svmud.lysator.liu.se 2043
Swedish language MUD.
                                                 svmud.lysator.liu.se 2046
http://www.kuai.se/~wizard/svmud.html

The Palace
(VR MOO from Time Warner) http://www.thepalace.com/

The Sprawl   sprawl.sensemedia.net 7777
ChibaMOO. Uses the WOO protocol to provide WWW access
to the MOO. http://sensemedia.net/sprawl/

UNItopia   UNItopia.uni-stuttgart.de 3333
German MUD. http://unitopia.uni-stuttgart.de/

UT Austin OWL   babbage.cwrl.utexas.edu 8888
http://piglet.cc.utexas.edu/~blkangel/OWLWeb/
http://ccwf.cc.utexas.edu/~blkangel/OWLWeb/

Virtual Writing Center MOO (VWCMOO)   bessie.englab.slcc.edu 7777
An educational space where people come to talk and learn
about writing
http://bessie.englab.slcc.edu:7777/

VOU (Virtual On-Line University)   athena.edu 8888
http://www.athena.edu/ or http://www.vousi.com/

VUW MOO   watarts.uwaterloo.ca 7777
Virtual campus at the University of Waterloo.
http://colinmoock.iceinc.com/nostalgia/moo1.html

Walden Pond   olympus.lang.arts.ualberta.ca 8888
http://www.ualberta.ca/CNS/PUBS/WaldenPond.html

ZooMOO   moo.missouri.edu 8888
University of Missouri's MOO
http://www.missouri.edu:80/~moo/

Chapter 10

A Server for the Joint Production of Documents on the World Wide Web

Alain Karsenty and Bernard Merialdo[*]

This chapter presents a server allowing the Joint Production of Documents on the World Wide Web. While much research has been done in the field of synchronous and asynchronous shared editing, the integration of such techniques in the WWW environment raises a number of open issues, both on interface behaviour and coordination mechanisms. In this chapter, we present the features and the implementation issues that arise during the design of the server, as well as potential areas for future improvements.

10.1 Introduction

This chapter presents the current status of a project to build a server for the Joint Production of Documents (JPD) on the World Wide Web. This work is part of a European project Weg4Groups which aims to provide Web-based asynchronous group collaboration tools.

Recently, much work has been done in the field of shared editing, i.e. the possibility for a set of users to edit synchronously or asynchronously the same document. There are many user interface and technical issues that arise when implementing such systems. Indeed, human computer interaction has been focused on the relationship between one user and a machine, whereas in shared editing many users interact through computers. Therefore, the computer becomes more of a communication tool than a simple machine computing numbers. From the

[*] Institut Eurecom, 2229, route des Cretes, PB 193, 06904 Sophia Antipolis, FRANCE
Email:{karsenty, merialdo}@eurecom.fr

technical point of view, the designers of the system must find an appropriate architecture (e.g. whether data and control are replicated or centralised) and specific algorithms that fit the needs of such a distributed application.

The research in shared editing leads to a number of interesting results and prototypes. However, applying these results in the WWW environment is not straightforward. The constraints that are imposed by the WWW tools and protocols raise specific issues, both on the user interface and on the coordination mechanisms. For instance, designing an interface that can be supported by existing Web browsers imposes many constraints, and it is difficult to allow real-time updating or drag-and-drop interaction (although the expansion of JAVA is improving the situation rapidly).

In the following sections, we will give an overview of the Web4Groups project, then describe our server for the Joint Production of Documents (JPD). Next, we will outline potential areas for improvement. Finally, we will review existing work, and how it relates to our system.

10.2   The Web4Groups Project

The purpose of the Web4Groups project is to provide, demonstrate and establish a commonly available standard service for a fluent transfer of knowledge for Internet users. The project is funded by the Commission of the European Community within the Telematics Application Program. The project started in December 1995 and ended in December 1997.

The coordinator of the project is Omega Generation (Bologna, Italy). Partners of the project are organized in three groups according to their role and competence:

Developers:

*   Kapsch AG, Vienna, Austria

*   Stockholm University, Department of Computer and System Sciences, Stockholm, Sweden

*   Institut Eurecom, Sophia-Antipolis, France

*   Swiss Federal Institute for Forest, Snow and Landscape Research.

Technology assessment:

*   Research Unit for Socio-Economics, Austrian Academy of Sciences, Vienna, Austria.

User organizations:

*   European Forest Institute, Joensuu, Finland

*   Swiss Federal Institute for Forest, Snow and Landscape Research

- European Information Technology Association, Gateshead, Tyne and Wear, United Kingdom

- Community of Bologna, Italy.

The project is developing a service for asynchronous group collaboration. In the first phase, the service will include basic functionalities:

- asynchronous collaboration through discussions on message boards

- links between Web-pages and discussions

- basic security

- email and fax gateways.

The service will allow for the creation of message boards. These boards will be either public or private. The manager of the board will be able to assign roles to users corresponding to their authorization pattern. Users will browse boards and messages, and will eventually respond or extend a discussion by submitting new messages.

In the second phase of the project, more advanced functionality will be developed:

- support for multi-language discussions

- intelligent filters

- joint production of documents

- voting and rating tools.

The responsibility of Eurecom within the Web4Group project is to develop the joint document production service[14].

10.3 Principles of Joint Production of Documents (JPD)

In this section, we survey the major issues that arise in the design of the JPD server, and we discuss the orientations that we have chosen.

The role of the JPD server is to provide a facility by which a group of users can collaborate in the production of a single document. This means that users can create parts of the document, insert them in single structure, browse other users' contributions and comment on them, modify parts of the document (either content or structure) and retrieve part or all of the document's content.

---

[14] More details can be found on the Web4Groups WWW server at:
http://www.web4groups.at/

In the World Wide Web environment, users already have tools to create local documents (word processors such as Microsoft Word) and to access remote services (Web browsers such as Netscape Navigator). The JPD server must be integrated with these tools. Since there is a great variety of such tools, it is important to rely heavily on standard formats and protocols to exchange information. We permit users to create document parts using their favourite word processor, then use their Web browser to access the service that will allow them to insert these parts inside the global document. Modifications to the document are permitted with a similar mechanism.

In the process of creating a document (for example a paper or a book), there are generally two steps: first getting the contents right, second presenting this content in a manner that respects the typographical constraints of the publication (such as page length, number of columns, font sizes etc...). We assume that these two processes are separated, and that the server is only responsible for the first part, that is to manage the content of the document through the input of several users, but not for the second (getting the final presentation of the whole document). When the various parts of a document have been created by the authors, one user (the publisher) will retrieve the whole document and perform the last refinements that are required to get the presentable version of the document.

Users in the WWW are generally working asynchronously. However it might happen that two users want to modify the same part of the document at the same time. In this case a conflict arises that the server has to support efficiently. While the server could take hard actions such as locking document parts or erasing older versions, we have taken the view that users are mature and that the server's role is only to report such situations to the users involved and obey their instructions.

When a document is written collaboratively, it is often the case that users provide comments on parts written by others. Therefore it is useful that the server contains an annotation mechanism that allows users to attach comments, suggestions, evaluations to the various parts of the document being composed.

10.3.1 Document Structure

In this section, we describe some design choices that we have made in the design and construction of our JPD server.
We assume that a document follows a tree-based model: a document is a tree structure that contains nodes and leaves. Nodes contain a title and an ordered list of pointers to other nodes and leaves. Leaves contain only text.

The tree structure strictly follows the logical structure of the document into sections, subsections, subsubsections... so that each level of the tree corresponds to a level of headings. This constraint is used to facilitate partial views of the document, which will be obtained by displaying parts of the tree structure. This also facilitates modifications to the document structure, as they are directly mapped into modifications of the tree structure.

Within such a structure, we consider for now that the name of the node is the title of the section. For instance, the following structure:

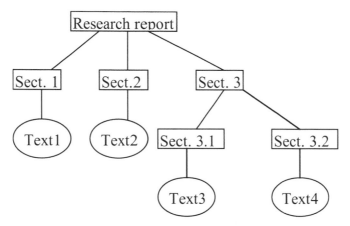

Figure 10.1. Logical structure.

would generate this text:

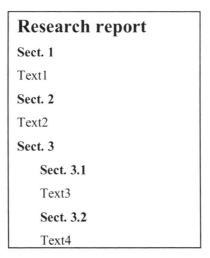

Figure 10.2. Physical representation of a logical structure.

10.3.2 Server Architecture

The Web4Groups server is implemented as two main modules (Figure 10.3): the KOM server manages the database of distributed objects. These objects can be messages, forums (boards), users, groups, and their associated methods and properties. There might be several KOM servers in various locations on the Internet. Objects can be linked together, either on the same or on different KOM servers. For example, a message contains a link to the forum where it was published and another link to the user who created it. The Interface Gateway (written in Java) makes the interface between the user and the objects accessible in the KOM database. Thus, when a client sends a request to the Web4Groups server, the Interface Gateway translates the HTTP request into a KOM request which it sends to the KOM server, retrieves the results from the server, builds the response to the user as an HTML page and sends this page back to the client. The JPD server uses specific KOM objects (nodes and leaves), and is implemented as specific procedures in the Interface Gateway.

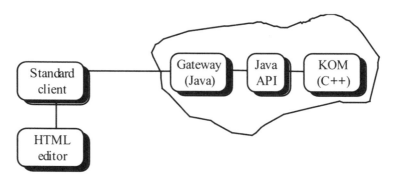

Figure 10.3. Architecture.

10.3.3 Server Functionalities

The basic functions of the JPD server are to create, modify, and delete the document structure and contents in an asynchronous way. The following functions are available:

- *create*

- *delete*

- *see*: allows the user to obtain a copy of the object for visualisation only (the client interface should ensure that)

- *take*: allows the user to obtain a copy while instructing the server that he intends to modify it. The server can then take appropriate actions to avoid or manage potential conflicts (explained below)

- *write*.

It is also possible to copy a document (or part of the document). This is useful for creating frozen versions of documents.

10.3.4 Format

As we said previously, the purpose of the JPD server is not to produce the final presentable form of the document, but rather to build the content of the document and its structure. Final formatting will be done separately by one user (the publisher) when the content is ready. Thus we need to have a common format for the document, which most word processors can import and export. We chose HTML to be this common format, because of a number of advantages. The HTML language is easy to learn, so that is it possible to write HTML even with a simple text editor, without advanced word processing facilities. It is also easy to read, so that you can easily understand the source of an HTML document. Most word processors currently have or will shortly have an import/export HTML feature, making such documents easy to produce and read by everyone. Finally, it is fairly easy to concatenate multiple HTML files into one HTML file, which is an important feature when we want to merge the various parts of the document into a single file.

As part of the Web4Groups base system, we have developed a « smart text » filter which smartly converts text into HTML. For instance, underlined text is formatted as a Heading, indented text is converted into List Items, tables can be inserted etc. This feature is also available in the JPD server, and can be used to create text quickly with a text editor or with the Web browser itself.

10.3.5 Upload

Uploading a section of a document is done either through the Form Upload method [13] or by inputting the text directly into a text form. The issue that arises is how to upload an HTML file that contains graphics and references to other HTML files. Indeed, the inline graphics also need to be sent; however, for security reasons, the server cannot ask the client to upload the necessary inline graphic objects. Our simple solution is to let the user select all the files necessary to upload (HTML files and graphics) when uploading a given file. The name of the graphics files should, however, match the referenced name in the HTML files. This is a manual solution, but an automatic one is discussed in the second part of this document.

In the next section we discuss another upload issue, the problem of references.

10.3.6 Hypertext Handling

The next problem we address is how to store documents in the server that include references to other objects. If the JPD server simply stores a document, without scanning the content for references, it will not be visualized properly afterwards. For instance, a gif file referenced as *file:/homes/karsenty/image.gif* will not be found when visualized by another user.

Thus, when copying a file onto the Web4Groups server, a number of operations must be performed:

1. generate new names for the files

2. scan recursively for references and change them appropriately

3. when encountering the same references, do not generate a new file each time

4. garbage collection: eliminate files that are no longer referenced.

Issue 1 does not raise any difficulties. Issue 3 can be addressed by storing the initial reference and its new name in a two-dimensional array in the server. When scanning a document, the fact that the reference has not been already scanned must be checked. However, the content of the file must also be checked since the reference to a file can point to different content (for instance, if the reference is a meteorological image that is updated every hour).

Issue 4 only leads to the observation that garbage collection should be done when the system is quiescent (i.e. nobody is editing a file). Otherwise, there is a risk that a referenced file will be deleted.

The most difficult problem is issue 2. It can be resolved in different ways in order to ensure that a document visualized locally can be visualized the same way by any user. Three kinds of references can be found:

*   absolute Web references, such as http://www.netscape.com/index.html

*   relative Web references, such as href="../toto.gif "

*   local references, such as file://homes/karsenty/toto.gif

Absolute references do not raise any issue, except if they are used instead of local references. For instance, one could write:

    <IMG SRC = "http://www.eurecom.fr/~karsenty/toto.gif">

instead of:

    <IMG SRC = "toto.gif">

This case should be handled as a relative reference.

In order to handle relative and local Web references, we can have different approaches:

- *pictures only mode:* if we look at joint editing as a means to produce printable rather than hypertext documents, there will be difficulties. The only references we have to deal with are included pictures. In this case, when uploading/downloading a document, the references to pictures should be translated from one system to another, and the object that is referenced should also be uploaded/downloaded.

- *absolute/relative2local:* the other possibility is to transfer the references to other objects into local references in the Web4Groups server and transfer all the referenced documents in the Web4Groups server. However, the translation should be limited to the local server, at most. For instance, if one were editing a document at Eurecom which contained the following references, they would be translated as shown after the arrow →:

  - Eurecom server (http://www.eurecom.fr) → http://www.eurecom.fr

  - my home directory at Eurecom (http://www.eurecom.fr/~karsenty/index.html) →

    file:/homes/w4g/id1.html

  - another server (http://www.netscape.com) → http://www.netscape.com

  - absolute files (file://homes/karsenty/test.gif) → file://home/w4g/id2.gif

  - relative Web reference "image.gif" → file:/homes/w4g/id2.gif

The absolute/relative2local algorithm is not trivial. It is recursive and must take into account loops that are frequent in Web documents. An appropriate naming convention should also be used for storing documents in the Web4Groups server:

- *customizable absolute/relative2local:* since we cannot always guess what the user wants to translate into absolute/local, one way to figure it out is to ask him/her. When creating a hyperlink, it must be specified whether the link should be saved as absolute or local. This solution, however, burdens the user, and should only be an option.

- *absolute/relative2absolute:* a more simple, if inelegant, solution consists of turning all references into absolute references; consequently, it is not necessary to download the referenced objects. It is, however, difficult to maintain the state of a document with such a solution. The elements (pictures, hypertext links) will be dispatched at different sites and it is difficult to ensure that the elements will not move or be destroyed.

To summarise, absolute/relative2local is the most suitable solution, since it allows hypertext documents to be saved.

10.3.7 Annotations

An annotation service is provided as part of the base Web4Groups server. A user can create a forum that is linked to any WWW page (URL), even if this page is not on the Web4Groups server itself, but at another site. Other users may join this forum and discuss by appending messages. The annotation service allows one to ask whether any forum has been linked to a particular page, or to a page nearby (with a similar URL). If it is the case, the appropriate page is shown so that the user may see the last contributions and eventually participate in the discussion. This service may annotate any existing WWW page in the world, but can only be used by users connecting to a Web4Groups server.

The JPD server directly benefits from this annotation facility. Since document elements (nodes representing sections and leaves representing text) are Web4Groups objects, they are identified by a Web4Groups address and can be annotated as regular WWW pages. This allows an annotation at the level of each section or piece of text.

There are currently two limitations :
- the user has to specifically ask if an annotation is available for a given section (it is not yet sent automatically to him when he consults an annotated page).
- annotations are attached to the tree structure and not to the content of the tree itself. For example it is not yet possible to attach an annotation to a specific word within a paragraph.

10.4 User Interface

The design of a good user interface is crucial for the adoption of the system by final users. It has to be both fast and clear to understand. The current implementation (Figure 10.4) is based on HTML forms and the CGI-bin protocol. Forms allow the users to select multiple objects or options, to activate functions and to enter text directly. When forms are filled and sent by the users, the Interface Gateway receives the request, decodes the arguments according to the CGI-bin protocol, and executes the corresponding commands. The results are returned as an HTML page to the user.

Most JPD functions are easy to activate using an HTML interface. The most difficult operation is the one that moves objects, because one has to specify both the origin (which section) and the destination (location between two sections and level of heading). This operation is performed in two steps: an initial page shows an outline of the document where each section is associated to a checkbox. The user selects the section he wants to move and pushes the « move » button. Another page is then displayed where checkboxes have been added between sections showing all the possible destination locations. The user selects the proper destination and activates the operation. To reduce the number of operations required, it is planned that future implementations will use a Java user interface, which will be discussed at the end of this chapter.

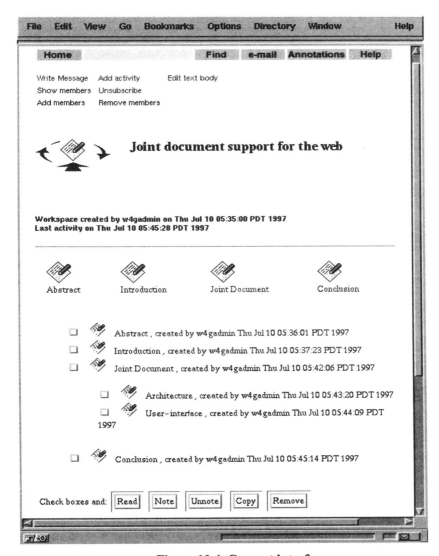

Figure 10.4. Current interface.

The Web4Groups server also allows users to access the system using a line-oriented interface (mainly for local debugging), an email interface as well as a fax and voice-mail interface. However, those other interfaces are limited and only a few number of JPD operations will be accessible in that manner (e.g. put and get sections, get document, etc).

10.5   Extensions

10.5.1 Features

In this final section, we discuss features which are not yet implemented in the software but which are being considered for implementation in subsequent releases.

Versions

The server maintains several versions of the objects (nodes, leaves) as they are modified. The maximum number of versions is specified for the whole document at creation time. Each time a modification is made to an object, a new version is created.

Because we trust users, the last version is always the valid one. The role of the other version is to facilitate discussion and provide support for an undo function.

Merging and conflicts

An important role of the server is to facilitate the management of conflicts, when a user makes a modification over another user's modifications.

Conflict management is handled by a soft-lock mechanism, since we consider this method more flexible for the user. The soft-lock rules are as follows:

- when user A requests an object for modification, this object is soft-locked by the server. This means that, whenever a user B requests the same object for modification, he will receive a warning message stating that this object is being modified by A.

- as users are supposed to be mature, user B may still modify this object and submit his modifications to the server.

- when a user submits a new version of an object, this request is always accepted by the server (provided that the user has write permission for the document) and the soft-lock flag is reset (Figure 10.5).

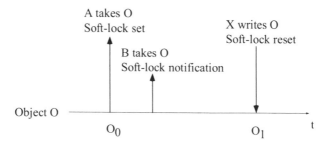

Figure 10.5. Soft-lock notification and reset.

Rule for the soft-lock:

The soft-lock belongs to an object and not a version. It is set when:

- a user requests an object for modification, and

- the soft-lock is clear.

The soft-lock is cleared when a user writes a new version of the object.

When the soft-lock is set, the server also remembers the user name and the date/time of the *take* operation. When a user submits a new version of an object, and this object has been modified by someone else in the meantime, the server creates a new version, but also raises a conflict flag for this object and warns the last user (Figure 10.6). It is up to this user, or to any other user that will later modify this object, to resolve the conflict.

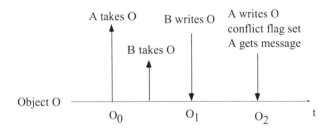

Figure 10.6. Conflict flag.

Rules for the conflict flag:

The conflict flag belongs to an object and not a version. The conflict flag is set (Figure 10.7) when a user writes a new version that is a modification of a version older than the current one. The conflict flag is cleared (Figure 10.8) when a user writes a new version that is a modification of the current version.

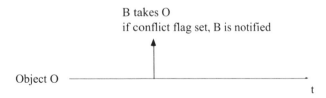

Figure 10.7. Conflict notification.

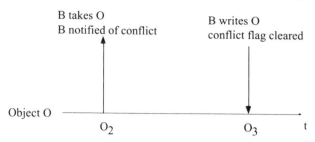

Figure 10.8. Conflict flag cleared.

When a user sends a *see* or *take* request, he gets the current version of the object, together with an indication of the status of the soft-lock and conflict flags.

Annotations

We designed a scheme to support the annotation of documents at the word level. A prototype implementation of this scheme has been done, but is not yet integrated in the server. It is currently based on a set of CGI-bin scripts that receives requests from the users (through the form interface) and creates, updates and deletes local files accordingly.

The procedure involves the following steps:

- an editable document contains a button with a label "Annotate document" that calls a script with certain specific parameters (such as the real filename of the document).

- this script will parse the document, filter HTML tags, and assign a token number to each word of the text. The script will produce a document with the same physical layout, but where each word of text is an anchor that calls the annotation script with the proper token number.

- the user selects the word of text where he wants to place the annotation. The annotation server will answer with a form interface that contains a text area that the user will fill with the content of the annotation.

- the content of the annotation is then sent to the server which creates a new file to contain the annotation, and modifies the original document by adding a hypertext reference to this file at the proper position, as indicated by the token number. The anchor for this reference is a special annotation widget.

- by clicking on this widget, users will browse the content of the annotation. They also have the option to remove the annotation, in which case the corresponding file is deleted and the document is modified to remove the hypertext reference.

One advantage of this scheme is that it allows placement of annotations at every word of the document. Since the modifications of the documents are done by CGI-bin scripts, it is relatively easy to ensure that the integrity of the document is preserved (the content of the document cannot be destroyed by malicious or erroneous operations of users).

The current implementation is still an exploratory prototype that is only used for experimentation. It lacks several features needed for serving as a production system with real users.

First, it uses documents contained in files rather than Web4Groups objects. Second, there is currently no user authorisation checking.

Within the Web4Groups project, an extension of the annotation mechanism using Javascript is planned to automate the process of querying for annotations for a given page. The new service will be activated by accessing a page (for convenience it should be stored in the bookmark file) which contains a Javascript that will retrieve the last page in the history (the page the user is looking for annotations to) and will automatically query the annotation service about this page. This facility could easily be integrated in the JPD server as well.

10.5.2 Upload Extensions

Currently, files are uploaded manually; however, using a helper application is one way to overcome this issue. The helper can scan the uploaded HTML file and automatically upload the inline graphics. However, depending on which HTML editor is used and how it can be parameterised, this process can be done in a number of ways.

The first solution is that the helper is launched before a section is edited (Figure 10.9). The helper then starts the HTML editor and waits until the user quits the editor, at which point the document is sent to the server.

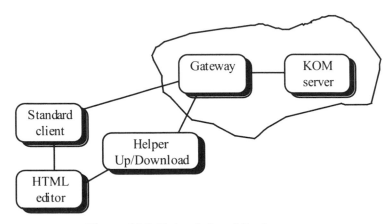

Figure 10.9. Extended architecture.

The other solution is that the HTML editor is launched first and, when quitting it, the helper is launched in order to save the file in the server. However, the HTML editor must be customised to be able to launch the helper application when needed.

No matter which solution is used, an application must be launched automatically when getting a file to be edited. One way to do it is to create an HTML/edit MIME type and configure the browser to launch the application when getting this MIME type (this is possible in Netscape, for instance).

An important and complex function performed by the helper is translating references, which we discussed in an earlier section.

10.5.3 Generic Model

Currently, the logical model maps directly onto the physical model. However, we plan to develop a more flexible system where the logical and physical models are independent. With such a structure, the name of the node is independent of the real name of the section attached to the node. For instance, let us consider the example described earlier on Figure 10.. In that case, the resulting document produced would be Figure 10.10.

```
Text1

Text2

Text3

Text4
```

10.10. Physical representation of a logical structure.

Whether we adopt a more generic model or not would depend on the user groups' feedback, since both options can be implemented. Our choice of a less generic model was made because it seemed more intuitive to understand.

10.5.4 User Interface

The current user interface is intended to be used by most browsers. However, things change quickly in this field, and we are exploring in parallel the use of Frames and the use of Java.

With regard to the Java implementation, we are currently developing a Tree applet that will allow the easy visualisation and modification of the outline view.

Although in beta version, JDK already makes available a tree class and drag-and-drop extension. This way, users can easily modify the outline structure by drag-and-drop instead of going through multiple pages. Moreover, they can customise the level of headings very quickly.

10.6   Related Work

From the non-Web related research, we can separate asynchronous and synchronous shared editors. Asynchronous systems clearly separate the text from comments/versions from other users, e.g. ForComments [1], Griffon [2] and Word 5.1[3]. Other systems deal with how to merge different versions of the same document. For instance, Prep [4] is a shared text editor that smartly compares different versions and shows users what has been removed/added.

Synchronous shared editors, such as the text editors GROVE [5] and Sasse [6] or the drawing systems GROUPDRAW, GROUPSKETCH [7] and CaveDraw [8], allow multiple users to modify a document simultaneously. SASSE (Synchronous Asynchronous Structured Shared Editor) also provides asynchronous features such as annotations.

As said earlier, although those systems provide interesting features and innovative implementation, they cannot be directly applied to the Web. With regard to Web-related research, BSCW [9] allows a set of users to exchange documents in different formats. The interface provides interesting information, such as the owner of the document, what document is new, etc. The implementation is based on CGI scripts and uses the PUT feature of the server to upload documents. However, BSCW does not really deal with shared editing; it is mostly a sophisticated file server.

Another interesting approach is the definition of transformation language [10] that allows interactive restructuring of HTML documents. It has been used to implement an authoring environment wired on the World Wide Web, Tamaya [11].

Finally, with regard to versioning systems, VTML [12] is a new content-type that has been proposed to communicate version information between Web-browsers and clients.

Despite the existence of these various systems, there is not, as yet, a joint production tool available for the Web.

10.7   Conclusion

We have presented a server for the Joint Production of Documents on the World Wide Web, part of the Web4Groups project, a European initiative for setting up non-simultaneous group communication service for the World Wide Web. We have described the features and the many implementation issues that arise during the design of such a system.

In future, the user groups will help us refine the prototype. Indeed, this is a TELEMATICS European project that therefore strongly emphasises user needs. At this point we have performed the user requirements phase and are ready to submit a first prototype for testing by the user-groups.

Future work will continue by refining user-needs and developing, in parallel, a Java interface in order to have a more powerful user interface for Joint Production of Documents.

References

1. Opper, S. (1988) A groupware toolbox. *Byte*, December.

2. Decouchant, D., Quint, V. and Vatton, I. (1992) L'édition coopérative de documents avec Griffon. dans les actes des Quatrième Journée sur l'Ingénierie *des Interfaces Homme-Machine (IHM '92)*, Décembre 1992, 137-142.

3. Microsoft (1992) *Microsoft Word User's Guide*, Microsoft_Corporation.

4. Neuwirth, C.M., Chandhok, R., Kaufer, D.S., Erion, P., Morris, J. and Miller, D. (1992) Flexible DIFF-ing in a Collaborative Writing System. *Proc. ACM Conference on Computer Supported Collaborative Work (CSCW)*, 147-154.

5. Ellis , C.A., Gibbs, S.J. and Rein, G.L. (1991) Groupware, Some Issues and Experiences. *Communications of the ACM*, 34, 1, 38–58.

6. Baecker, R.M., Nastos, D., Posner, L.R., and Mawby, K.L. (1992) The user-centred iterative design of collaborative writing software *Proceedings of the Workshop on Real Time Group Drawing and Writing Tools held at CSCW '92*, Toronto, Ontario, October 31, 1992.

7. Greenberg, S., Roseman, M. and Webster, D. (1992) Human and Technical Factors of Distributed Group Drawing Tools, *Interacting with Computers*, 4, 3, 364-392.

8. Lu, I.M. and Mantei, M.M. (1991) Idea Management in a Shared Drawing Tool *Proceedings of the Second European Conference on Computer-Supported Cooperative Work*, September 25-27, 97-112.

9. Bentley, R., Horstmann, T., Sikhel, K. and Trevor, J. (1995) Supporting Collaborative Information Sharing with the World Wide Web: The BSCW Shared Workspace System. *Proc. of the 4th World Wide Web Conference*, Boston.

10. Bonhomme, S. and Roisin, C. (1996) Interactively Restructuring HTML Documents. *Proc. of the 5th International World Wide Web Conference*, Paris.

11. Quint, V., Roisin, C. and Vatton, I. (1995) A Structured Authoring Environment for the World Wide Web. *Computer Networks and ISDN Systems*, 27, 6 (April), 831-840.

12. Vitali, F. and Durand, D. (1995) Using versioning to support collaboration on the WWW. *Proc. of the 4th World Wide Web Conference*, Boston.

13. Nebel, E. and Masinter L. (1995), rfc1867, Network Working Group , Request For Comments: 1867, Nov. 1995. http://www.cis.ohio-state.edu/htbin/rfc/rfc1867.html

Chapter 11

Support for Authoring and Managing Web-based Coursework: The TACO Project

Martina Angela Sasse, Christopher Harris, Ismail Ismail and

*Peter Monthienvichienchai**

The aim of the TACO (Teaching And Coursework Online) project was to develop a generic system for distributed authoring and management of computer-based coursework. The requirements for such a system were established in requirements capture workshops with lecturers from a range of academic departments. Lecturers can create Web-based self-learning exercises and assessed coursework - without knowledge of HTML or other authoring languages. A form-based user interface allows lecturers to choose from a range of question types, marking schemes and weightings, including confidence assessment. Students completing coursework receive immediate feedback in the form of marks, and comments or explanations associated with questions. Lecturers and students interact with TACO through a Web browser. The system itself consists of a Java Web server and a commercial database; the only code written for the project is a number of Java "servlets" which manage the interaction between these. Lecturers from different departments at UCL used the first implementation of TACO to author sets of self-learning exercises and assessed assignments for one of their courses. The results of this pilot study - involving 4 lecturers and 500 students - are encouraging; additional functionality and improvements to the user interface have been identified.

* Department of Computer Science, University College London, Gower Street, London, WC1E 6BT, U.K., A.Sasse@cs.ucl.ac.uk

11.1   Introduction

Student numbers in most UK Higher Education Institutions (HEIs) have increased considerably over the past few years, and in most, this has not been matched by an increase in the number of teaching staff. At the same time, the perception of how teaching in HEIs should be delivered has changed. Teaching Quality Assessment (TQA), and rules for accreditation by professional bodies in science and engineering, suggest that good courses provide students with regular feedback on their progress, and assess student knowledge and skills throughout a course, rather than just in end-of-year exams. Both feedback and continuous assessment can - and is in many HEIs - provided through coursework. For coursework to provide effective feedback and assessment, it has:

- to be assessed and returned to students quickly

- to point out discrepancies between an individual student's expected and actual knowledge and skills; and

- to suggest how the student can remedy shortcomings identified.

Providing such coursework on a regular basis requires considerable time and effort. This poses a problem in the current situation, where most teaching staff have *less* time per student than previously. It is therefore not surprising that the HEIs are keen to utilise computer-assisted learning (CAL) solutions to improve the efficiency of course delivery. Most CAL applications to date, however, fall into the category of *primary courseware*: they deliver materials containing knowledge about a subject to the student [1, 2]. Laurillard [3] states that educational technology which only "pushes" information in this one-way manner does not provide effective support for the learning process. Yet, there are far fewer commercial CAL systems that provide feedback to the learner, and/or support assessment. Systems which include self-testing exercises are often not adopted by HEIs because the content and assessment cannot be easily tailored to the requirements of a particular course. If a standard set of questions on a topic is widely used for assessed coursework, the possibility of plagiarism is a further concern.

There are examples of lecturers writing their own computer-based systems to distribute self-teaching exercises and/or assessed coursework for their particular courses and topics (e.g. [4, 5]). The majority of lecturers, however, lack the expertise required to write their own systems from scratch. It is also self-evident that, from a HEI's point of view, the construction and maintenance of a myriad of systems for coursework in different subjects or courses cannot be an efficient solution. The aim of the work reported in this chapter was therefore to investigate whether it is possible to provide a generic system for authoring, distribution, marking and administration of assignments for student feedback and assessment.

The World Wide Web (WWW) provides a good platform for such a system:

- It is widely deployed and used in HEIs in the UK (and elsewhere)

- Most teaching staff and students are familiar with Web browsers

- It can be accessed from a wide range of different hardware platforms and operating systems

- Remote access is possible – there is an increasing requirement to support:

  - teaching staff and students working from home

  - HEIs with geographically distributed-sites

  - HEIs who collaborate and deliver joint courses

  - HEIs who deliver courses to commercial organisations.

TACO (Teaching And Coursework Online) was created to provide a generic Web-based coursework authoring and delivery system. Lectures and students interact with the system via Web browsers (see Figure 11.1).

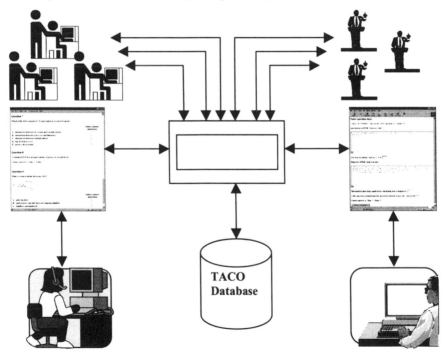

Figure 11.1. Lecturers and students interact with TACO via Web browsers.

The authoring tool enables lecturers of any subject to create learning exercises and assessed coursework without using HTML or other Web programming tools. They can choose from a range of question types and marking schemes, and assign weightings and add confidence assessments. The requirements for these features had been identified during the requirements capture phase (described in more detail in Section 11.2). Apart from marks, lecturers can attach comments or explanations to any question, to further students' understanding. Since an increasing number of lecturers provide course materials – authored by themselves or others – via the Web, integration of those materials with the coursework system was deemed to be desirable. TACO supports this because courseworks are accessed via URLs, and URLs can be incorporated into comments (see Section 11.3 for a detailed description of TACO's architecture and implementation). TACO has been used by 4 lecturers in UCL in autumn 1997 to author and distribute coursework to their students - Section 4 reports the results of the evaluation by lecturers and students. A discussion of the experiences gained during the project, and an outline of further development proposed for the system, is provided in Section 11.5.

11.2 Background

Like in many other HEIs, a number of systems for student feedback and assessment had been developed by individual lecturers in various departments of UCL. The Higher Education Research and Development Unit (HERDU) conducted a survey of such systems, and arranged a number of exhibitions and workshops to raise awareness amongst other teaching staff about the availability of these systems. Some systems, such as LAPT [10,14] (developed by Anthony Garner-Medwin in the Department of Physiology), met the requirements of lecturers teaching related subjects and have been adopted for courses in other departments – e.g. Pharmacology. A recurring concern among teaching staff, however, was the difficulty of adapting existing systems to the pedagogical and administrative requirements of other courses.

Two existing Web-based systems for self-teaching exercises and assessed coursework (developed by Kevin Boone in the Department of Physiology, and by M. Angela Sasse and Chris Harris in the Department of Computer Science, respectively) created most interest during those workshops. The main reasons for the interest in Web-based solutions were lecturers' and students' familiarity with Web-browers, and the ability to access such systems from a wide range of systems throughout UCL and from home (see also Section 11.1).

HERDU offered three workshops for those lecturers who had expressed an interest in using a Web-based system to create student exercises and assessments. The aim of those workshops was:

- To provide lecturers with a detailed understanding of the functionality provided by the two existing systems.

- To give lecturers hands-on experience of authoring and completing sample assignments by their own courses using the existing systems.

- To identify requirements for a generic system for authoring and distributing coursework.

These workshops were, therefore, organised as requirements capture workshops in the tradition of *participatory design* [6, 7], a design approach which is being adopted by an increasing number of projects developing educational technology [8, 9]. Of the 25 lecturers who had expressed an interest in using a Web-based system and were invited to the workshop, 6 attended the workshop and one sent a detailed wish-list by email. The workshops were moderated by Kim Issroff of HERDU, with the designers of the existing systems (Kevin Boone and M. Angela Sasse) explaining functionality offered by existing systems, and discussing ways of implementing requirements raised by lecturers. Despite the small number of lecturers participating, the organiser felt that a sufficient range of subjects and requirements was represented (Biochemistry and Molecular Biology, Dutch, Electrical and Electronic Engineering, Greek and Latin, Mathematics, Pharmacology, Primary Care and Population Sciences). The discussions during the workshops were recorded (with lecturers' permission) and transcribed; the transcripts provided the basis for the requirements specification. The draft set of requirements was circulated for comment to the 25 lecturers on a the mailing list; 3 lecturers provided detailed comments and feedback. The final set of requirements (see Section 11.2.1) formed the basis of the system specification, and the system was implemented over a period of 8 weeks.

The first implementation of TACO was then submitted to a pilot study. Four lecturers (3 who had contributed to the requirements, and one of the designers, M. Angela Sasse) used TACO to author sets of assignments for courses running in the autumn term of 1997. Almost 500 students were registered for the courses in which the sets of assignments were used (see Section 11.4 for details of the evaluation and results).

11.2.1 Requirements for a Web-based Coursework System

The requirements identified in the workshop can be divided into 4 different aspects: *authoring, distribution, marking* and *administration* of coursework. A detailed list of the requirements elicited are shown in Appendix 11.A. (Requirements not addressed in the first implementation of TACO - because of limited time available before the start of the pilot - are printed in italics.)

One of the major concerns we expected to be raised in connection with *authoring* of coursework was whether lecturers would have to use the Hypertext Markup Language (HTML) or another Web authoring tool. Whilst some of the participants had used HTML previously, there was a general consensus that having to learn and use HTML would deter many lecturers from adopting a Web-based coursework system. Other systems such as CASTLE [13] and QUASI [15] have addressed this by providing form-based user interfaces which generate the HMTL code for the assignments. These existing systems do not, however, support the range of *question types* which lecturers want to use, since they tend to focus on supporting binary and multiple choice questions (MCQs).

Like many other lecturers, the participants in this project felt that these question types can encourage the "wrong" type of student learning. Students may try to guess the right answer when they do not know it. With repeated practice, students may simply learn which answer is the "correct" one for a particular question (*"The correct answer to Question 5 is B"*). Despite these concerns, MCQs have been used extensively over a considerable period of time, and a number of techniques have been developed to combat these problems:

1. Penalty *weightings* for incorrect answers can deter students from taking a guess when they do not know the correct answer.

2. Creating a *pool of question variants*, and selecting variants randomly, can make learning the "correct" answer more difficult.

3. The addition of *confidence assessment* can encourage students to assess how well they have understood topics covered in the course, and thus provide meaningful feedback [4, 10].

4. Making students *assess each answer* (instead of asking them to chose one or more answers) can encourage students to compare answers and reflection on their merits; this type of reflection leads to deeper understanding of the topics [11].

The merits and drawbacks of these techniques were discussed in some detail during the requirements capture phase. It emerged that individual lecturers have very strong convictions as to:

•   which question types are suitable for particular topics and students, and

•   which of the techniques available will encourage the desired type of learning and behaviour amongst particular students.

Consequently, any system which aims to support authoring of assignments for a large number of lecturers and academic disciplines has to offer a great deal of *flexibility*: a wide range of preferred question types has to be supported. The same is true for *marking* and *feedback*: a wide range of marking schemes, weightings and associated techniques has to be supported. All lecturers agreed that providing feedback to students is important. The form and extent of feedback lecturers want to give, however, varies widely. Some lecturers want to:

•   display the correct answer to the student - others do not

•   provide comments or explanations as well as marks

•   display detailed feedback irrespective of student performance - others want to direct student effort towards topics where their knowledge is weak

•   integrate assessment with other materials, such as lecture notes, textbooks, lab exercises.

Support for *distribution* of electronic coursework is inherent in the chosen platform. Like many HEIs, UCL has a wide range of hardware platforms and operating systems, but the vast majority of computers are networked and have Web browsers installed. All lecturers in the workshops had use of a suitable machine in UCL, and a significant number had Web access from home. An increasing number of students also have Web access from home, and thus can access and complete assignments without taking up a machine in UCL. One group whose requirements could not be addressed in the first implementation are students who have a computer, but no Internet access. It is, in principle, possible to download assignments onto disk. However, lecturers were wary of the *security* implications of allowing students to download questions - and answers - which are part of assessed coursework.

Increasing student numbers and TQA are likely to be at the root of the detailed *administrative* support requirements elicited in this study. One obvious requirement is to obtain student marks at the end of the course in a format that is suitable for further processing (e.g. in lecturers' spreadsheets or an HEIs' examination records). But lecturers also wanted to monitor individual students' effort and performance *during* the course, in order to identify those who are not practicing or performing well enough. Statistics on assignments and questions were seen as an essential feature to weed out "bad" questions (too easy, too difficult, ambiguously phrased). They could also be used to identify topics where student performance across the board indicates lack of understanding (e.g. because of the way in which the material was delivered). Administrative support features allow lecturers to intervene whilst a course is in progress to improve the fate of individual students, and the quality of the course.

A final but fundamental point emerging from the discussion is many lecturers' perception of computer-based coursework as an efficient, but somewhat inferior, means of providing feedback and conducting assessment. Computer-based assessment is seen by many as a *necessary* means of coping with increased numbers of students and coursework, rather a *desirable* tool for supporting student learning. The distinction may be a subtle one from a system developer's point of view. However, we can infer from previous case studies of technology and change [6, 12] that this type of perception is likely to have a major impact on the rate of adoption, and the quality of coursework produced with such a system. From the evidence obtained in this study, we believe that what is required to change this perception of computer-based assessment is support for more *active* ways student interact with the system. Lecturers believe asking students to enter text, numbers or drawings in response to a question requires that students understand the material they have been taught. Actively constructing an answer requires a "deeper" understanding of what is required than choosing options from a list of answers. From the developers' point of view, the problem is that these types of questions require more elaborate technical solutions than MCQs. Active images and student submission of drawings via the Web require a Java-based system. A marking facility for numerical and text submissions which can identify partially correct answers requires pattern-matching.

11.3 The TACO System

The design team realised early in the project that the high degree of flexibility requested by lecturers (see 11.2.1) ruled out using existing systems such as CASTLE and QUASI as a basis for implementing a generic coursework authoring and management system. This section presents a summary technical description of the software and processes that constitute the TACO system. Supporting active images and submission of drawings by students via the Web can only be implemented in Java; even though the first implementation of TACO does not support these features, the platform was chosen so that they can be implemented later. Lecturers and students interact with the system via a Web browser; the choice of platform means that the browser has to be Java-compatible (e.g Netscape 3 or 4).

The TACO architecture consists of a Java Web server, which facilitates the interaction between student and lecturer clients, and the TACO Web server and a database (Oracle[15]) [16]. These requests are made using CGI (Common Gateway Interface) requests to a number of specially designed *servlets* (described below). The reason for adopting a CGI-based design is grounded in the fact that very few machines, around the University, were running Java-enabled versions of the Netscape Navigator browser. Subsequently, it was decided to address this constraint by using a CGI-based interface to TACO, which works independently of Java on the client machine.

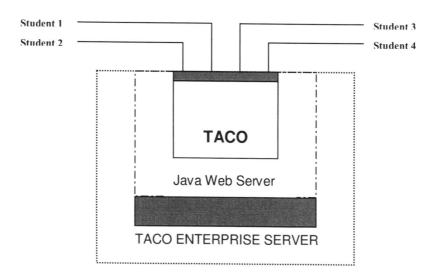

Figure 11.2. A TACO servlet with 4 treads.

---

[15] TACO uses ORACLE, but any other commercial database can be used.
[16] TACO runs on an ENTERPRISE II Server with 2X300 MHz processors, 256 megabytes of RAM and 4.2 Gb of disk space.

A Java Web servlet (see Figure 11.2) is a program that responds, in this context, to requests made by student and lecturer Web clients. When, for example, a student wishes to start an assignment, they submit their authentication details via a Web page to the TACO system. The TACO servlet (in this case TacoQuestionSetGenerator) receives a HTTP request containing the student's user ID and password in form of a CGI stream. This stream is broken down to extract the student user ID and password; this allows the servlet to deal with the student's request. Similarly, when a student submits an assignment the appropriate servlet (TacoQuestionSetMarker) receives a CGI stream containing the answers entered by the student. Again, this stream is used to extract the relevant answers and apply the appropriate marking schema to it. The Java Web server contains three servlets that handle the *lecturer authoring tool*, the *question set generator* and *the question set marker*. These servlets are briefly described below:

- *TacoDisplayFrontEnd*: allows lecturers to interact with the TACO authoring tool. Lecturer ID and passwords are validated, then a list of existing courses, courseworks, questions and variants are presented to the lecturer's client (see Figure 11.3) along with the authoring options. If there are no existing courses, for a particular lecturer, the authoring options are presented on their own.

- *TacoQuestionSetGenerator*: authenticates student ID and passwords, and retrieves a random set of questions from the database, for the appropriate coursework assignment, to present to the student's client.

- *TacoQuestionSetMarker*: receives the student's answers, stores them in the database and applies the appropriate marking scheme to produce the student's results. A breakdown of the marks, on a question-by-question basis, along with relevant lecturer comments is presented to the student (and the final score).

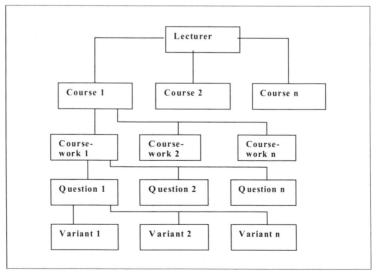

Figure 11.3. Hierachical Structure of Courseworks and Questions in TACO.

These three servlets work in conjunction with an Oracle database. The database stores:

- lecturer and student user IDs and passwords

- course/coursework/question/variant data (see Figure 11.3) and associated comments/feedback

- student answers and marks.

The dialogue between these two subsystems is achieved through the use of a JDBC (Java Database Connectivity) connection. The rationale used to isolate the database and external connections from clients is based in the growing concern for Internet security. By establishing connections with the database through an explicit set of servlets, the TACO system maintains a secure firewall between the database and the outside world.

The interactions between the various TACO system components are illustrated in Figure 11.4.

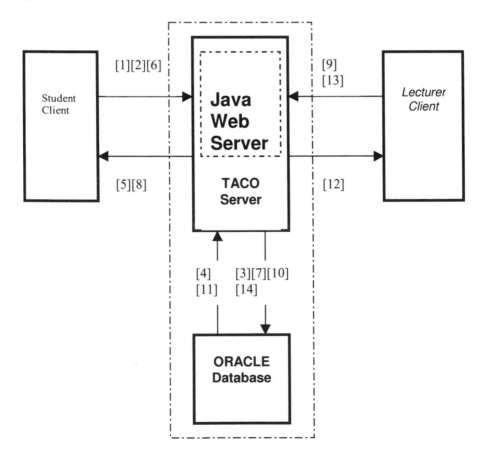

1.   Log into TACO with student ID and password

2.   Request coursework assignment

3.   Authenticate student ID and password

4.   Get questions from database

5.   Issue coursework assignment to student

6.   Submit completed coursework assignment

7.   Mark coursework assignment and store student results

8.   Issue student mark and lecturer's comments

9.   Log into TACO authoring tool with lecturer ID and password

10. Authenticate lecturer ID and password

11. Get existing course/coursework/question/variant information

12. Issue authoring options and present existing course/coursework/question/variant information

13. Request creation of course/coursework/question/variant entry

14. Store course/coursework/question/variant entry

Figure 11.4. TACO architecture diagram.

11.3.1 The TACO Authoring Interface

As discussed in Section 11.2.1, a key requirement for any Web-based coursework system is to allow lecturers to author questions and assignments without knowledge of HTML, CGI, etc.

In TACO, lecturers set up courses and assignments via menus and dialogue boxes. This determines the type of assignment (practice or assessed), and the way in which it is administered (question-by question or set of questions).

Questions (or variants) are authored or edited through forms. After selecting a question type (see Appendix 11.A), lecturers add question text, comment text and answers into the form displayed (see Figure 11.5). They can add confidence assessments and choose scoring and weighting for each individual question, and mark a question as compulsory. Default values are set for those who do not want to apply any of these options.

Access to a lecturer's assignments, questions and marks is protected (see above). Furthermore, only students registered for a particular course can complete the assignments, unless the lecturer chooses to make it an open one.

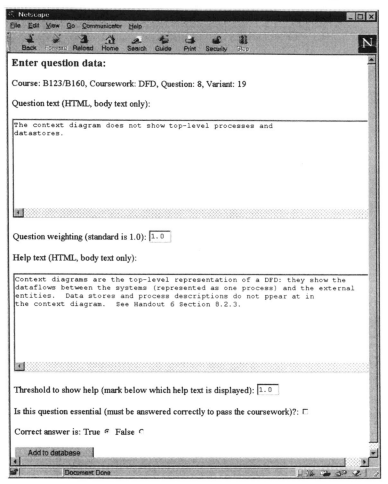

Figure 11.5. TACO question form for a binary question.

11.3.2 The TACO Student Interface

Students completing assignments via TACO only need to know how to use a Web browser. After connecting to the HTTP address for a particular assignment, they have to identify themselves through a TACO username and password[17].

If more than one assignment is active, they choose the assignment they want to work on from a list. If an assignment can be completed both as practice and assessed coursework, student have to chose between these two modes; most lecturers allow students to complete assessed coursework once.

---

[17] This can be set to be identical with their system login ID and password to avoid extra memory load.

Once an assignment has been chosen, questions are displayed to the student (see Figure 11.6 for an example).

When an individual question (or a whole assignment) is submitted by the student, it is returned to the TACO server for marking. Answers selected or entered are compared with the answers selected by lecturers. Marks and are then displayed to the student; if the lecturer has added comments or explanation, and the mark achieved by the student falls below a specified levels, these will be displayed as well (see Figure 11.7 for an example).

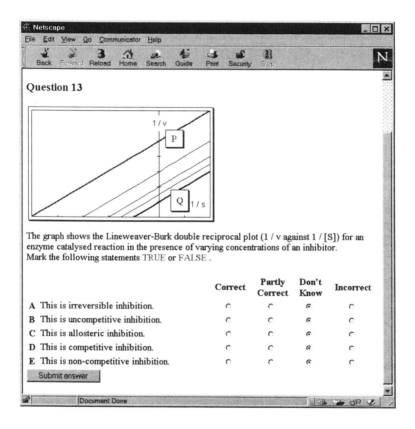

Figure 11.6. Question displayed to student (assignment on a *question-by-question* basis, question type *evaluate each answer*).

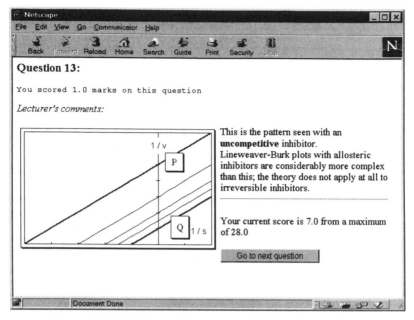

Figure 11.7. Marks and comments displayed to student.

11.4 Results from the Pilot Study

The first implementation of TACO was evaluated through a pilot project in the Autumn term of 1997. Four lecturers from different academic departments (Biochemistry, Computer Science, Greek and Latin, Mathematics) authored sets of assignments for courses on which over 500 students were registered. It has to be emphasised that the results were collected during the pilot study, and are mainly based on user reports – a more detailed evaluation is currently being undertaken. Nevertheless, the results provide important input for the further implementation of TACO and a re-design of user and student interfaces. We first report results from interviews with two of the lecturers. We then summarise results from a questionnaire study with students, and some of the statistics on student use of the system.

11.4.1 Evaluation by Lecturers

Interviews with two of the pilot lecturers (from Biochemistry and Mathematics) were conducted in an unstructured manner to allow lecturers to raise any observations or criticism. Lecturers were asked to provide a general assessment of the first implementation, and to raise any problems encountered with the system, and make suggestions for improvements.

General impression

The first implementation provided adequate functionality for the purpose of authoring assignments in these two subjects. Assignments can be created speedily and easily through the structured approach which the authoring interface prescribes.

However, the lecturers felt that the "look-and-feel" of the form-based user interface was out-of-date, mainly because every screen was text-based where transitions were triggered by clicking on a piece of text. It was also somewhat "clumsy" to use, because question and answer text on the current form were separated (see Figure 11.5).

Reliability of the system was the other major issue - i.e., the server was down sufficiently often in the pilot phase to give students the impression that it was not reliable.

Suggested improvements

Both lectures wanted a WYSIWYG *(What You See Is What You Get)* editor, or at least a *preview* facility, when authoring questions – immediate feedback as to what the question looks like is essential to check and correct questions. Ideally, lecturers want to interact with the authoring system using *direct manipulation*, i.e. move variants, questions and assignments by *drag-and-drop*. Other amenities of a Windows interface, such as a toolbar, online documentation and help, were missing.

A simple improvement was that it should be possible to attach a label to questions to indicate what they are about (rather than just Question 1, Question 2).

11.4.2 Evaluation by Students

The student evaluation was conducted via a Web-based questionnaire. Students were encouraged to participate in the anonymous questionnaire study (it was conducted by a final year student, rather than the lecturer) by raffling 3 book vouchers among those who completed the questionnaire. 40 students – i.e. less than 10% of the total number of users - completed the questionnaire over a period of one week.

General impression

The general impression was Web-based feedback and assessment was "a good idea"; the majority of respondents stated that completing Web-based assignments took less time and was easier to complete than paper-based coursework, and felt they identified the essential concepts of the course faster than they would have otherwise. 20% of the respondents said they had used similar systems before. Reliability of the server during the pilot was an issue – half of the respondents had been unable to access a coursework at some point.

Suggested improvements

The vast majority of respondents in this sample (80%) had completed their assignments using machines in UCL. Even though most of them indicated that they had no problem finding a terminal when they wanted to complete an exercise, the single most frequently suggested improvement was "to be able to take practice exercises home on disk". This may indicates that there is a substantial number of students who have computers at home, but either have no Internet access, or are unwilling to use it because of the associated cost.

Students also realised that the usefulness of the system to support their learning activity very much depended on the quality of the authoring: complaints raised included:

- ambiguous phrasing of questions

- typing errors in questions

- "incorrect" marking (including receiving no marks at all for mis-spelt or partly correct answers on free-text or numerical answers)

- lack of integration with other materials.

11.4.3 Observation on Student Behaviour

A quick analysis of system logs for students on one course (Computer Science) revealed something that many lecturers have suspected: students' use of the system is very much deadline-driven. On courseworks announced 10-14 working days before the deadline, the vast majority of students started their first practice coursework 3 days before. Most completed 2-3 practice runs before submitting assessed coursework.

11.5   Conclusions

At the review workshop held at the end of the pilot phase, all participants agreed that the TACO system had achieved the original aim of the project: it demonstrated that it is possible to provide a generic system to support authoring, distribution, marking and administration of computer-based coursework. Lecturers' and students' use of the system, and subsequent feedback, identified many possible changes and additions that would improve the effectiveness, efficiency and usability of TACO. The project also provided a more detailed understanding of the overall process of authoring and completing computer-based coursework in a distributed environment. This improved understanding will not only lead to improvements in the system itself, but will be (a) incorporated in guidelines for the development and use of computer-based coursework; and (b) brought to the attention of those in charge of UCL's IT strategy and planning. The development team learnt some extremely valuable lessons about the advantages and drawbacks of a participatory design project, which involves early trials and evaluation, in the context of a HEI. The detailed conclusions are reported and discussed under these 4 points.

11.5.1 Improvements to the TACO System

As reported in Section 11.4.1, the authoring user interface to TACO requires considerable improvement. During the requirements capture phase, lecturers' main concern was that the system should have a "really simple" user interface. That was exactly what TACO provided. Once lecturers started to use the simple, form-based user interface, however, it became clear they wanted something that was simple to use, i.e. shielded them from HTML or other programming-style authoring tools. But, like many users today, they expected the look-and-feel and functionality offered by contemporary Windows interfaces: WYSIWYG, menus, icons, moving files by "drag-and-drop", search function, and bubble help. From the developers' point of view, these features are not technically difficult, but require considerable time and effort to implement. One major problem with the user interface from the students' point of view was that pressing the return key submitted the coursework for marking. Several students accidentally submitted their coursework before they had completed all questions; since assessed coursework can only be submitted once, lecturers had to remove the "accidental" mark from the database to allow the student to complete the assignment properly.

11.5.2 The Process of Authoring Coursework

Both lecturers and developers discovered early during the pilot that some aspects of authoring coursework had not been considered in the requirements capture phase. The process of authoring coursework was described as a top-down approach. Each lecturer is responsible for a number of courses, and plans a number of assignments for a particular course. For each assignment, the lecturer writes a number of questions, and maybe a number of variants for each question. When all questions are written, the assignment is released to the students. Whilst lecturers started to author assignments in this manner, it quickly emerged that questions, rather than assignments, are the level of granularity at which authoring is done. Lecturers were more inclined to write a number of questions and variants, and then put together an assignment by selecting a number of questions. Lecturers also discovered that they wanted to re-use questions in assignments on different courses. The model of authoring which emerged from these observations was that lecturers could create a library or pool of questions, from which they then put together assignments.

Furthermore, the re-use or adaptation of other lecturers' questions. Some courses cover similar material, but from a different perspective. Some assignments have more than one author. This problem became evident with one of the pilot courses, which taught mathematics to geology students. A perennial problem with such service courses is that, whilst it is desirable to have the subject taught by an expert mathematician, students often fail to relate the material taught to their own subject. Ideally, mathematical knowledge should be presented in the context of problems arising from the students' subject. Such questions could be created as a joint effort between two lecturers - the expert mathematician and an expert in the other subject. Since this requirement exists for many other subjects, the expert mathematician could create sets of questions on a range of topics, which could then be adapted for use in different subjects. Implementation of both suggestions - question libraries and joint authoring - will require modifications to the design of TACO: the current model has a virtual Web server owned by each lecturer, and the hierarchical model of course, coursework and questions (see Figure 11.3).

11.5.3 Coping with Distributed System Environments in HEIs

As outlined in Section 11.1, most HEIs have a variety of hardware and operating systems. One of the main reasons for choosing a Web-based system was that it could be accessed from a wide range of hardware platforms and operating systems. During the pilot, all students could access their coursework, but there were still a number of problems arising from the distributed and heterogeneous nature of the terminals:

- some of the machines were not very powerful, and as a result, scrolling through long sets of coursework was slow

- network access from some clusters was slow

- some machines had several version of Web browsers installed - students using very old versions found that not all features of the coursework (e.g. colour) were supported.

It is easy for lecturers to forget that the coursework they author may have a different look-and-feel on some students' screen. Guidelines for authoring coursework should point out features which tend to cause problems, and recommend that lecturers test assignments on machines which are used by their students in the HEI. This will help to detect some, but not all, potential problems, since some students (and many lecturers) prefer to complete (or author) coursework from home. Whilst this reduces the demand for machines in the HEI, we found that it can create other problems. Since telephone costs are lower outside normal working hours, most outside access to the system occurred in the evenings and at weekends. Unfortunately, there is no support available if any technical problem or query about an assignment arises during those hours. Even though students had been made aware that this was the case, they were still upset when they encountered a problem and found they had to wait until normal working hours to have it dealt with. Similarly, lecturers' planning was badly upset when a night or weekend authoring session could not be completed as planned.

11.5.4 Participatory Design in the Development of Educational Technology

Participatory Design advocates the use of early prototypes to (a) help users to envision how they will work with the system, and (b) to detect omissions in the requirement, or problems in the use of the system, at an early stage. In many projects, user interaction with prototypes takes place in a series of short lab sessions, where the designers observe users "walk through" a small number of selected tasks (Bødker, 1991). This type of evaluation is, however, not sufficient to validate requirements for, and identify potential problems with, a large distributed system. It is also unlikely that a short session with simulated tasks gives users sufficient opportunity to discover all major problems which may arise in everyday use of the system.

The evaluation of the first implementation of TACO - the prototype in this project - was therefore conducted as a field trial. In retrospect, it did yield additional requirements and helped to identify some problems which had not been anticipated by lecturers and the development team. It is difficult to imagine that the development of the type of technology which will support the Digital University can be undertaken without this type of field study, where a large number of potential users evaluate a new system in the context of real courses. Developers should, however, be aware that some users find it difficult to distinguish between prototypes and fully developed systems.

The pilot study with real users completing real tasks was extremely valuable, but it was also resource-intensive and occasionally straining. Many students (especially those on the Computer Science course) did not appreciate the difference between a prototype and a fully tested and stable system. Reports of problems with or failure of the system early in the pilot were sometimes accompanied by derogatory comments about the technical abilities of those who had developed it. The developers were able to recognise that these comments were born out of temporary frustration, and the unique combination of arrogance and ignorance with which some first year computer science students tend to view other people's software. But there is a danger that users may form a tainted view of a system through interaction with a prototype. Lecturers also have to prepare themselves to receive haughty comments from some students who discover any mistakes in questions or scoring. This poses a dilemma for any development project as to when to submit the system to a field trial: running it too early may create a negative response which kills the project; running it late may mean fundamental omissions or problems are only discovered very late in the design process.

Acknowledgements

TACO is a UCL-internal project, funded by the Department of Computer Science and the Education and Information Support Division (EISD). Sun Microsystems UK generously donated the Enterprise II server, Java Server and Java development kit. Dr Kevin Boone (now at the University of Middlesex) helped the development team by giving feedback on the design and implementation planning, as well as contributing to the requirements specification. Nadav Zin helped with setting up of the Oracle Database, and writing SQL queries for retrieving results.

Dr Kim Issroff from the Higher Education Research and Development Unit (HERDU) has been involved in the project from the beginning; the setting up of a UCL-wide project and the arrangements for funding are due to her ideas and initiative. Many UCL lecturers contributed through the requirements capture workshops, and comments on the requirements specification; others helped by evaluating the first version of TACO. The three "pilots" were Dr David Bender (Department of Biochemistry and Molecular Biology), Dr Rowena Bowles (Department of Mathematics) and Professor Bob Sharples (Department of Greek and Latin). All three made very important contributions throughout the project and developed substantial coursework sets for their students.

References

1.   Mayes, J. T. and Fowler, C. (in press) Learning Technology and Usability: A Framework for Understanding Courseware. *Interacting with Computers*.

2.   Mayes, J. T. (1995) Learning Technology and Groundhog Day *Hypermedia at Work: Practice and Theory in Higher Education*. Strang, W., Simpson V.B. and Slater D. [Eds.]University of Kent Press.

3.   Laurillard, D. (1993) *Rethinking University Teaching: A Framework for the Effective Use of Educational Technology*. Routledge.

4.   Gardner-Medwin, A.R. (1995) Confidence Assessment in the Teaching of Basic Science. *ALT-J*, 3, 80-85.

5.   Cann, A. J. (1996) On-Line Interactive Computer-Assisted Learning in Biology and Medicine. *Computers in Biology Education* (vCUBE) 96.

6.   Bødker, S. (1991) *Through the Interface: A Human Activity Approach to User Interface Design*. Lawrence Erlbaum Associates.

7.   Schuler, D. and Namioka, A. [Eds.] (1993) *Participatory Design: Principles and Practices*. Lawrence Erlbaum Associates.

8.   Bellamy, R. (1996) Designing Educational Technology: Computer-Mediated Change. *Context and Consciousness: Activity Theory and Human-Computer Interaction*. Nardi, B. [Ed.], MIT Press.

9.   Hughes, J. and Sasse, M. A. (1998) Design to Instruct: Lessons for Training Through Involving Teachers in Design. *Proceedings of SITE98, Annual Conference on Technology and Teacher Education.* Washington, DC, March 10-14.

10.   Gardner-Medwin, A.R. and Curtin, N.A. (1996) Confidence Assessment in the Teaching of Physiology. *Journal of Physiology*, 494:74P.

11.   Paul, J. (1994) Improving Education Trough Computer-Based Alternative Assessment Methods. *People and Computers IX: Proceedings of HCI'94*, Cockton, G. *et al.* [Eds.], Glasgow August 1994. Cambridge University Press.

12.   Grudin, J. (1991) Interactive Systems: Bridging the Gaps Between Developers and Users. *IEEE Computer*, April 1991, 59-69.

13.   CASTLE (Computer Assisted Teaching and Learning) Project at Leicester University. URL http://www.le.ac.uk/cc/ltg/castle/

14.   LAPT (London Agreed Protocol for Teaching) Project at University College London. URL: http://www.ucl.ac.uk/~cusplap

15.   QUASI (Question and Answer System for the Internet). URL:

      http://www.physiol.ucl.ac.uk/quasi/

16.   TACO (Teaching and Coursework Online) Project at University College London. URL: http://taco.cs.ucl.ac.uk:8080/taco/www/

Appendix 11.A List of Requirements for a Web-based System (Requirements not Implemented in the First Version of TACO are Printed in Italics)

1 Question Types

1.1 Multiple-choice questions

- student selects one of n
- student selects n of n
- student has to evaluate each answer

1.2 Binary questions (true/false)

1.3 Numerical response (student enters value+unit)

- *Accommodate acceptable range of answers*

1.4 Text response

- one-word responses
- short (1 line) freeform text
  - *approximate phrase-matching*
  - *spell-checking and feedback of error*
- long text answers
  - stored for hand-marking by lecturer
  - *automatic marking (using pattern matching)*

1.5 Image-based questions

- displaying figures/formulas/tables
- selecting images
- *active images 1 (hotspots - student selects region on image)*
- *active image 2 (student annotates/edits or drawing*
- *student draws image from scratch*

2 Confidence Assessment

2.1 Option of adding confidence assessment to any question

2.2 Provide range of weighting scheme for confidence assessment

2.3 Make confidence assessment scheme transparent to students

3 Marking Schemes

3.1 Straight count

3.2 Questions weighted (weighting specified by lecturer)

3.3 Essential questions (assignment failed if question failed)

3.4 Dynamic scoring

- *multiple attempts at questions allowed, scoring adjusted accordingly*

- *recommend switching to certain levels depending on progress*

3.6 Scaling marks

- *scale marks to achieve normal distribution*

4 Feedback to Student

4.1 Display score

4.2 Display correct answer

4.3 Display explanation (pre-stored by lecturer

4.4 Return explanation depending on score achieved

4.5 Feedback on whole assignments (assessed coursework)

4.6 Compilation (histogram) of scoring during testing

5 Assignment Types

5.1 Self-learning exercises

5.2 Assessed coursework

5.3 Assignment display

- sheet-based (student completes all questions before submitting)

- question-by-question (student completes and submits answer before next question is displayed)

6 Authoring Assignments

6.1 Authoring via form (no knowledge of HTML, CGI, Java required)

6.2 Choice of

- Question types (see 1)

- Confidence Assessment (see 2)

- Marking schemes (see 3)

- Feedback (see 4)

- Assignment type (see 5)

6.3 Random selection from pool of questions

6.4 Links to other online documents

6.5 Automatic transfer of existing MCQ documents (e.g. MS Word files)

6.6 Preview facility when authoring questions

6.7 Spell-checking

6.8 Basic syntax and consistency checking

6.9 Support for Maths/Greek symbols

7 Reports and Feedback to Lecturers

7.1 Every student interaction with system logged

7.2 Reports on students

- registration of student details
- which assignment completed when (see 7.1)
- where assignment was completed from
- assignment results
- files results for import into spreadsheets
- which questions attempted
- time spent on questions
- where assessment was completed form

7.3 Reports on questions

- how many attempts
- which answers chosen
- student comments on questions

8 Security

8.1 No student access to questions or marks

8.2 Time limits for completing assessed coursework

8.3 Notification when assignment started

9 Students Take Exercises Home on Disk

Chapter 12

Groupware Support for Asynchronous Collaborative Knowledge Work

Peter J.H. Hinssen[*]

In this chapter we discuss how Lotus Notes supports the information exchange among group members, one of the basic processes underlying collaborative work. The discussion is based on the results of interviews we conducted among members of five groups using Notes. All group tasks involved asynchronous knowledge work with clear, short-term outcomes. We conclude that Notes stimulates the provision of relevant information to a group as a whole, enables group members to deal with information in a more creative way and promotes the exchange of relevant information, although the facilitation provided by Notes is less successful in other respects. We also conclude that more attention should be paid to how individual group members experience task inter-dependence and sharing of information.

12.1 Introduction

There is a growing need for asynchronous collaboration in various fields, including learning environments. This often involves the creation and sharing of information within small groups of employees or students. At the same time we can observe an increasing supply of groupware applications intended to support such collaborative knowledge work. A well-known example is Lotus Notes, which combines, among other things, electronic mail, replicated databases, a group scheduling function and application development tools. Based on the results of interviews we conducted among members of five groups using Notes, we discuss whether and how Notes

[*] Telematics Institute, P.O. Box 589, 7500 AN Enschede, The Netherlands
Email: p.hinssen@wxs.nl

can support asynchronous collaboration. We thereby focus on the extent to which Notes facilitates the exchange of different types of information, and eventually contributes to the overall quality of information exchange within the group.

The context of our work lies within the field of computer supported cooperative work (CSCW). The development of this field thus far has shown examples of positive and negative effects of various groupware applications on (distributed) group work. Following this stage of development, more insight has to be gained into the relevant characteristics by which computer supported group work varies [1]. In our research work we distinguish such characteristics. Basically, we start from the assumption that four, inter-related sets of characteristics (groupware, group task, group culture, and personal characteristics) influence the quality of information exchange among members of (small) groups, which in turn has an impact on group performance [2]. In this chapter, we focus on one part of our work only. We study how the group task, in relation to the groupware support provided (limited to Lotus Notes here), influences the quality of information exchange. This does not mean that we consider the other aspects as less relevant. Both cultural characteristics, such as group members' willingness to collaborate and to share information (see, e.g., [3]), and personal characteristics, such as attitudes about and experience with technological support, shape relevant conditions for successful information exchange and group performance (e.g., outcome quality, satisfaction-related variables and inter-personal variables). These issues, however, are dealt with elsewhere [2].

Below, we discuss the theoretical background for this chapter in more detail, through the distinction of relevant characteristics of the group task, the groupware application (i.e., Notes) and the quality of information exchange. Next, we discuss the results of the interviews we conducted among the members of five groups. We end with a few conclusions.

12.2   Group Task Characteristics

Why the distinction of group task characteristics at all? As Olson *et al.* [1, p. 120] argue: "When we understand the details of the tasks people are engaged in, [...] we can better design systems to support the work". This understanding is important as the type of task determines the need for information exchange [4]. A few classifications of task types already exist, the best-known probably being the one by McGrath (see, e.g., [5]). What we are in particular looking for is a taxonomy that can be used to describe *any* group task in terms of meaningful characteristics.

For the distinction of relevant group task characteristics we start by using an information exchange perspective. By adopting such a perspective, we explicitly focus on the process of information exchange within a group. This leads us to define five characteristics which determine the amount and nature of information exchange within a group. These five characteristics are in turn dependent on the type of task inter-dependence among group members. Below, we discuss (a) the information exchange perspective as well as the five characteristics that can be derived from this perspective, and (b) group task inter-dependence.

12.2.1   Adopting an Information Exchange Perspective

Supporting group work actually means supporting the processes that allow or facilitate collaboration among group members. The processes that are generally the target of computer support within the CSCW field are communication and coordination (e.g. [6, 7]), of which communication or information exchange (which we regard here as synonyms) is the most basic group process. Coordination, the other basic group process, can be defined as managing dependencies between activities [8], involving the allocation, planning and integration of the tasks of individual group members [9]. Its quality depends to a high degree on the quality of information exchange. As we focus on the support of the information exchange among group members we adopt an information exchange perspective (e.g. [4]). From this perspective, group performance depends on the fit between task information exchange demands and task information exchange capacity (cf. [10]). In order to meet information exchange demands, information exchange capacity has to be provided or increased, for instance by means of procedures, databases and adequate media (such as groupware in general and Notes in particular).

A concept central to the information exchange perspective is the information richness of a medium (e.g. [5, 11]), which is defined as a medium's "capacity to facilitate shared meaning" [12]. It refers to a medium's ability to support the exchange of information resulting from task uncertainty and task equivocality. *Equivocality* is the degree of confusion and lack of understanding among group members as they may interpret the available information in different ways [e.g., 11]. The exchange of information resulting from equivocality is aimed at removing such confusion and bridging conflicting opinions. *Uncertainty* is the absence of information which is required to carry out the group task [11]. Such information may be obtained in a simple way and comprises ideas, explanations and answers to (simple) work-related questions.

It is also necessary to support the exchange of information that is directly related to the product a group is working on (e.g. [13, 14]). In fact, this type of information comprises (parts of) the product itself, such as an outline or sections in case the product is a document (as an outcome of knowledge work). Not meeting such *technical demands* was found to affect information exchange negatively [13].

Other information that may be exchanged among group members results from *demands for social interaction*. Social interaction can influence the longevity and (long-term) productivity of a group. Communication media vary in the extent to which they support the exchange of social information (see, e.g., [15]).

Finally, we examine the extent to which groupware supports the exchange of information related to Schmidt and Bannon's coordination [9], that is, information resulting from *coordination demands*. Of the different kinds of dependencies

Malone and Crowston mention, each requiring a different kind of coordination [8], we focus on task inter-dependence. We particularly focus on the degree to which the activities (i.e., parts of the overall group task) of members of a group are inter-dependent. We will discuss group task inter-dependence in more detail below.

The *amount and nature of information exchange* now strongly depend on how the task varies along the five group task characteristics (i.e., the five different information exchange demands) described above. Furthermore, we suppose that the ability of a groupware application to meet these five characteristics eventually affects the quality of information exchange (cf. [16, 17]).

12.2.2 Group Task Inter-dependence

The emphasis on group task inter-dependence (e.g., [10, 18, 19]) is not strange, given the fact that group members are likely to depend on each other in their collaborative efforts. In fact, the level of inter-dependence influences the demands for exchanging the different types of information and as a result the performance of a group [18]. We distinguish four forms, in increasing levels of inter-dependence: pooled, sequential, reciprocal (cf. Thompson, in [20]) and team inter-dependence [18]. *Pooled* inter-dependence means that two or more group members work with relative independence, but their individual outputs have to be combined to one output being the contribution of the group as a whole. *Sequential* inter-dependence means that the output of one group member serves as the input to a second member, etc. *Reciprocal* inter-dependence means that the output of one group member not only serves as the input to a second member, but the output of this second member is also the input to the first one. *Team inter-dependence*, finally, means that "group members jointly diagnose, problem solve, and collaborate to complete a task" ([18], p. 63). In comparison to the other forms, the group as a whole has more autonomy.

12.3 Groupware Characteristics: Support of Information Exchange

With respect to groupware characteristics, we first examine which *functions* of Notes are used by group members. Next, we use one other, more subjective, characteristic of groupware: *perceived usefulness*. As an example, the perceived usefulness of a computer system has been found to be positively related to the use of this system (e.g., [21]).

We will discuss the groupware characteristics further on when we discuss the results of the interviews.

12.4   The Quality of Information Exchange

For a description of the quality of the information exchange process we start from Nunamaker et al.'s "sources of *group process gains and losses*" ([16] p. 724]). Although these gains and losses are specific to the field of group decision support, several of them can be used to describe (general) communication gains and losses.

In Table 12.1 relevant communication gains and losses are listed and described. Resulting from the amount and nature of information exchange and depending on the support provided by the groupware application, they provide a description of the quality of the information exchange process.

Communication gain	Description
More information	Relevant information is provided to the group as a whole
Synergy	Information is dealt with in a creative way
Communication loss	**Description**
Failure to trace information	It is difficult to trace who is the source of information
Information overload	Information overload occurs Much irrelevant information is exchanged
Coordination problems	It is difficult to integrate individual contributions
Incomplete use of information	There is insufficient access to relevant information There is insufficient use of relevant information

Table 12.1. Overview of communication gains and losses (adapted from [16]).

12.5   Method

We conducted 15 interviews to gain insight into how Lotus Notes is used in practice. For the discussion of the results, we start from the model shown in Figure 12.1.

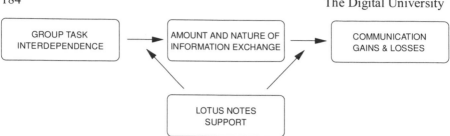

Figure 12.1. Model depicting relationships between group task inter-dependence, amount and nature of information exchange, communication gains and losses, and support provided by Lotus Notes.

We used an interview scheme comprising both questionnaire items and open-ended questions (the item scores and answers were written down by the interviewer). The data were collected through interviewing 15 members of 5 groups, belonging to 4 organisations. All group tasks involved knowledge work with clear, short-term outcomes: three group tasks (group size: 2, 4 and 5 persons, respectively) involved the development (and filling) of databases for mostly external clients (mainly consultants), using Notes as a development platform, while the other two group tasks (group size: 2 persons in both cases) involved the writing and editing of documents. The members of two groups (the 2-person development group and one of the document writing/editing groups) were working at different locations most of the time. The members of another group (the other document writing/editing group) were sometimes working from home. In the other cases, group members had the possibility to communicate face-to-face with the other group members because they worked at the same location (though sometimes in different rooms). All respondents used a Notes version with a Windows interface.

A decision had to be made regarding the level of data analysis. The results of the case studies, which we will discuss further on, seem to indicate that members of a single group differ considerably in their answers. This was confirmed by the outcomes of simple one-way analyses of variance (with groups as factor): for most communication gains and losses from Table 12.1 there is no evidence of non-independence due to group membership. Based on these outcomes, as well as the consideration that a single group score results in a loss of information about individual thoughts and outcomes, we have decided to analyse the data at the individual level (see [2]).

12.6   Results and Discussion

We now describe and discuss several variables and relationships between them, starting from the model depicted in Figure 12.3. We should keep in mind, however, that the number of respondents reported in this chapter is relatively small, which may be an impediment to the use of statistical analyses and obtaining statistically significant results. Therefore, we restrict the analyses to the calculation of mean scores, (Spearman) correlation coefficients, and a single reliability analysis. The (quantitative) analyses are complemented with qualitative data (i.e., answers to the open-ended questions). Finally, we do not pretend all of the results are generalisable to other groups, but rather want to give insight into the process of information exchange among group members and into the ways Notes does and does not support such a process. This insight can also be benificial when applying Notes in learning environments, depending on the level of similarity to the group work reported here.

12.6.1 Overall Support by Lotus Notes

The respondents answered several general questions regarding the support with which Lotus Notes provides them. Most respondents distinguish the following main functions of Notes:

- *Electronic mail* for the support of asynchronous communication; also (to be) used as an archive (through categorising of messages).

- *Replicated databases* to store, retrieve and share various kinds of documents/information. Depending on their purpose, such databases may contain information about projects, clients and procedures as well as (other) task-related information (articles, dictionaries, etc.). These databases are not only used to support actual task performance but, in a wider context, also for administrative purposes (planning, workflow, etc.) and for announcements and discussions.

- *Scheduling function*, which may also be used for administrative purposes.

- *Platform for developing* Notes applications (in fact, Notes *is* a platform, with various end-user functions on top of it, including the ones mentioned above). Such applications are developed both for (external) clients and for internal use.

On average, the respondents perceive the overall *usefulness* of Notes as high (a mean score of 4.1, on a questionnaire item scale of 1 to 5), because Notes can be used as a (database) source for their daily work, it allows them to communicate by email and to work remotely with others, and especially replication of databases and desktop integration are considered useful.

More specific findings regarding the support that Notes provides are discussed in the remainder of this chapter.

12.6.2 Group Task Inter-dependence

The six questionnaire items concerning task inter-dependence that were propounded to the respondents can be summarised on one scale (Cronbach's α = 0.75), indicating the degree of task inter-dependence, varying from "1 = pooled inter-dependence" to "5 = team inter-dependence".[18] As the group tasks were strongly information-oriented, task inter-dependence actually refers to inter-dependence with respect to information resulting from technical demands. The mean score is 3.1, which implies that on average neither pooled nor team inter-dependence occurred.[19] However, from observations by the interviewer it appeared that, although all kinds of information were exchanged among members of the different groups, strictly speaking mainly pooled inter-dependence occurred. Taking into account the information-oriented character of the group tasks as well as the media available to exchange all kinds of information in an informal and ad-hoc way (Notes/email, phone, fax, face-to-face), it is not surprising that respondents do not perceive themselves to be relatively independent of other group members (i.e., pooled inter-dependence). Several respondents state that, during their work on a group task, they continuously exchange information in an ad-hoc and unstructured way.

12.6.3 Amount and Nature of Information Exchange

We calculated the correlations between task inter-dependence and the amounts of information exchanged (for each type); see Table 12.2. From this table we can conclude that coordination indeed is a basic group process, as it appears to be common to strong (i.e., team) group task inter-dependence. Moreover, the exchange of (additional) information is required in order to meet the concerning coordination demands. All other correlation coefficients are not significant.

Information resulting from:	Technical demands	Coordinatin demands	Uncertainty	Equivocality	Demands for social interaction
Group task inter-dependence	0.43	0.78*			

Correlations listed only if $p < 0.1$.

* Significant at 0.001.

Table 12.2. Correlations between group task inter-dependence and amounts of information exchanged.

[18] The six items measured, respectively:
1. dependence of respondent on information from other group members;
2. dependence of other group members on information of respondent;
3. pooled inter-dependence among group members;
4. sequential inter-dependence among group members;
5. reciprocal inter-dependence among group members;
6. team inter-dependence among group members.

[19] The standard deviation is 0.88.

Of course, beside group task inter-dependence, *other factors* may affect the amount and nature of information exchange among group members. As the answers to the open-ended question show, such factors may include the degree of communication with (external) clients, the way the group is managed, and the knowledge and skills of individual group members which may or may not require additional information exchange.

Furthermore, the *use of Notes* may have altered the relationship between inter-dependence and information exchange. Much information previously at the disposal of individual group members only, may be shared with other group members through the use of Notes. Indeed, the majority of the respondents said they appreciate sharing knowledge, opinions and experiences of others. Apart from the question of whether all group members actually do share information, Notes offers the (technical) possibility to do so. It has the potential to make certain types of information exchange superfluous or less necessary. Typical of this role of Notes is the remark of one of the respondents who said that Notes removes dependencies between people, as people are provided with the opportunity to obtain information by themselves (i.e., through groupware support). This may be regarded as an advantage by several other respondents who said they appreciate collaborating with others, but only on the condition that working independently remains possible.

Next, we examine in more detail the amounts of information exchanged by the members of the groups studied and the extent to which Notes is used, again per type; see Table 12.3. On average, information resulting from technical demands and uncertainty make the largest contributions to the total amount of information exchanged (see the second column).[20] Information resulting from equivocality makes the smallest contribution, which means that little disagreement exists among group members.

This table (third column) also demonstrates that Notes is often used to support the exchange of technical information (note that the concerning scale has three points), and sometimes for the support of information resulting from coordination demands and uncertainty. Notes is seldom used to support the exchange of information that has an informal and personal character, considering the low mean scores for the use of Notes to meet equivocality and social interaction demands.

Finally, respondents find that Notes in particular facilitates the exchange of technical information. Not surprisingly from the perspective of information richness, Notes is considered not to facilitate the exchange of informal and personal information. It is questionable whether Notes can be used to meet the increased coordination demands in the case of strong group task inter-dependence, as it only moderately facilitates the exchange of information from such demands.

---

[20] In a statistical sense, both types are closely related (correlation coefficient of 0.65, p < 0.01).

Information resulting from	Amount of information exchanged (per type, relative to total amount of information exchanged)*	Degree to which Notes is used for the exchange of information (per type, regardless the amount exchanged)**	Degree to which Notes facilitates the exchange of information (per type, regardless the amount exchanged)***
Technical demands	3.5	2.7	4.5
Coordination demands	2.5	1.7	3.2
Uncertainty	3.3	1.9	3.6
Equivocality	1.4	1.3	2.0
Demands for social interaction	1.8	1.1	1.6

KEY

*   These variables correspond to questionnaire items (1 = very small amount, 5 = very large amount).

**   These variables are calculated from the answers to open-ended questions (1 = Notes seldom used, 3 = Notes often used).

***   These variables correspond to questionnaire items (1 = hinders exchange to a high degree, 5 = facilitates exchange to a high degree).

Table 12.3. Exchange of different types of information and the use of Notes (n=15).

12.6.4 Communication Gains and Losses

The quality of information exchange can be described in terms of the communication gains and losses. The respondents' ratings can be found in Table 12.4. On average, respondents think that the quality of information exchange is high. They rate the provision of relevant information to the group as a whole and the ease of tracing who is the source of information most positively.

It is interesting to know whether the facilitation of the exchange of each type of information increases the quality of information exchange, that is, whether the use of Notes indeed results in communication gains. To this purpose, we calculated the correlations between the degree to which Notes facilitates the exchange of each type of information and the communication gains; see Table 12.5.

Communication gain*	Mean score	Communication gain*	Mean score
Relevant information is provided to the group as a whole	4.6	There is sufficient access to information required for the task	4.1
Information is dealt with in a creative way (n=13)	3.6	It is easy to integrate individual contributions**	4.1
It is easy to trace who is the source of information**	4.5	Only relevant information is exchanged**	3.9
No information overload occurs**	3.7	There is sufficient use of information required for the task	4.1

KEY

*   The variables correspond to questionnaire items (1 = strongly disagree, 5 = strongly agree).

**   For the purpose of data presentation, all items are formulated in the table as gains. The items indicated with ** were presented in the interviews as losses.

Table 12.4. Rating of communication gains (n=15, unless indicated otherwise).

	Communication gain (see Table 12.4 for a description of each gain):							
Degree of facilitation of information resulting from:	Gain 1	Gain 2	Gain 3	Gain 4	Gain 5	Gain 6	Gain 7	Gain 8
Technical demands								
Coordination demands								-0.79**
Uncertainty	0.63*	0.92***				0.45	0.70**	
Equivocality				0.56				
Demands for social interaction			-0.59					-0.59

Correlations listed only if p < 0.1.	**	Significant at 0.01.
* Significant at 0.05.	***	Significant at 0.001.

Table 12.5. Correlations between the degree to which Notes facilitates the exchange of information and ease of data import on the one hand, and communication gains on the other hand.

It appears that on average especially the *facilitation of the exchange of information resulting from uncertainty* is related to the quality of information exchange, considering the three significant and positive correlation coefficients.

First, this kind of facilitation stimulates the provision of relevant information to the group as a whole. Notes may support the respondents with obtaining information which is required for delivering the end-product, either through access to shared information stored in replicated databases or through supporting the exchange of email messages.

Second, it enables group members to deal with information in a more creative way. According to some respondents, this has to do with more possibilities (in comparison with a situation without Notes) and with the sharing of information and ideas between people of different backgrounds. It is striking, however, that a few (other) respondents think that Notes has not really resulted in more creativity. They argue that group members are not stimulated to invent things themselves, as they now have sufficient information of all kinds at their disposal.

Third, Notes promotes the exchange of information that is relevant. Probably, information resulting from uncertainty is considered as such as it is more or less directly related to the end-product (i.e., it is to the point). From this point of view, it is not strange that one of the respondents who thinks too much irrelevant information is exchanged, imputes this to the exchange of social information.

Finally, the more Notes *facilitates the exchange of information for coordination purposes* the more the sufficient use of information required for the task is hindered (a significant correlation of -0.79 in Table 12.5). This is a finding that cannot be easily interpreted and that requires further study. Possibly, in situations in which the exchange of information from coordination demands is facilitated, there is too strong a focus on this type of information, which may be at the expense of the use of information required for actual task performance (although such information might be available).

On the whole, although not all possible communication gains were achieved, the facilitation of the different types of information did not lead to communication losses either, apart from a possible insufficient use of relevant information. Thus, considering the nonsignificant correlations, the facilitation by Notes *did not* significantly:

- make it more difficult to trace who is the source of information

- result in information overload

- prevent group members from having sufficient access to information required for the task

- make it more difficult to integrate individual contributions.

12.7   Conclusions

To what extent now does Lotus Notes support asynchronous collaborative knowledge work? In some respects Notes does support information exchange among group members, one of the basic processes underlying collaborative knowledge work. That is, Notes in particular supports the exchange of technical information (e.g., parts of a document) and information resulting from uncertainty (e.g., ideas about the structure or contents of a document). Notes' facilitation of the exchange of the latter type of information increases the quality of information exchange, especially when Notes supports (individual) group members with the import of data from other applications. More specifically, Notes was found to stimulate the provision of relevant information to the group as a whole, to enable the group members to deal with information in a more creative way, and to promote the exchange of relevant information. However, Notes is less successful with the facilitation of information resulting from coordination demands, as this was found to be related to insufficient use of information required for the task. All these findings may be translated to academic environments, when we know in what respects such an environment is similar to the group work reported here.

Another important question is the following one: what is the essence of asynchronous collaboration? From the interviews it appeared that the asynchronous character of the groupware support enables many persons to keep working relatively independently of others, relying on the information provided by Notes rather than on other persons. Although possible strong inter-dependence leads to the exchange of more information related to coordination, other types of information are not exchanged to a higher degree among group members, at least not as a result of strong inter-dependence. Keeping in mind that several respondents preferred to work independently, it seems as if coordination takes place in order to ensure that inter-dependence does not get too strong. Another indication of an individual orientation towards collaboration is that group membership as such generally has little or no influence on individual group members' ratings of communication gains (which apply to the group as a whole). More insight is needed into the willingness of individuals to collaborate and share information with others and how this affects the successful use of groupware support for asynchronous collaboration.

Finally, more groups with varying group tasks have to be studied in future, in order to be able to obtain more detailed and generalisable findings about the support that Notes as well as other groupware applications provide. Such studies should also include other factors that affect both the quality of information exchange and the performance of groups.

References

1. Olson, J.S., Card, S.K., Landauer, T.K., Olson, G.M., Malone, T. and Leggett, J. (1993) Computer supported cooperative work: research issues for the 90s, *Behaviour & Information Technology*, 12, 2, 115-129.

2. Hinssen, P.J.H. (1996) Validation of a conceptual model of CSCW in groups: rationale, design and results of a multiple-case study. Report (N019/V00) of the PLATINUM project (PLATform providing Integrated services to New Users of Multimedia). Enschede: Telematics Research Centre.

3. Orlikowski, W.J. (1992) Learning from Notes: organizational issues in groupware implementation, *Proceedings CSCW'92*, 362-369.

4. DeSanctis, G. and Gallupe, R.B. (1987) A foundation for the study of group decision support systems, *Management Science,* 33, 5, 589-609.

5. McGrath, J.E., and Hollingshead, A.B. (1993) Putting the "group" back in group support systems: some theoretical issues about dynamic processes in groups with technological enhancements. *Group support systems: new perspectives* Jessup, L.M. and Valacich, J.S. (Eds.), New York: Macmillan, 78-96.

6. Ellis, C.A., Gibbs, S.J. and Rein, G.L. (1991) Groupware: some issues and experiences, *Communications of the ACM,* 34, 1, 38-58.

7. Galegher, J., Kraut, R.E. (1990) Technology for intellectual teamwork: perspectives on research and design. *Intellectual teamwork: social and technological foundations of cooperative work,* Galegher, J., Kraut, R.E., and Egido, C. (Eds.), Hillsdale, NJ, USA: Lawrence Erbaum Associates, 1-20.

8. Malone, T.W. and Crowston, K. (1994) The interdisciplinary study of coordination. *ACM Computing Surveys,* 26, 1, 87-119.

9. Schmidt, K. and Bannon, L. (1992) Taking CSCW seriously: supporting articulation work. *Computer Supported Cooperative Work (CSCW),* 1, 1, 7-40.

10. Tushman, M.L., Nadler, D.A. (1978) Information processing as an integrating concept in organizational design. *Academy of Management Review,* 3, 613-624.

11. Daft, R.L. and Lengel, R.H. (1986) Organizational information requirements, media richness and structural design. *Management Science,* 32, 5, 554-571.

12. Trevino, L.K., Daft, R.L. and Lengel, R.H. (1990) Understanding managers' media choices: a symbolic interactionist perspective. *Organizations and communication technology.* Fulk, J. and Steinfield, C. (Eds.), Newbury Park, CA: Sage, 71-94.

13. Farmer, S.M. and Hyatt, C.W. (1994) Effects of task language demands and task complexity on computer mediated work groups, *Small Group Research*, 25, 3, 331-366.

14. Kraut, R.E., Rice, R.E., Cool, C. and Fish, R.S. (1994) Life and death of new technology: task, utility and social influences on the use of a communication medium. *Proceedings CSCW'94*, 13-21.

15. Galegher, J. and Kraut, R.E. (1994) Computer mediated communication for intellectual teamwork: an experiment in group writing. *Information Systems Research,* 5, 2, 110-138.

16. Nunamaker, J.F., Dennis, A.R., Valacich, J.S., Vogel, D.R. and George, J.F. (1991) Electronic meeting systems to support group work. *Communications of the ACM,* 34, 7, 40-61.

17. Pinsonneault, A., Kraemer, K.L. (1989) The impact of technological support on groups: an assessment of the empirical research. *Decision Support Systems*, 5, 2, 197-216.

18. Saavedra, R., Earley, P.C. and Van Dyne, L. (1993) Complex interdependence in task-performing groups. *Journal of Applied Psychology*, 78, 1, 61-72.

19. Straus, S.G. and McGrath, J.E. (1994), Does the medium matter? The interaction of task type and technology on group performance and member reactions, *Journal of Applied Psychology,* 79, 1, 87-97.

20. Moorhead, G. and Griffin, R.W. (1989) *Organizational behavior.* Boston: Houghton Mifflin.

21. Thompson, R.L., Higgins, C.A. and Howell, J.M. (1991) Personal computing: toward a conceptual model of utilization, *MIS Quarterly*, 15, 1, 125-143.

Chapter 13

Using Lotus Notes for Asynchronous, Collaborative Learning and Research

*Susan Armitage and Mark Bryson**

A touchstone of Lancaster University's learning technology strategy is the use of IT to support collaborative learning. The University has been using asynchronous computer-mediated communication to support collaboration in teaching, learning and research since 1988. Since 1993, Lotus Notes [1] has been in use at the University and in April 1995 was adopted as the University's centrally supported conference system.

This chapter describes completed work and work in progress that uses Notes, now also known as 'Domino', as the support environment for asynchronous collaboration and information sharing. The factors affecting the choice of Lotus Notes as the centrally supported system are outlined, along with some of the practical support implications. The potential Notes provides to support robust and secure use of the Web for collaborative working is also explored.

13.1 Asynchronous Collaboration

This area of activity takes two distinct forms where asynchronous collaboration (Notes) is used either as an integral part of an academic course of study or for research support. The following sections describe the characteristics of each of these forms.

* Learning Technology Support, Information Systems Services, Library Building, Lancaster University, LANCS LA1 4YW
Email: m.bryson@notes.lancs.ac.uk , s.armitage@lancaster.ac.uk

13.2   Academic Courses

There are three cases used to illustrate this category, two involving part-time
Masters level courses and one a campus-based undergraduate level course.

The Masters level courses have a number of common features, most critically a
need to support part-time distance learners, in a flexible way to fit with their
working practice. The student body comprises for the most busy professionals who
wish to pursue a course of study for professional or personal development. As
such, academic programmes with constraints of time and place are unsuitable for
them.

There are a variety of models for CMC participation [2, 3, 4] some of which are
shown below:

Query and Response - problem centered communication, with all participants able
to see the question and suggested solution(s).

Electronic Seminar - the discussion is started with a short written presentation or
question relevant to the area to be discussed. Students then participate in ongoing
debate about this area.

Electronic Learning Sets - takes the idea of face-to-face learning sets and translates
it to an electronic medium. Learners explain their own current problem or task
(generally with a work-based focus). The set then acts as a resource to assist them
in thinking through their course of action or understanding of the problem/task.

13.2.1   Case 1 - Professional Development for Practicing
Management Developers

This course took its 'traditional' face-to-face course design and looked at how CMC
could be used to support the course in order to open up more opportunities for
participation in the programme. The traditional course has a series of week long
residential workshops that focus on different aspects of Management Development.
At these workshops, learning sets are formed, between 5-7 participants in size.
These sets then meet once or twice between the workshops, at a convenient time
and place with a tutor, to discuss their course work. As can be imagined, the
difficulties of negotiating the time and place can become overwhelming as work
pressures take over from commitment to the course.

A computer-mediated version of this course has been offered since 1992, initially
using a text-only system called Caucus and now using Lotus Notes. The residential
workshops still take place as before. However, the face-to-face set meetings are
replaced with Electronic Learning Sets. Each set has its own discussion database,
with read access for other members of the larger group being allowed by some sets.
There is also a group discussion database, where whole group issues can be raised
and discussed. This is also the main place for communication with the Notes
support staff.

Previously, participants exchanged their written work using postal means, but commented on the work using the conference system. Now, since Notes allows them to attach files containing their papers, this process can also be speeded up.

Since 1995, they have also instigated an initial 24 hour (lunch time to lunch time) workshop to get participants up to speed with the use of Notes. They feel this has significantly speeded up the process for people to get on-line and focusing on the course content, rather than on their initial experiences with the technology.

On the move from Caucus to Notes, one student commented that it was "like changing from driving a Reliant Robin to a Ferrari". Altogether about 150 conferences have been moved from Caucus into Lotus Notes, so earlier discussions are still available.

13.2.2 Case 2 - A Modular Programme for the Development of Learning Technology Professionals

This programme of study is based around a set of modules, introductory face-to-face residential sessions and exchange of knowledge and experience between tutors and learners using CMC. This course has also made the move from Caucus to Lotus Notes. Each module begins with a 24 hour residential session. Where necessary, the module also includes hands-on sessions with Lotus Notes.

The residential is followed by a 12 week period of home/work-based independent study. A resource pack is supplied to support this study period, consisting of reading, audio-visual material etc. Lotus Notes is used to support tutorial discussion and learner interaction, with different discussion databases being created for different discussion topics. Resources are developed around learner's queries and discussions, with remedial information and updates being quickly disseminated through the electronic discussion space. Learner collaboration and sharing of professional concerns and expertise is encouraged [5].

13.2.3 Case 3 - Second Year Law Undergraduates

This course recently conducted its case-based negotiations unit via Lotus Notes. In the past, getting face-to-face inter-team meetings was problematic due to constraints of time and space. Using a Web client to access the discussion areas meant that students could participate from any PC lab on-campus and off-campus if they had Internet provision. The lecturers who participated commented that, although participation was variable, in those instances where students engaged enthusiastically the quality of the interaction and role-playing was of a significantly higher standard than they had experienced in previous years when the activities were confined to the classroom. Students also found the medium useful for general communication with tutors over both academic and administrative queries.

13.3   Research Support

Notes and its predecessor at Lancaster were both initially used in distributed research projects rather than in support of taught courses. For a discussion of on-line distributed research issues see [6]. Two ongoing research projects are described here to illustrate what is possible.

13.3.1 Case 4 - Learning Company and Re-view

The Learning Company is a personal, professional and organisational development programme based on the assumption that improved learning processes will help organisations better achieve their objectives and purposes for the benefit of all stakeholders. Re-View is a European organisation aiming to explore collective learning processes and democratic collaboration in an on-line environment.

So far Notes has been used almost exclusively for on-line discussion but other more specialised applications are planned. Participants in these projects may use Notes from their place of work but many connect from home either by direct dial or using a dialled Internet connection.

13.3.2 Case 5 - Virtual Student Mobility

This is a two year European funded project, currently half way through, involving universities in Aarhus (Denmark), Athens (Greece), Lancaster (UK), Lyon (France), Porto (Portugal) and Rome (Italy). One Management course will be run on-line for between 6 to 12 weeks by each institution and students from the other institutions will be able to participate. ECTS credits for each of the courses have been agreed. This means students will have a wider choice of possible courses plus exposure to Management culture and practices in another European country.

Two Domino-hosted Web discussions have been used during the development stage of the project, one for general project communication and one for discussions of a more technical nature. Notification of fresh conference contributions by electronic mail to participants was added to the Web conferences because there was not enough activity to make daily checking a worthwhile practice.

Each of the 6 institutions runs a Notes (Domino) server providing students and staff with HTTP client (Netscape Navigator or Internet Explorer) access to their course materials and discussions. Each institution has designed one or more Notes (Web) applications appropriate to its own course requirements. Lancaster is using 3 linked applications, namely a discussion, a resource centre (for readings, papers etc.) and a bibliography.

Where appropriate Notes server-server replication is used to distribute a course deriving from one institution to the others, so providing students with local access to all courses and reducing congestion-induced delays and overall Internet traffic.

13.4   Asynchronous Information Sharing

Domino is a Notes server *and* a Web server, a Domino server will interact with a normal Web client to provide access to both standard HTML files and Notes databases. Notes databases are displayed on the Web in a very similar format to the way they appear in Notes itself, with the possibility of having different views of the same information, for example documents can be organised by author, creation date, keyword etc. Notes automatically generates the HTML code both for displaying documents and for the links between the documents effectively acting as a secure, multi-platform, multi-user Web authoring environment.

This approach has been particularly appropriate for information sharing, since many users are familiar with Web technology, but have neither the time nor the inclination to learn how to use Notes. It also ameliorates the cost of requiring a Notes license per user, a not insignificant sum when talking > 9,000 users at several pounds per person.

Again, case studies are used to illustrate how Notes and the Web have been used.

13.4.1 Case 6 - Teaching Developments Database and Discussion

This is an ongoing project aimed at disseminating examples of good teaching practice around the University. A Notes database has been custom designed to act as a repository of the information. Since the main aim of the project is dissemination, publication of the information held in Notes onto the Web is essential to the success of the project. At present this happens using the Domino HHTP server. This provides a development environment that is simple for data entry using a forms-based interface and manages both addition and deletion of material without the need to understand HTML code or keep track of local links etc.

Links can be made from Notes to other Web accessible information e.g. a lecturer's or department's own Web page or other useful Web resources.

Associated with the teaching developments' database is a discussion database, designed as a talking shop for those who wish to ask questions, either about the information held in the database or about teaching and learning in general. The discussion database is an example of the bi-directional possibilities, with both

Notes and Web users completing Main Topic or Response forms to participate in the discussion.

13.4.2 Case 7 - Notes Calls

Notes Calls is a tracking database used by the authors to assign, note and track any support calls received from learners (either on or off campus). This allows us to provide a better support service for a number of reasons:

- we can quickly see if a problem is recurring for many users and take remedial action.

- we are building up a database of problems and solutions. This can be interrogated when other people report problems and speed up solution time.

- it provides a shared knowledge-base that allows cover when holidays/courses etc. take people out of the office for extended periods.

13.5   Future Developments

The models of pedagogic integration of computer conferences into courses, outlined in case studies 1, 2 and 3 are being promoted and adopted by other departments in the University. Two areas of development are described.

13.5.1 The Networking Academy

This project has two main goals:

- to create innovative, cross-campus and cross-cultural learning partnerships

- to develop models of effective participation in networked environments for learning across the curriculum.

The project aims to harness multimedia and hypertext for teaching and learning events in inter and intra-university collaboration and to base their application on effective pedagogical models and recognised styles of learning [7, 8].

Notes supports iterative development (prototyping in response to user requirements), automates several Web-related activities (avoiding a barrier to exploitation by unskilled users) and integrates well with the existing IT infrastructure which should facilitate the longer term uptake of any successful outcomes.

13.5.2 Showcase for Notes/Web

The most exciting and attractive feature of Notes at present is the possibility it offers for supporting Web applications. A showcase of possibilities for this development is currently under development and involves:

- a notice board, with automatic publication and embargo dates

- interactive forms e.g. for student degree application forms

- discussions

- reference materials e.g. User Guides.

13.6 Support Issues

Offering any centrally supported service necessarily raises issues concerning the type and level of support offered. Perhaps one of the main disadvantages of Lotus Notes is caused by its great flexibility, paradoxically one of the main reasons for choosing Notes in the first place. This flexibility exacerbates the problem of being clear to users about the level of support offered. Since the system has been chosen to be the conference system, not the groupware system, for the university, support could legitimately be restricted to conference activities. However, to allow users to remain in ignorance of the other possibilities offered by Notes would also be a disservice to the user community.

In the first instance however, we have restricted workshops and user support documentation to conference activity. As the user base grows and some of the case studies reported above reach fruition, we feel sure that Notes will play an increasingly important role in supporting staff and students in this time of the declining unit of resource. The following sections outline briefly the support activities currently undertaken with two support staff, both of whom have other work responsibilities.

13.6.1 Administration

User management
Users require their names to be registered with Notes and an initial password to be issued. The possibility of incorporating this user registration with the university's automatic registration system is currently being investigated. Support for the inevitable lost or forgotten passwords is made more complex by Notes' security which requires a expirable personal identity disc file to be used in addition to the case-sensitive password.

Licensing

Each user is required to have a license allocated to them, although these are transferable from one user to another. Ordering licenses is easy. Maintaining records of which departments have licenses and how many are in use at any given time is not!

Application development

As mentioned above, as people become aware of the power of Notes, they wish to harness that power to their own advantage. Where the standard Notes templates provide the system functionality and behaviour as required, this is a simple matter of creating a new database, giving it a suitable name and icon and setting access controls. However, where something more tailored is required Notes application development work is necessary. One member of staff is entirely funded by departments wishing to have such development undertaken.

Notes flexibility and functionality means more requests for customised installation sets, application design (e.g. conferences, Web publishing, document archives) and data integration (e.g. ODBC, OLE); all complicated somewhat by the wide range of client platforms. The possibilities for enhancement are virtually endless when compared to Lancaster's earlier text-based conference system in which opportunities for local improvements were limited to development of new commands and command menu hierarchies.

Staff development

For Notes to be used successfully, staff need to be made aware of the possibilities it offers and how, pedagogically, they should incorporate this technology into their educational provision [9, 10, 11], they also need to think through their role and to develop skills on-line, as distinct from face-to-face, tutors [12, 13]. Also, some users of the previous conference system, Caucus, expressed a reluctance for people to change to Notes. Rogers [14] refers to this as the gradient of resistance experienced in most cases when introducing computer supported collaborative working into an organisation. In association with university Staff Development officers, courses have and will continue to be offered. The courses cover best practice in the use of conference systems to support learners, using examples from UK Higher Education, not just Lancaster-based examples. We are fortunate that Lancaster was the host to the computer mediated communication in Higher Education scheme, a British Telecom University Development Award winner. Thus we have a local source of expertise [15].

Staff/student training

Once a member of staff has decided to incorporate Notes into their course in some way, there is then an additional training need for any other members of teaching staff and students. To date, the central support staff have provided about 50% of the training required for staff and students. Again as use increases, the IT trainers are likely to take on responsibility for offering courses.

Supporting users on- and off-campus

A help-line is offered to both on- and off-campus users. At present, this does not take up a great deal of time since there a user base of around 200 people. However as use increases, this will have implications for support. Again it is likely that the training group, who run the general computer help desk, will take on some of this role for routine inquiries, referring more problematic inquiries to the specialist support staff.

Development of support materials

One way of alleviating calls is to provide comprehensive support materials for both on- and off-campus users. This has proved successful so far, with only 5% of off-campus users needing to call the help-line (usually the problems are associated with setting up the initial modem connection either by direct dial or Internet dial-up.)

13.7   Problems Encountered in Supporting Distance Learner Use of Notes

Initial installation has so far run smoothly for most users, supporting paper-based documentation being a critical element in helping learners through the process. Installation has occasionally caused difficulty and getting the software to people is often non-trivial simply because of the number of disks involved.

Most commonly problems concern modems, usually when the modem is not a type supported by Notes. Notes is supplied with many purpose-written modem scripts but it can still be more fussy about modem connections than some other communication systems; probably because, unlike a typical terminal dial-up connection, Notes is designed to make and break 'out-of-hours' connections without human intervention. In our experience once initial problems have been solved, client-server and server-server dial-up connections are usually very reliable.

13.7.1 Replication

Perhaps one of the main difficulties is the initial conceptual understanding of the process of Replication. This is where an identical copy of a database, held on the Notes server, is made on a learner's own machine. A learner can then work on the database locally i.e. not incurring any network connection charges, an important consideration for distance learners. After this initial copy is made, the learner must regularly update the server copy (replicate with it) to register comments they have made and 'collect' any comments that have been made by others. Since the on- and off-line working environments in Notes are so similar, learners sometimes forget to replicate and wonder why things are so quiet. The importance of regular replication is stressed in the supporting documentation and demonstration and practice of the process at residential workshops appears to ease this problem.

13.7.2 The Groupware Mind Set

Another conceptual hiccup tends to be to get people away from the e-mail mentality to the groupware mind set. Since many users are familiar with e-mail they expect conferences to be an extension of that, which of course in some ways they are. The main difference is to ensure people understand that all people with access to a discussion space can read what is written, even if they are not writing anything. There have been instances of personal messages being placed in a public discussion space because the person had forgotten that this was not private e-mail.

13.7.3 Hardware

Notes V4.0 requires a minimum specification of a 486, 8 Mb RAM and at least 20 Mb HD space for installation. Anyone purchasing a new machine should meet this specification easily. However, learners who have inherited old PCs may have to participate using Notes V3, which can run on a 386 with 4 Mb RAM and takes less disk space. This has a support implication, since user's guides are required for both versions, some V4.0 database designs cannot be accessed by V3 etc. The same is true of Notes on a Mac and there was great disappointment when V4 turned out to be very resource-hungry requiring a minimum 12 Mb RAM. Ideally, installation on all platforms would be done from CD-ROM because the numbers of disks required can range from 17 to more than 50.

Notes support for multiple client platforms is a boon but it also makes for more complex support issues, particularly when many client machines are remote from Lancaster and the range of client software supported is so diverse. Some types of client machine and client software may not even be available to support staff.

13.7.4 Development vs Stability

The very rapid evolution of HTTP-related technology and universities inherent interest in keeping up with developments and trends means that new ways of supporting and enhancing opportunities for collaboration are appearing all the time. On the other hand, many of the people actually collaborating on-line do not appreciate repeated alterations to their on-line environment or frequent requests to change their client software. This can create tension. Of course at some stage decisions have to be taken to cease support for legacy systems, for example 386 PCs and Notes 3.x clients.

13.8   Advantages of Using Notes to Support Learners

A touchstone of Lancaster University's learning technology strategy is the use of IT to support collaborative learning. As such the choice of a robust, flexible conference system is seen as an essential element in implementing that strategy. Initially, consultation with the user-base was undertaken to form evaluation criteria to apply to the various conference systems on offer at the time (early 1995) and an extensive review of these systems was then undertaken against criteria generated by the user community consultation.

The advantages of using Notes were identified and implementation in various scenarios has shown that these are in fact the case. The main ones as far as *distance learners* are concerned is the integrated support for off-line working, the ability to share documents electronically, the multiple media possibilities that Notes can support compared to the old text-only system, for example, sound files, graphics, video clips, Screencam movies for training etc. Recent developments and announcements relating to Domino, tighter integration with Windows NTAS and the proposed Internet Calendar Access Protocol further endorse the original decision.

Replication over long distances can be by telephone (direct dial PSTN), Internet (TCP/IP) or ISDN. At the time of writing Lancaster's Notes servers are available to remote Notes client users by one dedicated PSTN modem and by Internet. Lancaster University provides a dial-up Internet access service but many off-campus users still connect to Notes by direct dial-up. Typical remote connections average only 3 to 4 minutes so a single modem is well able to service the existing community of users. Connections are typically so short because of Notes built-in off-line working environment and replication capability. Users can schedule replication to occur during quiet periods (typically at night) or click a button to begin an ad-hoc replication whenever they feel like it. In both cases their Notes client connects to their server, exchanges changes and disconnects all automatically. People need to work on-line only briefly when initiating the first replication of a conference.

Currently, in our opinion some of the main strengths of Notes to support collaborative learning and research are:

- the support it offers for off-line working

- Web integration

- integration with mail systems, including support for POP mail clients

- secure access control to conferences

- structure of discussion clearly presented

- the flexibility to support different forms of collaboration (not just discussions)

- foreign language working

- potential for adaptation for specific requirements, e.g. in research projects
- extensibility through the API and integrated development environment
- the potential to integrate other sources of data, e.g. Usenet News and Video
- desktop 'folders' for managing conferences
- buttons for simple operations in conferences (e.g. Display next response etc.).

Experimenting with leading edge conference technology was not a goal. Programming support is expensive and very new technology changes quickly.

References

1. Lotus Notes http://www.lotus.com

2. Steeples C. (1995) Models for CMC Participation. *CMC. HE Newsletter*, 2, C SALT publication, Lancaster University, UK.

3. Davies, D. (1991) Learning Network Design: Coordinating Group Interactions in Formal Learning Environments Over Time and Distance. *Computer Supported Collaborative Learning*, O'Malley, C. (Ed), NATO ASI series, Berlin, Springer-Verlag.

4. Paulsen, M. (1995) The On-line Report on Pedagogical Techniques for Computer-Mediated Communication. http://www.nki.no/~morten.

5. Goodyear, P. (1994) Telematics, flexible and distance learning in postgraduate education: the MSc in Information Technology and Learning at Lancaster University, *The CTISS File*, 17.

6. Lewis, R. and Collis, B. (1995) Virtual mobility in distributed laboratories: Supporting collaborative research with knowledge technology. *Innovative adult learning with innovative technologies*, Collis B. and Davies G. (Eds.), Amsterdam: Elsevier Science, 163-173.

7. Eastmond, D. (1992) Learning approaches of adult students taking computer conferencing courses. *Annual conference of the Northeastern Education Research Association*. Ellensville, New York.

8. Tagg, A. (1994) Leadership from within: Student moderation of computer conferences. *The American Journal of Distance Education*, 8, 3, 40-50.

9. Wells, R. (1993) Computer-Mediated Communication for Distance Education. *An International Review of Design, Teaching and Institutional Issues, Research Monograph No. 6*, American Centre for the Study of Distance Education, College of Education, The Pennsylvania State University, USA.

10. McConnell, D. (1994) *Implementing Computer Supported Cooperative Learning*, London, Kogan Page.

11. Hiltz, S.R. (1993) Correlates of Learning in a Virtual Classroom. *International Journal of Man-Machine Studies*, 39, 71-98.

12. Perkins, J. (1995) E-Discourse in Education, *World Conference on Computers in Education*, Birmingham. 24-28th July 1995.

Available from: perkins@fhs.mcmaster.ca.

13. Eastmond, D. (1992) Effective facilitation of computer conferencing. *Continuing Higher Education Review*, 56, 1-2, 23-34.

14. Rogers, Y. (1994) Exploring Obstacles: Integrating CSCW in Evolving Organisations, *Proceedings of CSCW'94*, ACM, Chapel Hill, NC, USA. 67-77.

15. Steeples, C. (1994) Broadening Access to Higher Education, *CMC in HE Newsletter 1*, C SALT publication, Lancaster University, UK.

Chapter 14

Supporting Asynchronous Collaboration in Academia

Reza Hazemi, Stephen Hailes and Steve Wilbur[*]

Numerous groupware products are now in use in many commercial environments. These systems typically integrate a number of tools for communication, workflow, database-sharing, contact management, and group scheduling, and operate across a variety of environments. This chapter looks at the use of groupware in organisations, and looks at a range of groupware which supports asynchronous collaboration. It identifies three categories of asynchronous collaboration in an academic environment: teaching; research; and support for teaching and research. It then looks at how the groupware tools could be used to support asynchronous collaboration in academia.

14.1   Introduction

The domain of Computer Supported Collaborative Work (CSCW) can be separated into four areas [1] based on whether users are working at the same place or different places and whether they are working synchronously or asynchronously [2]. This chapter looks at groupware and asynchronous collaboration in academic environments. It looks at the groupware market and looks at the impact of groupware in organisations. It also identifies the products that could support asynchronous collaboration amongst academics.

---

[*] Department of Computer Science, University College London, Gower Street, London, WC1E 6BT, U.K.
Email: {R.Hazemi, S.Hailes, S.Wilbur}@cs.ucl.ac.uk

Asynchronous collaboration can be defined as two or more people working on the same task at different times. Research and development in CSCW and groupware has produced a large number of experimental software infrastructures, services, and applications [3]. Many CSCW systems have remained in the research and scientific community, where they continue to evolve in line with technological developments. A few systems, such as gIbis [4] and rIbis [5] have been adapted to meet the needs of the commercial sector. However, while CSCW systems have not, on the whole, been enthusiastically adopted by industry, the principles and key ideas of workgroup support have influenced the design of products, such as Lotus Notes, Microsoft Exchange and Collabra Share. In these systems, asynchronous collaboration is the target area, building on existing email services and database concepts. There is a growing market for these products in line with business trends towards team-based working practices and distributed organisations.

14.2   Asynchronous Collaboration

Asynchronous collaboration in an academic environment can be divided into three categories; teaching; research; teaching and research support. The information gathered for these tasks should ideally be available for students' colleagues' or administrative staff's use.

Teaching could include: preparing course material; supervision of undergraduate and postgraduate students; marking student assignments; marking exam papers; writing references; and preparing students progress report.

Research is usually done on an individual basis, with colleagues, assistants, students or external bodies. During the course of a research project, a series of reports, deliverables, and papers are produced. There could be internal and external meetings for which agendas and minutes have to be produced. There might be seminars or workshops to attend or organise. If the research is funded externally, it includes application for research funding.

Research support includes preparation of application for research funding, and administration of project funding and personnel during the project. It also includes support for hardware, software and help desks.

Teaching support includes student management (admissions and administration), finance management, timetabling and scheduling of students and lecture theatres, administration of course work and lecture notes, liaison with internal and external examiners; preparation of agendas and minutes for meetings, etc.

Asynchronous collaboration activities in all three categories (teaching, research and support) can be classified into three groups: information sharing and document management, contact management and workflow management. This categorisation is useful as groupware products are aimed at providing support for these activities.

The exchange of timely information and management of group documents are activities at the core of group work. Groups of individuals working together need a means of sharing and pooling the information relevant to their shared goals and tasks. A group database permits members to enter, store, index, access and modify this data, which can include plain text or formatted word processed documents, spreadsheet data with embedded formulae, graphics, images, video clips, and audio files. The information that is entered into the database can be tagged as being for either public or private use.

Contact management can be achieved using such tools as electronic group diaries, group calendars, and meeting schedulers. Group diaries furnish group members with their own diaries, detailing their appointments and commitments, and the capability to access the public parts of other group members' diaries. These diaries can be used to help identify individuals' availability and set up suitable times for meetings. Central resources (such as meeting rooms, audio visual or catering facilities) can be booked through these systems.

Studies of workgroups show that many team activities follow established patterns or procedures. Examples are forms-processing (e.g. travel claims) and production of regular group reports. Workflow works best with well-established, highly-structured tasks, where a description of how to route electronic data from one user to the next is not difficult to automate.

Three categories of asynchronous collaboration (information sharing and document management; contact management; and workflow management) are common to both business and academic environments. The next section will look at the impact of groupware in organisations, results of which could be useful in academic environments.

14.3 Groupware and Asynchronous Collaboration

Groupware success factors [6] and social impacts of groupware [4] in organisations have been the subject of numerous studies. Determining the conditions of success and continuation has been much less clear [7]. One school of thought associates the use of groupware with user satisfaction while others argue that management and IT groups are the most influential. It can be argued that social, technical and economic factors are the major success factors or inhibitors of groupware products.

Turrell [8] carried out a study of how companies in the UK were using groupware in their organisations. His study found that many companies are getting tangible benefits from using groupware products, but the resistance from the IT organisation and a lack of knowledge of what groupware can do limits the potential benefits to only a few areas in most businesses. The findings also provide some insight into implementation strategies, technical issues, groupware personalities and the impact of other groupware systems. Turrell reports that companies benefit from using groupware. However, most problems arise when companies try to apply groupware in a way that conflicts with the existing corporate culture. Culture change can be a lengthy process with no guarantee of success. Users are found to be more willing to adopt an application which fits their current way of working. As they become familiar with the groupware environment, they quickly demand changes to the application and actively look for ways of improving the underlying business process.

Adoption of groupware products is reported to be fairly simple for small companies who have got a good technical infrastructure as they can use their existing infrastructure with little financial investment. On the other hand, it is a critical limiting factor for companies who need to make substantial investments in hardware which makes groupware a more serious financial decision.

There are some perceived benefits from linking groupware to strategic objectives, but most companies have only realised significant returns on investments through specific business applications. It is possible to use groupware to support strategic objectives but usually groupware is employed as an afterthought in a company's business strategy.

Turrell [8] provides substantial evidence of business benefits in most organisations, irrespective of their size or industry, and argues that there are tremendous opportunities for further return of investments by applying the technology to different areas of business. The major barrier is reported to come from the IT organisation and a general lack of education on the business possibilities for groupware. He found the key determinant of success to be the existence and use of business applications. In order to realise the benefits of groupware, applications have to fit the existing culture.

Orlikowski [9] carried out a field study which examined the implementation of Lotus Notes into an office of a large organisation. Her studies suggest that two organisational elements influence the effective utilisation of groupware:

- people's cognitive or mental models about technology and their work, and

- the structural properties of the organisation such as policies, norms, and reward systems.

The findings suggest that where people's mental models do not understand or appreciate the collaborative nature of groupware, such technologies will be interpreted and used as if they were personal stand-alone software such as spreadsheets or word-processing programs. The findings further suggest that where the premises underlying the groupware technology (shared effort, cooperation, collaboration) are counter-cultural to an organisation where competitiveness and individualistic culture is important, the technology will be unlikely to be of great value. That is, where there are few incentives for cooperating or sharing expertise, groupware technology alone can not engender these.

Conversely, where the structural properties do support shared effort, cooperation, and collaboration, it is likely that the technology will be used cooperatively and it will be another medium within which those values and norms are expressed. Recognising the significant influence of these organisational elements appears critical to groupware developers, users and researchers.

Orlikowski's report also emphasises the proper training of users. Individuals try to understand the new technology in terms of their existing technological frames. If the technology is sufficiently different their existing frames may be inappropriate and individuals will need to significantly modify their technological frames in response to a new technology. The way users change their technology frames in response to a new technology is influenced by: the kind and amount of product information communicated to them, and the nature and form of training they receive about the product.

Bowers [10] acknowledges the necessity of the organisational fit and argues that it is important to consider individual's goals, shared understanding and system affordance, he also argues that the system assumptions cannot be contrary to the reward scheme and mental maps of the organisation.

A recent Groupware report [11] comments that there appear to be two distinct migration paths that companies follow when they move towards groupware. The first is the organisation that implements a LAN-based PC network and then moves towards email, conferencing and scheduling packages, partly to fill a need and partly to maximise the benefit of their initial investment in the LAN and its infrastructure. The additional costs of moving to groupware are relatively low in this situation, and the tendency is towards 'shrink-wrapped' solutions introduced by the IS department. The other path that organisations take is at the opposite end of the market where they are undertaking a business re-engineering process and wish to use groupware technology to help them achieve the benefits they have identified. Because of the high level of financial and organisational commitment involved, these decisions are made at board level in the organisation.

14.4   Relevance to Academia

Groupware enables a number of organisational changes. These changes are technology-enabled and evolve over time through a series of technological and organisational adaptions. Some of these changes are planned but others emerge as organisations evolve in their understanding and experience of the technology. The changes are significant and affect the nature and distribution of work, the form of collaboration and interaction, the coordination between different parts of the organisation, and the utilisation of knowledge accumulating in the groupware repository.

The main conclusion drawn from business sector is that the social, technical and economic factors are the major success factors of groupware products. Problems arise when existing corporate culture conflicts with deployment of groupware. To avoid this problem, the applications have to fit the existing culture. Existing culture in an academic environment is likely to conflict with the new culture which implies that deployment of groupware may not lead to all the benefits it might otherwise.

The authors' experience suggests that the culture change and problems with differences between the existing technology and the new technology are common to both business and academic environments. Email is used extensively in academic environments and encouraging the academic community to migrate from email to more comprehensive groupware products can be difficult. This would suggest that groupware products are only likely to be successful in academic environments if they were compatible with existing email systems.

The next section will compare the leading groupware products currently available in the market that could be employed to support asynchronous collaboration.

14.5   Groupware Market

Three main competing platforms in the area of groupware and asynchronous collaboration are: Lotus Notes, Microsoft Exchange and the World Wide Web. Other platforms include Novell's Groupwise and Netscape bundled with Collabra Share. The main components to ship are fax, email, calendering/scheduling, document sharing including spreadsheets, images, mobile computing, etc.

Lotus Notes is a complete infrastructure and development environment for groupware applications that runs on a variety of platforms and includes directory services, message transport services, a distributed object store, management services and numerous APIs. It provides good security management. Information retrieval, storage and modification is easy and efficient and database *replication* enhances information sharing. Notes combined with Domino technology has also created an environment where Web browsing and Internet access have become easy.

Microsoft Exchange provides email, group scheduling and electronic forms. It is a glamorised email system. It is designed to sit on top of Microsoft NT taking advantage of NT's tools and security. The mail features are an extension to Microsoft Mail and include rule-based message processing, filing of messages in private folders, and public and private directory browsing, it also supports mail clients written to MAPI 1.0. Exchange does not contain any groupware elements, but has three broad groupware capabilities: information sharing which provides users with public folders for sharing documents, messages, threaded discussions with support for conferencing; calendaring and scheduling; and custom applications include an Exchange form designer, and rules and hooks to Visual Basics. Microsoft Exchange is expected to become the obvious choice for companies using Windows clients and NT servers. Its strategy is different to Lotus. It may well be a more important competitor to Lotus Notes in future but, at present, it is more difficult to use than Lotus Notes and has less functionality.

Novell's GroupWise tightly integrates mail, calendaring/scheduling, and task management, but it falls short as an application development or workflow platform. Novell's group of products does not currently add anything new to what Lotus and Microsoft already offer.

Collabra-Share bundled with Netscape navigator belongs to a group of products that focus on individual pieces of groupware. Collabra Share was designed as an addition to existing email systems. Collabra Share works with all existing email systems that support VIM or MAPI. Netscape navigator provides other functionality such as bulletin boards, usenet news, on-line chat and email.

These products aim to solve the problems associated with information sharing and document management discussed earlier in this chapter. Contact management, workflow and integrated environments are being increasingly incorporated within integrated office products, of these, Lotus Notes seems to have achieved the greatest success.

The main advantages of Lotus Notes over the Web are its security features, ease in application development and the fact that it has a centralised database. Lotus Notes and the Web are viewed as competitors and enemies, but the best strategy might be to combine the best of Notes and the Web rather than picking one technology over the other. This is the approach that Lotus has taken.

Latest browsers based on Java provide a good environment for creating Web-based applications. Java, JDBC and proprietary databases such as Oracle can now be used to develop application similar to Notes applications.

14.6   Groupware and Academia: a Case Study

This section describes a case study carried out in the Department of Computer Science, University College London in collaboration with the Department of Computer Science, Queen Mary and Westfied College.

It was argued in the previous section that Lotus Notes represents the state of the art in document sharing and asynchronous collaboration. For this reason, it was selected for application development.

Most academic environments are multi-platform environments and UCL and QMW are no exception. For this reason, it was decided that the architecture had to be a multi-platform one. Implementation of Lotus Notes using all possible combinations of servers and workstations was investigated during the case study.

During the case study, a number of tasks were identified as asynchronous collaboration. They include: help desk, student management, processing of research proposals, student supervision, etc. Requirements capture was carried out for these tasks and several applications were implemented using Lotus Notes. One of the implemented applications was help desk.

In the caase study, the help desk is manned by two groups of people (Systems Group and Hardware Group). Reported problems fall into three categories: systems software faults, hardware faults and network faults. The Systems Group deals with the first category of faults (systems software faults) and hardware group handles the other two.

Upon discovery of a fault, the user contacts the help desk, either by phone or email. If it is reported by phone, the person in charge of the help desk resolves the problem himself or assigns it to the appropriate person.

If it is reported by email, the system sends an automated response to the sender of the message acknowledging their problem. The person in charge of the help desk monitors the system regularly and, when a message is received, s/he takes responsibility for the fault. A log is kept of how long the user has been waiting for the fault to be fixed, when they last received a response and how long they have been waiting for the fault to be fixed. Figure 14.1 represents the workflow for the help desk.

Job Scheduling Work Flow Diagram - Version 1.0

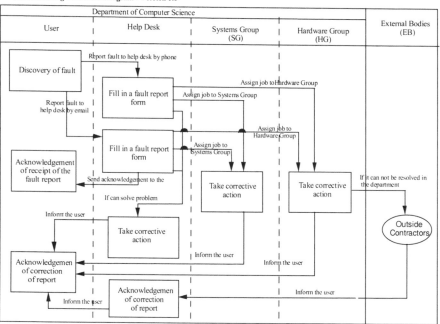

Figure 14.1. Workflow for Help Desk.

The help desk application was implemented using Lotus Notes in a short period of time (4 weeks). The implemented application automates the workflow presented in Figure 14.1. In this application, a user can report the fault by filling a form using Lotus Notes. The form is designed to include all the required detail about the fault, eliminating lack of information and possible delay when the help desk receives the form. When the form is filled and saved in the database, it is automatically forwarded to the help desk. Notes assigns the fault a job number and follows the progress of the work until it is resolved. The user (fault reporter) can use the database to check the status of the job.

The results of the evaluation were encouraging. Lotus Notes was easy to learn and to develop applications in a short period of time, however, we feel there is a need for basic training in application development since Notes is not a programming language and uses its own scripting language which is tedious and inflexible. Feedback from users for improvements, modifications and enhancements could be incorporated into the application easily. Users liked the new application and preferred it to the email-based application.

14.7 Conclusions

The principal lessons already learnt from experiences with groupware systems are that users need their groupware tools to be integrated within a single environment, enabling them to make use of documents and applications from their existing single-user systems wherever possible. Furthermore, users need interoperability across different platforms. These requirements are now being reflected in a trend towards integrated groupware products operating across a variety of platforms, as provided increasingly by groupware products.

These are lessons already familiar to the network community, who struggle to keep track of different systems providing them with access to private mailboxes, global newsgroups, conferencing systems, and the World Wide Web. Integration and interoperability are probably the most important problems to be solved for both individual and group communication needs.

This chapter looked at groupware and use of groupware for asynchronous collaboration. A survey of products revealed that Lotus Notes has been the front runner in groupware products. There are other competitors such as Microsoft Exchange; Novell's GroupWise; and Netscape and CollabraShare. Notes is currently integrated with the Web, after Exchange's integration with the Web and next generation of Netscape, the competition is expected to be between the three products. Lotus Notes is fast becoming the industry standard because of its capabilities but Java-based Web browsers are a major competitor.

The authors have developed applications using Lotus Notes which support asynchronous collaboration for teaching, research and administration. The result of the investigation is encouraging because development of the prototypes were done in a relatively short period of time. The users who took part in requirements capture, evaluation and use of the prototypes generally like the system, they found the system easy to learn and use.

A major restricting factor in use of the groupware products in an academic environment is the financial commitments and cost of licensing. This could be a more restricting factor in an academic environment than in business environments. Justifying the cost of licensing groupware products is more difficult in academic environments as there is little or no financial incentive in doing so.

Comparison of business and academic environments reveals that asynchronous collaborative activities are common to both environments; and social, technical and economic factors are the major success factors of groupware products. However, groupware products are expected to be used more widely in commercial environments than in academic environments. The first reason is the difficulty of migrating from email culture to groupware culture. The second reason is the fact the academic environments are more relaxed than commercial environments and corporal policies take longer to take effect. Finally the cost of licensing is difficult to justify in academic environments.

Acknowledgements

The ACOL project was a joint project between the University College London (UCL) and the Queen Mary and Westfield College and the authors would like to thank their partners at QMW for their collaboration. Funding for the project was provided by UKERNA.

References

1. Ellis, C.A., Gibbs S.J. and Rein G.L. (1991) Groupware: some issues and experiences. *Communications of the ACM*, 34, 1 , ACM Press, 38-58.

2. Ruhleder, K. and King, J.L. (1991) Computer support for work across space, time, and social worlds. *Journal of Organizational Computing*, 1, 4, 341-355.

3. Rodden, T. (1991) A survey of CSCW systems. *Interacting with Computers*, 3, 3, 319-353.

4. Randall, D. and Hughes, J.A. (1995) Sociology, CSCW, and working with customers. *The Social and International Dimentsions of Human-Computer Interaction*, Thomas, P.J. (Ed), Cambridge University Press.

5. Rein, G.L. and Ellis, C.A. (1991) rIBIS: A real-time group- hypertext system. *Interntional Journal of Man-Machine studies*, 34, 349-367.

6. Grudin, J. and Palen, L. (1995) Groupware success factors: A study of meeting scheduling. *Proceedings of ECSCW Conference*.

7. Ackerman, M.S. and Palen, L. (1996) The Zephyr Help Instance: Promoting ongoing activity in a CSCW system. *Proceedings of the CHI conference*, ACM Press, 268-275.

8. Turrell, M.C. (1995) Learning from experience: How companies are really using Lotus Notes. *Groupware'95 Conference Proceedings*, D.Coleman (Ed.), 149-163.

9. Orlikowski, W.J. (1992) Learning from Notes: Organisation Issues in Groupware Implementation. *CSCW '92 Conference Proceedings*, ACM Press, 362-369.

10. Bowers, J. (1994) The work to make a network work: Studying CSCW in action. *Proceedings of CSCW'94*, ACM Press, 287-298.

11. Cambell, R., Craig, C. and Wilbur, S. (1994) *Groupware Report*. Cambridge Market Intelligence Limited.

Chapter 15

Using Asynchronous Computer-Conferencing to Encourage Interaction in Seminar Discussions

Jacqueline Taylor[*]

This chapter describes an evaluation of students' experiences when seminars were conducted asynchronously using a text-based computer-conferencing system. It was anticipated that by conducting seminars which were not constrained by time or location this would encourage participation and would lead to higher quality contributions. A secondary aim of the evaluation was to investigate whether 'quieter' students were encouraged to interact more during the computer-mediated seminar discussions than they would normally do in face-to-face seminars. Examination of the transcripts revealed that there was 100% participation in the majority of discussions. The responses to an evaluation questionnaire indicated that the more introverted students were, the more they perceived the computer-mediated seminars as satisfying and enjoyable. The results also indicated that because there was no need to respond immediately, students were able to research an area in detail before contributing, leading to a more informed discussion. Other individual differences are examined, for example, communication and group working skills and preferences. In conclusion, although computer-mediated seminars can offer flexibility and encourage interaction, it is suggested here that individual differences may also play a part in their perception and use.

[*] Department of Applied Psychology, Bournemouth University, Fern Barrow, POOLE, Dorset, BH12 5BB, UK.
Email: jtaylor@bournemouth.ac.uk

15.1   Introduction

Although Universities are being encouraged to use new technology in teaching, so far the potential for asynchronous computer-mediated communication (CMC) systems to support collaborative learning has received less attention than other forms of computer-aided learning. As Crook [1] notes, "little attention is given to distributed computing; and (it is) curious how slow educational practitioners have been to recognise the relevance of networking to the support of collaborative practices" (p. 197). This may be because lecturers fail to see computer networks as offering anything more than an efficient means to co-ordinate teaching activities and the administrative tasks associated with teaching. However, CMC systems can be used in a number of ways to support teaching and learning. The main ways can be summarised as: (i) to enhance communication between staff and students [2] and between students [3]; (ii) to teach computing skills [4]; (iii) to improve the availability of research resources [5]; (iv) to deliver teaching materials in new and exciting ways [6]; (v) to expand the availability of distance education via the 'electronic campus' [7] and connecting remote learners together [8], and (vi) to improve the speed and efficiency of carrying out the administrative tasks associated with teaching [2]. Although lecturers are beginning to use CMC in their teaching, so far there is very little empirical research evaluating the effectiveness of this; in terms of students learning the required material and developing the required skills, and in terms of the way learners use and perceive CMC in this context.

The remainder of this Introduction will first discuss some of the ways that CMC systems have been used to support teaching and the implications this may have for a more flexible learning environment; then it will discuss the impact that individual differences may have on the use and perception of CMC within the learning environment.

15.1.1   Using CMC Systems to Support Teaching and Learning

It seems that the predictions of Hiltz [9] regarding the 'virtual classroom' are now finally being realised on a large scale. CMC can extend and diversify those who are to be educated, for example, disabled students and part-time students are finding it easier to take part in Higher and Further Education programmes. The flexibility of CMC allows a unit or a full degree to be completed entirely online [10]. In addition, CMC can improve communication channels between students, and between lecturers and students, taking part in distance learning programmes. For example, institutions like the Open University in the UK are recognising the opportunity that computer-conferencing offers to the distance learner; conferencing is being used to bring contact and interaction to the isolated learner. While the work by Riel [8] focuses on bringing lecturers and students working remotely together using 'learning circles'.

CMC can also be used to assist teaching in the 'traditional' university in a number of ways. Lecturers keen to enhance communication between students and staff have set up 'virtual' notice boards, which can be more easily accessed by students and items can be easily updated [11]. A computer-mediated format for tutorials and seminars allows more flexibility for both student and lecturer. This could be important in maintaining communication with students who, due to increasing financial pressures, are undertaking paid employment while studying and are therefore less able to attend seminars and tutorials. For example, Duffy, Arnold and Henderson [12] replaced traditional face-to-face seminars with computer-conferencing in a music department. They found that two of the main advantages of these were that there was 100% attendance (as the seminars were open 24 hours per day) and students perceived there to be easier access to the lecturer. Browning and Williams [6] suggest that CMC systems could be used to improve the effectiveness of lectures. Rather than replace lectures they propose that online material could be available before and after the face-to-face lecture; then in the lecture, the lecturer could go through the material, glossing over the easy bits and dwelling on the difficult areas. However, as Pickering [13] warns, if CMC is seen as merely a way to do what teachers do now, only quicker, an exciting opportunity will be missed. CMC has the potential to not only encourage interaction but also to improve the quality of that interaction. For example, because of the asyncronicity there is time for reflection, critical thinking and additional research to take place between interactions [14].

There have been a number of ambitious claims regarding the way that the use of CMC will change the way students learn. Pickering [13] believes that many educational establishments impose teaching and destroy learning. He proposes that CMC, specifically the Internet, can help to encourage autonomous learning, while reducing the authoritative nature of teaching. However, this view assumes that all students are self-motivated and are willing to accept responsibility for their learning. Similarly, Browning and Williams [6] propose that if such a change in teaching were to be adopted "...given the responsibility for their learning rather than being continually spoon-fed...[would students]...actually be prepared to work in this way?" (p. 37). Also, it is not clear whether the student body is suitably computer-literate to take on a new computer-mediated form of learning and some students may find it more difficult to adapt to the use of such technology. This leads us on to consider the impact that individual differences between students may have on the perception and use of CMC-assisted teaching and learning.

15.1.2 Individual Differences and the Use of CMC in Education

Although educational psychologists maintain that teachers should acknowledge and accommodate the individuality of their students [15], this has rarely amounted to more than lip service when implementing computer-assisted learning (CAL) techniques. Recently however, the importance of considering individual differences has begun to be recognised [16]. Individual differences studied so far within the CAL literature include age, gender, computer experience and cognitive style. However, only differences in communication skills and preferences between individuals will be considered here. Such differences are likely to affect the use and perception of computer-mediated seminars and ultimately the learning outcome and therefore need to be considered prior to widespread implementation of CMC within education. For example, it may be that the reduced social context and non-verbal cues in CMC may encourage participation for some students, while others may be unsettled by the lack of face-to-face interaction with lecturers and peers.

There has been very little research relating face-to-face communication skills and preferences with the use and perception of CMC. McCroskey [17] proposed that individuals who are highly apprehensive about communicating face-to-face are fearful about being negatively evaluated by others. CMC, through the lack of social context cues, is thought to reduce evaluation anxiety [18] and it has been suggested [19] that individuals with high levels of communication apprehension (CA) may prefer to use CMC and be more expressive using this medium. In contrast, individuals who are extravert or who are confident verbal communicators may feel restricted using only text-based media. To investigate these suggestions, Oxley [19] compared individuals with high, medium and low levels of CA in face-to-face and computer-mediated discussions. The results showed that individuals with high levels of CA were significantly less anxious when communicating via CMC, compared to when they took part in face-to-face discussion, and also these individuals participated more in the computer-mediated discussions. In an earlier study, Taylor [20] found that perceived fluency when speaking (compared to writing) correlated with a more negative attitude towards email, but frequency of use of email was not related to this. However, both these studies were conducted in laboratory environments and therefore it is not clear how far the findings can be generalised to 'real' CMC use. Two recent reports which discuss the relationship between communication style and use of CMC were based on observations of CMC use within educational settings. Hoare and Race [2] found that when using a computer-conferencing system students felt able to address topics which they would have been reluctant to do through normal conversation or correspondence, and that "shy students were able to express themselves in a voluble manner". Similarly, when Duffy, Arnold and Henderson [12] used computer-conferencing to replace traditional seminars, they found that there was more active debate because "quieter group members found it easier to contribute". They proposed that this was because lack of face-to-face cues reduced the pressure for instant communication and allowed time to phrase responses. However, neither of these reports collected measures of students' communication preferences to support these proposals.

Giving seminar presentations and contributing to group discussion help students to develop many useful transferable skills; effective group communication skills are recognised as important and valuable in the workplace [21]. However, many students either fail to attend seminars or do not participate fully in them. In addition to the individual differences already discussed, another reason why students may fail to contribute to seminar discussion is that vocal and more confident students often dominate the available 'talk time'. This is where CMC is able to encourage interaction, by enabling all communicators an equal opportunity to communicate, without interruption. Empirical research has frequently shown that there is more balanced participation in computer-mediated group discussion, compared to face-to-face group discussion [22]. This is thought to be due to both the lack of social context cues (e.g. status and gender information) and non-verbal cues in CMC which are proposed to 'equalise' participation.

The study reported next investigates the way that computer-mediated seminars impact on student interaction and the relationship between individual differences in communication style and students' perceptions of the seminars.

15.2   Method

15.2.1 Participants

The participants in this study were final year students taking a CMC unit as part of a BSc (Hons) Applied Psychology and Computing degree. Questionnaires were distributed to all 46 students taking this unit and 29 were returned (63%). The majority of those completing the questionnaire (65%) were aged between 20 and 22, with 24% in the 23-39 age range and 10% were above 40 years of age. There was a 2:1 ratio of females to males. The sample was representative of the final year of the course in terms of age and gender. The majority of users considered themselves to be experienced computer users.

15.2.2   Apparatus and Materials

A closed network of 15 Macintosh computers and one server were installed with an asynchronous computer-conferencing software package called 'Inforum'. Inforum is a structured conferencing system consisting of 'forums', 'topics', 'statements' and 'responses'. A 'forum' is a meeting or discussion containing a list of 'topics' to be discussed, a list of 'statements' about each topic and a list of 'responses' to each statement. Each of these items has a title and message. File, clipboard contents and sound attachments can be added to each item. The system was set up to enable students to read items in all forums but they could only write messages to their own forum. An evaluation questionnaire requested information regarding students' perceptions of the seminars and of their own communication skills and preferences.

15.2.3   Procedure

Eleven groups of three to five students were formed through student choice. Before the seminar discussions began, students were provided with training sessions on the computer-conferencing system and a practice seminar was run for two weeks to allow students to experiment with the system. An advice and help forum was maintained throughout the series of seminars for students experiencing technical problems. Each group was allocated one member of staff who moderated discussions (where necessary). Five seminar titles were provided and each member of a group presented a seminar paper by submitting a 1000-word document to their forum on the conference system. Groups were given two weeks to debate issues raised in each seminar paper, communicating via the conferencing system only. Students were encouraged to use the Internet to obtain material to support their discussions and they were encouraged to join other discussion groups as guest members to compare the different presentations and assimilate the different contributions. Students were expected to make at least one contribution per week and presenters were asked to check their forum daily for new messages. After two weeks, the presenter summarised the debate in a concluding paragraph, then the next seminar would begin. The evaluation questionnaire was distributed at the end of the last computer-mediated seminar.

15.3   Results

The results are presented in three sections. The first section reports students' perceptions of the computer-mediated seminars, compared to face-to-face seminars. The second section describes the relationships between communication skills and preferences and these perceptions. Finally, the responses to an open-ended item requesting comments regarding the best and worst features of the seminars are described.

15.3.1   Perceptions of the Computer-mediated Seminars

Students were asked to compare their experiences of the computer-mediated seminars to face-to-face seminars on a number of bi-polar scales, where 1 indicated a more positive attitude and 5 a more negative attitude.

Students indicated that participating in the computer-mediated seminars had been a positive experience; as shown in Table 15.1, the mean scores for all items are below the mid-point score of 3. In particular, a number of the items elicited very positive responses, for example, the seminars were considered a good learning experience and more involving, beneficial and enjoyable than traditional seminars. Although, students did indicate that the computer-mediated seminars required more preparation than face-to-face seminars.

	1	2	3	4	5		Mean
More satisfying	5	10	8	4	2	Less satisfying	2.6
More creative	4	15	6	3	1	Less creative	2.4
More enjoyable	9	8	7	3	2	Less enjoyable	2.3
More stimulating	6	8	8	3	4	Less stimulating	2.7
More preparation	10	10	6	2	1	Less preparation	2.1
Beneficial	8	12	8	1	0	A waste of time	2.1
Involving	6	12	5	3	3	Uninvolving	2.5
A good learning experience	10	13	5	1	0	Not a good learning experience	1.9

Table 15.1. Frequency of responses to the item: 'Compared to face-to-face seminar discussion, do you feel that discussing the topics via CMC has been...'.

When asked how effective the computer-conferencing system was for carrying out specific tasks, it can be seen from Table 15.2 that it was perceived as very effective for giving and receiving information and exchanging opinions, but not so effective for the more 'interpersonal' tasks of resolving disagreements and getting to know each other.

	Effective			Ineffective		Mean
	1	2	3	4	5	
Give / receive info	7	14	5	2	1	2.2
Exchange opinions	10	17	2	0	0	1.7
Resolve disagreements	1	6	13	7	2	3.1·
Get to know others	1	4	9	7	8	3.6

Table 15.2. Frequency of responses to the item: 'How effective was CMC for the following tasks?'.

Discussion of each of the seminar topics was designed to coincide with the lectures, as far as possible. Three items assessed whether discussion of the seminar topics: prepared students for lectures; repeated material covered in lectures, and whether they covered new material or material from a different perspective compared to that covered in lectures. The results, presented in Table 15.3, show that 17% of students indicated that seminar discussions prepared them for lectures, 21% indicated that seminar discussions repeated material covered in lectures and 48% indicated that seminar discussions covered new material or material from a different perspective than that covered in lectures.

	Yes significantly	A little	No not at all
Preparation for lectures	5	22	2
Repeated lecture material	6	23	0
Covered new material or material from a different perspective	14	10	5

Table 15.3. Frequency of responses to items investigating the type of material covered in seminar discussions.

15.3.2 Communication Skills and Preferences

Participants were asked a number of questions relating to their communication style, in particular: how extrovert and self-conscious they perceived themselves to be; whether they felt that they were more eloquent when speaking or writing, and whether they preferred working individually or in groups. The results are presented in Table 15.4.

	1	2	3	4	5		Mean
Very extrovert	1	11	14	3	0	Very introvert	2.7
Very self-conscious	2	10	14	3	0	Not self-conscious	2.6
Writing more eloquent	7	10	7	4	1	Speaking more eloquent	2.4
Prefer group working	0	3	9	10	7	Prefer working individually	3.7

Table 15.4. Frequency of responses to communication items.

To identify the relationship between these communication items and perceptions of the computer-mediated seminars, those factors listed in Table 15.1 were correlated with those in Table 15.4. The results of the Spearman's correlation tests are presented in Table 15.5.[21]

---

[21] Please note because of the counter-intuitive direction of the scales used, low scores indicate more positive perception, not more negative.

	Extraversion	Self-conscious	Spoken	Group work
Satisfaction	r=-.47; p=.005**	r=.09; p=.306	r=.27; p=.080	r=-.58; p=.001**
Enjoyable	r=-.32; p=.046*	r=.08; p=.333	r=.17; p=.190	r=-.36; p=.029*
Stimulating	r=-.26; p=.090	r=.14; p=.241	r=.35; p=.029*	R=-.53; p=.002
Preparation	r=-.15; p=.223	r=.41; p=.014*	r=-.02; p=.448	r=-.26; p=.087
Involving	r=-.08; p=.334	r=.37; p=.024*	r=.28; p=.065	r=-.35; p=.033*

[* = significant at 5%, ** = significant at 1%]

Table 15.5. Correlations between responses to communication items and responses to items assessing perceptions of the seminars.

It can be seen from Table 15.4 that the majority of students perceived themselves as extrovert and self-conscious. The results presented in Table 15.5 show that the more extrovert that students were, the less likely they were to perceive the computer-mediated seminars as satisfying and enjoyable (compared to face-to-face seminars). In contrast, the more self-conscious that students were, the more likely they were to perceive the computer-mediated seminars as involving and to require more preparation than face-to-face seminars.

Table 15.4 shows that the majority of participants felt that they were more eloquent when writing, compared to speaking. This factor significantly correlated with one of the items assessing perceptions of the seminars. As shown in Table 15.5, participants who considered themselves to be more eloquent when writing perceived the computer-mediated seminars to be more stimulating (compared to face-to-face seminars). The responses in Table 15.4 indicate that the majority of participants preferred working individually, rather than in groups. When responses to this item were correlated with items assessing perceptions of the seminars, it can be seen from Table 15.5 that there were four significant correlations. The more that students preferred to work individually, the more that the computer-mediated seminars were perceived as satisfying, enjoyable, stimulating and involving than face-to-face seminars.

15.3.3   Responses to the Open-ended Item

The open-ended item asked students to indicate what they liked most and least about the computer-mediated seminars. Eleven students commented on the flexibility and convenience of the seminars, made possible by the asynchronous and text-based nature of CMC. These included the following comments:

"we had as much time as we wanted to develop our discussion"

"being able to contribute when it was convenient for me"

"there was a record of everything to refer back to"

"more time to consider replies; if someone mentioned research, there was time to go and look at it yourself before responding"

Four students indicated that the experience of using new technology and the novelty of communicating via CMC were useful experiences. Four students indicated that the seminars helped them to understand the topics better: one of these was impressed by the quantity and variety of information presented during the discussions. Finally, four students stated that they could express themselves better or were less anxious when using CMC. These included the following comments:

"I felt less anxious about putting ideas forward"

"chance to express myself in more detail and say things I wouldn't face-to-face"

"some interesting discussions came up and I could say what I liked"

"being able to say what I thought more easily than face-to-face"

Technical problems with the system dominated the negative responses, with 15 students commenting on these. Such comments included concerns regarding the slow speed of the network and the availability of computers during 'peak' hours (these 'technical' problems are discussed elsewhere [23]). The other main negative response, noted by six students, was the difficulty in sustaining a discussion, for example, in one group contributors responded only in the second week making it frustrating for the presenter who was checking for messages daily. Finally, three students complained about the extra preparation required, providing some support for the results previously presented.

15.4   Discussion

Discussion of the results will be presented in three sections. The first will discuss the ways that computer-mediated seminars encouraged interaction and the second will discuss the impact of prior individual differences regarding communication style on computer-mediated interaction. Finally, some suggestions for further research will be presented.

15.4.1 Computer-mediated Seminars and Student Interaction

Compared to traditional seminars, students perceived the computer-mediated seminars in generally positive terms: they were perceived as a good learning experience, more involving, more beneficial and more enjoyable. However, it must be noted that the computer-mediated seminars are not directly comparable to face-to-face seminars as the computer-mediated groups were smaller in size and were self-selected. Further research is planned to address this.

As predicted, the computer-mediated discussions did result in more active debate, there was nearly 100% participation in the majority of discussions. However, what is interesting here is that CMC not only encouraged more interaction, but it also appeared to encourage a different type and quality of interaction. For example, CMC was perceived as effective for interactions which involved giving and receiving information and discussing opinions, but not for those interactions which involved resolving disagreements or getting to know one another. This may be because students felt that social context and non-verbal cues, missing in CMC, were necessary for these 'interpersonal' tasks. Alternatively, it may be because the final year students were already relatively familiar with one another. The quality of contributions making up the interactions appeared to be higher than that frequently observed during face-to-face seminar discussions; there was evidence that many students researched topics before contributing to discussion, in line with the findings of Duffy, Arnold and Henderson [12]. For example, the majority of students indicated that the seminars required more preparation than traditional seminars and comments made in response to the open-ended item confirmed that because of the asynchronous nature of discussion, students were able to research an area before making their own contributions. Further analysis intends to examine in detail the content of contributions; this will use a qualitative methodology (e.g. conversation analysis) to compare contributions made in these computer-mediated seminars to comparable face-to-face seminar discussions to identify whether indeed the quality of contributions is higher. It was clear that the type of interactions taking place during the seminars was supporting the learning process, for example, it was most encouraging that 48% of students indicated that during the seminars they discussed new material or material from a different perspective than that covered in lectures. This is also supported by comments made in response to the open-ended item regarding the perceived increase in quantity and variety of information exchanged during the computer-mediated seminars, compared to face-to-face seminars. One of the important pedagogical reasons for running seminars is not just for students to be able to ask questions of the lecturer, but for students to discuss what they think about a topic and to listen to what others think. Students were encouraged to read the discussions of other groups and in line with the suggestions of Sangster [5] this, and the increased interaction, allowed students to be exposed to more views and different perspectives than would be possible in a traditional seminar. Further analysis is required to assess whether participation was more balanced, in terms of numbers of contributions from each group member, than is usually the case in face-to-face seminar discussions.

15.4.2 Individual Differences in Communication Style and Student Interaction

The results showed a significant relationship between low scores on the introversion-extraversion scale and high (i.e. negative) scores on scales assessing perceptions of satisfaction and enjoyability. The results also showed that the more self-conscious students were, the more they thought the seminars were involving. This suggests that quieter individuals may benefit the most from a computer-mediated format for discussion; similarly, more vocal students may benefit the least. Unfortunately, because questionnaires were completed anonymously it was not possible to relate questionnaire responses to contributions made during the seminars. It would be interesting in a future study to investigate whether quieter students contributed more to the discussions than more vocal students and to compare the quality of their contributions. Further research is also needed to collect more extensive measures of these two factors; the generalisability of these results is limited because they are based on the responses to just one questionnaire item assessing each factor.

Not surprisingly, those students perceiving their written skills to be more effective than their spoken skills perceived the computer-mediated discussions to be more stimulating than face-to-face discussions. Again, students who feel less eloquent when speaking may benefit more from a computer-mediated format for discussion than more confident verbal communicators. A preference for group working was related to lower levels of satisfaction, enjoyability and involvement in computer-mediated seminars, compared to face-to-face seminars. This may be because those students who enjoy working in groups do so as they enjoy the face-to-face interaction and perhaps therefore they did not enjoy the asynchronous and isolated nature of computer-mediated seminars. Alternatively, those students preferring normally to work individually may have found CMC more satisfying, more enjoyable, more stimulating and more involving as this medium allowed them an equal opportunity to participate in group discussions. Further research is needed to collect more extensive measures of individual and group communication skills and preferences (e.g. communication apprehension).

15.4.3 Further Research

Space limits a complete list of suggestions for further research, but three will be briefly discussed. A primary aim of implementing these computer-mediated seminars was to encourage intra-group interaction, however it would be beneficial if future computer-mediated seminars also encouraged more interaction between groups (e.g. individuals in some of the groups remained 'closed' to what was being discussed in other groups). This could be achieved by specifying inter-group communication as part of the seminar task or setting up membership so that individuals belonged to a number of groups concurrently. This study investigated the effects of using 'first-level' groupware (i.e. support for group communication), further research needs to investigate 'second-level' groupware, that is, systems which support collaboration rather than just communication (e.g. software which assists the organisation and synthesis of group members' ideas). This would clearly involve setting students more complex and / or more creative tasks, for example, more practical tasks could be set such as software design. Finally, it is intended to extend the work conducted here by setting up computer-mediated seminars as part of other university courses. In many cases the composition of these will mirror traditional seminar groups, i.e. they will be larger than those in this study and will be not be self-selected, thus allowing a more accurate comparison of computer-mediated and face-to-face seminars.

In conclusion, with financial constraints now limiting the times that many students are able to attend university, using asynchronous CMC to assist distance and open learning programmes may help encourage students to begin or to continue studying. A main consideration when deciding whether to use CMC to assist teaching and learning is to ensure that using CMC provides 'added value' to the learning experience. It seems that we are only just beginning to explore the potential of CMC to deliver improved learning experiences. As the results have shown, it is necessary to consider qualitative as well as quantitative differences when academic discussion is mediated via computer. In particular, it is important to consider that any improvements arising as a result of using CMC may vary according to individual differences between students.

References

1. Crook, C. (1994) *Computers and the Collaborative Experience of Learning*. Routledge.

2. Hoare, R. M. and Race, W. P. (1990) Computer conferencing: a versatile new undergraduate learning process. *University Computing*, 12, 13-17.

3. McCormick, N. B. and McCormick, J. W. (1992) Computer friends and foes: content of undergraduates' electronic mail. *Computers in Human Behavior*, 8, 379-405.

4. Bresler, L. (1990) Student perceptions of CMC: roles and experiences. *Journal of Mathematical Behaviour*, 9, 291-307.

5. Sangster, A. (1995) World Wide Web - what can it do for education. *Active Learning*, 2, 3-8.

6. Browning, P. and Williams, J. (1995) The geology@bristol experience. *Active Learning*, 2, 34-38.

7. Hiltz, S. R. (1990) Evaluating the virtual classroom. *Online Education: perspectives on a new environment*. Harasim L. (Ed.). Praeger.

8. Riel, M. (1993) Global education through learning circles. *Global Networks: computers and international communication*. Harasim, L. (Ed.), MIT Press.

9. Hiltz, S. R. (1985) *The Virtual Classroom: initial explorations of CMC systems as an interactive learning space*. New Jersey Institute of Technology.

10. Bryson, M. and Steeples, C. (1995) The BT CMC in HE project. *UCSG Summer Workshop on Conference Systems*. Lancaster University, July.

11. Philips, G. M. and Santoro, G. (1989) Teaching group discussion via computer-mediated communication. *Communication Education*. 38, 151-161.

12. Duffy, C., Arnold, S. and Henderson, F. (1995) NetSem - electrifying undergraduate seminars. *Active Learning*. 2, 42-48.

13. Pickering, J. (1995) Teaching on the Internet is learning. *Active Learning*. 2, 9-12

14. Newman, D. R., Johnson, C., Cochrane, C. and Webb, B. (1996) An experiment in group learning technology: evaluating critical thinking in face-to-face and computer-supported seminars. *Interpersonal Computing and Technology*. 4, 1, 57-74.

15. Biggs, J. B. (1979) Individual differences in study processes and the quality of learning outcomes. *Higher Education*. 8, 381-394.

16. Riding, R., Rees, G. and Sharratt, M. (1995) Cognitive style and personality in 12-year old children. *British Journal of Educational Psychology*, 65, 113-124.

17. McCroskey, J. C. Oral communication apprehension: a re conceptualisation. *Communication Yearbook*. Burgoon, M. (Ed.), Sage, 6, 136-170.

18. Adrianson, L. and Hjelmquist, E. (1988) Users' experiences of COM - a computer-mediated communication system. *Behaviour and Information Technology*. 7, 1, 79-99.

19. Oxley, J. (1995) The Effects of CMC on Communication Apprehension. Unpublished Undergraduate Thesis. Department of DEC, Bournemouth University.

20. Taylor, J. (1995) Electronic Mail, Communication and Social Identity. Unpublished PhD thesis. Department of Psychology, University of Portsmouth.

21. Newman, D. R. (1994) Computer supported co-operative learning. *Groupware in the 21st Century*, Lloyd, P. (Ed.), Adamtine Press, 211-219.

22. Dubrovsky, V., Kiesler, S. and Sethna, B. N. (1991) The equalisation phenomenon. *Human-Computer Interaction*, 6, 119-146.

23. McKee, A. (1995) The Usability of 'Inforum'. Unpublished Technical Report. Department of DEC, Bournemouth University.

Chapter 16

Quality of Use of Multimedia Learning Systems: Practical Considerations

J Kirakowski[*]

This is a practically-orientated chapter which outlines an approach for engineering the quality of use of multimedia learning systems, following the International Standards Organisation DIS 13 407 standard. It demonstrates the applicability of the standard to multimedia learning systems and gives references to sourcebooks of information on methods and procedures for carrying this out in practice. A case study from an anonymous source is given, showing how some of these principles were effectively integrated into a product development after development had started.

16.1   Introduction

There are at least two senses in which a learning system may be evaluated: one may evaluate it for content, and the effectiveness of the application as a way of approaching the content *(learning effectiveness);* and one may evaluate it for the ease with which it may be used *(quality of use)*. Good learning systems strive for *transparency*: that is, the learner is unaware of the application as such, and engages fully in exploration of the subject matter. For the learner, the application *is* the subject matter. Thus improving the *quality of use* will have a positive, beneficial effect on *learning effectiveness*. This chapter outlines some practical considerations

[*] Human Factors Research Group, University College, Cork, Ireland.
Email: jzk@ucc.ie

for developing multimedia learning systems for which quality of use is an important end goal.

16.2   Learning Effectiveness vs Quality of Use

This chapter has little to say about the evaluation of the *learning effectiveness* of an application as this is clearly bound up with subject matter and the teaching goals of the application. Although good, conscientious teachers are used to routinely checking on the progress of their students, strangely enough, when they enter the world of multimedia, some seem to relinquish responsibility for the learning process and stop measuring student progress or even end-testing the outcomes of the process. The multimedia process becomes an end in itself. This is a state of mind that should be avoided. It is not enough to include self-tests to be carried out during the course of interaction with the system: there should also be some assessment of how well the system facilitates the learner for applying or using the knowledge gained in the real world.

All too often, when organizations report savings resulting from the introduction of multimedia training they mean savings in the cost of staff, hours lost during work, time spent in travel, and so on. The amount of learning retained should also be entered into the cost equation as should on-the-job performance if this is relevant.

Evaluating the teaching application from the point of view of *quality of use* raises a completely different set of issues and should to some extent at least be considered independently of the content and other pedagogic considerations.

Quality of use evaluation when carried out at the end of the development process is of limited use unless the developers have the intention of creating an update soon. Thus evaluation, or *user-based validation* should be built in to all the stages of the design process, from the first prototypes till the pre-release stage. The forthcoming ISO 13 407 standard provides a framework for user-centered development activities that can be adapted to numerous development environments: from a straight *waterfall* type of development process (all too often the case when deadline pressures constrain the scope of development activities) to an iterative type of environment.

The ISO 13 407 standard as it is presented concentrates on the *process* of development. Two recently completed projects part-sponsored by the European Commission have produced sourcebooks of *methods* that can be used to implement the standard: the INUSE and RESPECT projects. These projects were concerned with gathering, testing, and promoting best practice methods for user-based evaluation, and user-based requirements elicitation and representation. Reference will be made to methods summarised and collected by these projects: Section 16.4 at the end of this chapter gives information about how these sourcebooks may be obtained.

16.3 Engineering Quality of Use Following ISO 13 407

In the past, statements about the adoption of *user centered design* tended to be strong on general philosophical orientations, but weak on guidance as to how these orientations should be implemented in the design process. This section outlines the model proposed by the draft standard in overview, adding comments and glosses in order to bring out the relevance of this model to the usability engineering of multimedia learning systems.

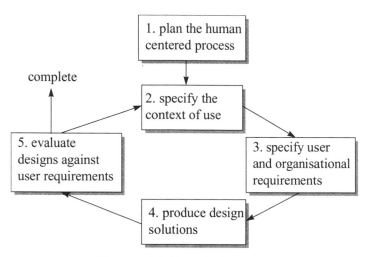

Figure 16.1. ISO 13 407 model.

The model comprises of five stages, four of which are implicitly joined in a loop. This section will examine each stage in turn. Although the process outlined above looks iterative, it need certainly not be so: it may be converted to a waterfall life-cycle model if required by simply going through once only (in this case, there is simply more focus on user needs and user evaluation than one would normally expect to find in a conventional system development) or a V-type lifecycle development (in which the evaluation phase is seen as signing off the specification phase). However, the true benefit of this model emerges when it is used to guide an iterative development process.

16.3.1 Plan the Human Centered Process

This first stage requires the gathering of the commitment of all concerned in the development process to the user-centered design philosophy, and to create a plan whereby there is ample time and opportunity for engaging in user requirements elicitation and testing as well as the more technical aspects of development.

The necessary side-effect of this first step should be to gain consensus among the design team that user involvement in the project is not simply at the end, that is, to 'baptise' the result with 'usability evaluation'. A **Validation Plan** is the outcome of this first stage. Such a plan specifies how many iterations will be carried out and time-lines for each. However, this plan should also list the success criteria to be reached at each stage and the methods to be adopted to attain these criteria and to check that the criteria have been reached. The BASELINE project (see Section 16.4) proposed and tested a *User-based Validation Assistant* which is a large pro-forma that enables an organisation to manage these concerns. Although the BASELINE *User-based Validation Assistant* was designed explicitly for use in projects involved in the Information Engineering domain of the EC's Telematics Application Programme it is orientated towards industrial usage outside of this programme, in line with the general objectives of the EC's Telematics Applications Programme as a whole.

Although the Validation Plan may appear to be outside the loop, in practice, the first draft will never be the last: it is more often a working document which is first produced in outline terms and which is then reviewed, maintained, extended and updated during the design and development process.

16.3.2 Specify the Context of Use

The quality of use of a system depends on understanding and planning for the characteristics of the users, tasks and the organisational and physical environment in which the system will be used. It is important to understand and identify the details of this context in order to guide early design decisions, and to provide a basis for specifying the context in which usability should be evaluated. Laboratory evaluations of the system by personnel intimately acquainted with it are likely to produce user acceptance results which are misleading when the system is later rolled out in the training room.

Where an existing system is to be upgraded or enhanced, the context may already be well understood. There may be extensive results from user feedback, help desk reports and other data which will provide a basis for prioritising user requirements for system modifications and changes. For new products or systems, it will be necessary to gather information about its context of use through interviews and meetings with project stakeholders.

The context in which the system will be used should be identified in terms of:

- *The characteristics of the intended users.* Of greatest relevance to the development of training systems is the realisation that there is usually more than one type of user. The learner, or the end user, is simply one potential user among many. Consideration should also be given to the role of:

- trainers

- managers of the learning process

- purchasers

- support technical staff

- knowledge providers

- evaluators.

- *The tasks the users will perform.* Clearly, the major goal of the learner is to acquire knowledge with the assistance of the system. A hierarchical breakdown of this global task is likely to be similar to the map of the learning domain to be covered. However, once the other kinds of users of the system are defined, it will be seen that they may have goals quite different from learning objectives alone, and the goals of these latter groups may well be phrased in standard task-description terminology. This kind of description should include the overall goals of use of the system for this category of user, as well as the characteristics of tasks which may influence usability in typical scenarios, e.g. the frequency and the duration of performance. The description should include the allocation of activities and operational steps between the human and technological resources. Tasks should not be described solely in terms of the functions or features provided by a product or system.

- *The environment in which the users will use the system.* With the availability of multimedia workstations of widely differing capabilities the design team faces an unenviable task: that of designing for run-time environments which may differ radically in unpredictable ways. In addition, delivery mechanisms (WWW, LAN, CD-ROM, or a combination of all of these) make the task of settling on one kind of technical environment even more complicated. It is, nevertheless, important at this early stage to set down some markers as to what the minimal as well as the optimal system requirements should be, with the intention to user-test in these environments before release. Relevant characteristics of the physical and social environment also need to be considered. Although an office environment may well be a standard to which the design is addressed, the legislative environment (e.g. laws, ordinances, directives and standards) and the social and cultural environment (e.g. work practices, organisational structure and attitudes) have also to be considered. Different parts of Europe have widely-differing expectations of the style of presentation that is expected; much more so different continents (c.f. for instance the difference between the degree of formality expected in the USA and that expected in, say, Germany or Sweden).

There are different methods which can be used for collecting information about the context of use. In the first instance it will usually be necessary to gather together a group of *stakeholders* in the product (such as the project manager, a developer, a marketing specialist, a representative of at least some of the various types of users specified earlier and a usability expert) to discuss and agree the details of the intended context of use. Where more detailed information is required, it may be necessary to conduct a task analysis which yields a systematic description of user activities.

The output from this activity may be summarised in a **Context of Use Description** which describes the relevant characteristics of the users, tasks and environment and identifies what aspects have an important impact on the system design. This too is unlikely to be a single document which is issued once. Some guidance on a well-tried method of Context of Use analysis will be given at the end of this chapter.

16.3.3 Specify the User and Organisational Requirements

In most design processes, there is a major activity in which the functional requirements for the product or system are specified. For user-centered design, it is essential to extend this to create an explicit statement of user and organisational requirements, in relation to the context of use description, in terms of:

- the quality of the human computer interface and workstation design.

- the quality and content of the tasks of the identified users (including the allocation of tasks between different categories of users - for instance, should learners be responsible for configuring optimal performance of the system as is the case in many home-based applications; as well as users' comfort, safety, health and especially motivation.

- effective task performance especially in terms of the transparency of the application to the learner.

- effective cooperation and communication between different categories of users and other relevant parties.

- required performance of new system against operational and financial objectives.

From this, usability criteria will be derived and objectives set with appropriate trade-offs identified between the different requirements. These requirements should be stated in terms which permit subsequent testing. In particular, the following objectives should be considered for each class of user, following the ISO 9241 part 11 model:

- *efficiency*: criteria whereby the attainment of a minimum level of effective performance may be determined (e.g. if it is envisaged that the application will be set up on clients' LAN systems, it must be possible for a reasonably competent operator to set up the system on their company's LAN within a certain stated expenditure of resources).

- *effectiveness*: criteria whereby the success or failure of task performance may be determined (e.g. regardless of whether a learner has achieved the educational objectives, it must be possible to state whether a learner has completed each module of a multi-part system and not left incomplete parts of the module because it was difficult to gain access to them).

- *satisfaction*: criteria by which the users may be judged to have interacted with the system to their internal degree of sufficiency: subjective ratings are frequently employed here, although few rating scales demonstrate enough internal consistency and validity to be of any practical use.

Usability objectives should be set for all of the major areas of user performance and acceptance. These agreed objectives should be set out in a **Specification of User and Organisational Requirements document.**

Requirements elicitation and analysis is widely accepted as the most crucial part of software development. Indeed, the success of the user-centred approach largely depends on how well this activity is done.

16.3.4 Produce Design Solutions

The next stage is to create potential design solutions by drawing on the established state of the art and the experience and knowledge of the participants. The process therefore involves:

- using existing knowledge (standards, guidelines etc.) to develop a proposed design solution

- making the design solution more concrete (using simulations, paper prototypes, mock-ups etc.)

- showing the prototypes to users and observing them as they perform specified tasks, with or without the assistance of evaluators

- using this feedback to improve the design

- iterating this process until design objectives (including usability objectives) are met.

The level of fidelity of prototype and the required amount of iteration will vary depending on several factors including the importance attached to optimising the design. In some developments, prototyping may start with paper visualisations of screen designs and progress through several stages of iteration to interactive software demonstrations with limited real life functionality. Later in design, prototypes can be evaluated in a more realistic context. When trying to improve a prototype to meet design objective such as usability, cooperative evaluation can be valuable, where an evaluator sits through a session with a user and discusses problems with the user as they occur. To obtain the maximum benefits, it is best to carry out such evaluations in several iterations with a few users, rather than fewer iterations with more users. At this stage, the emphasis is on qualitative feedback to the design. Expert-based evaluation is also useful, so long as the experts are experts in the domain of the application rather than technical design and multimedia experts.

Even if a straight 'waterfall' model is adopted (usually for reasons of time pressure) this stage simply begs for a number of small and fast iterations within the larger process. The greater the amount of confidence that user goals are being achieved with the prototypes, the more confidence there will be that the following stage of *evaluating designs against user requirements* will pass smoothly. Some guidance on user-based requirements techniques will be given at the end of this chapter.

One of the major problems in user-based work is to check the developing set of requirements against the experience and work practices of real end users. A set of technical requirements documents is not an adequate representation for most end users who will usually be unfamiliar with the methods and terminologies adopted. End users can appreciate a mockup, paper prototype, or storyboard, and can usually give meaningful feedback in reaction to such an *instantiated* statement of requirements. This has led in some companies to an inevitable blending of the stage summarised in this Section (16.2.4) with the preceeding one (summarised in Section 16.2.3). The degree to which this is desirable or possible depends on two factors: firstly, the work practices of the organisation carrying out the development, and secondly, the size and scope of the project. Small, relatively informal projects can blend these two stages to advantage; a large project in a formal development environment will of necessity see these stages as separate processes.

16.3.5 Evaluate Designs Against User Requirements

Evaluation is an essential activity in user-centred design. Evaluation can be used in at least two ways:

- *formative*: to provide feedback which can be used to improve design.

- *summative*: to assess whether user and organisational objectives have been achieved.

Whatever kind of evaluation is used, it is important to understand that evaluation results are only as meaningful as the context in which the system has been tested. If the system is tested only in unrealistic environments, with access to fast machines for instance, by users for whom tasks are specified 'by rote' in cookbook style, then the results are likely to be highly misleading when compared to realistic usage. In general, the following concept should be carefully considered:

context of evaluation ≅ context of use

If an iterative process is used, then early in design the emphasis will be on obtaining feedback (typically consisting of a list of usability defects) which can be used to improve the design, while later when a realistic prototype is available it will be possible to measure whether user and organisational objectives have been achieved.

The benefits of an iterative process are that in the early stages of the development and design process, changes are relatively inexpensive. The longer the process has progressed and the more fully the system is defined, the more expensive the introduction of changes will be. Bringing user evaluation in at the end of the process may be prohibitively expensive, and ignoring the results of user trials earlier in the process is just a waste of effort.

Evaluation techniques will vary in their degree of formality, rigour, and amount of involvement from designers and users, depending on the environment in which the evaluation is conducted. The choice will be determined by financial and time constraints, the stage of the development lifecycle and the nature of the system under development as well as the degree of maturity of the organisation with user-centered design. Thus organisations starting on the process maturity path may well wish to use evaluation tools and techniques which do not require a massive expenditure in time spent and expertise required. In fact, for such organisations, 'cheap and cheerful' methods of evaluation are strongly recommended (see Section 16.4).

All evaluations at this stage should be summarised in a **Usability Evaluation Report** which gives the reader progressively more detail as the report progresses, from *'design recommendations and summary'* at the front of the report, to statistically analysed data on which the recommendations are based at the back. All such reports should include a detailed *context of use* as well as a *context of evaluation* as appendices.

16.4   A Case Study in Quality of Use

In this section a case study will be presented. This is a fictional account based on recent experiences with two companies in Europe who sought HCI help at a fairly late stage in the process of designing a multimedia learning application. They have been merged to form a composite which we will call 'Company X'. However, each incident related below really did happen in one or other of the clients.

Company X had decided to produce a multimedia training package for a market which they had identified as a niche. The company is well known for its effective training courses in this market and has a good reputation for producing quality multimedia products for other niche international markets. The current project was the first time in which these two strands of the company's expertise had been drawn together.

By the time the HCI expert had been called in, the company had produced a machine prototype in which some of the modules were finished to a high degree of detail, others were present mainly as place markers. The overall system structure was well defined and implemented, and some parts, especially the opening screen sequences, looked very impressive. The system at this stage seemed to run fairly well without falling over so long as the end user stayed within the modules that were complete.

The company asked for help with a user-based evaluation. A series of tasks was drawn up, and a set of target learner users was recruited from a relevant postgraduate programme leading to a professional qualification in a nearby university. Users took approx. 30 minutes to carry out the required tasks, and they evaluated the software for satisfaction with the aid of a standardised user-perceived quality questionnaire, which was deemed suitable as it yielded not only a quantitative score but also opportunity for more specific user comments (satisfaction measure and user-elicited diagnoses). Some reservations were expressed that the version that would be user-tested was a prototype, and that it would be implicitly compared against completed market products in the standardisation database of the questionnaire. A record was also made of the number of steps in each task which had been achieved to pre-set criteria (effectiveness measure).

The results came as somewhat of a surprise for Company X who until then had felt fairly optimistic about progress and results. Overall satisfaction ratings were extremely low, and some tasks could not be finished without the explicit intervention of the evaluators. However, as the evaluation was starting up, company stakeholders had been drawn together in a Context of Use meeting, and it transpired from this meeting that a number of important issues about focusing the application development had been completely ignored: for instance, the optimal hardware platform; what users within the niche market were to be primary targets (e.g., trainers or learners); and the size of company at which the application was addressed, since there was a considerable difference in emphasis between small-SMEs and medium-SMEs in the way the issues should be covered.

In setting up the criteria for the successful completion of tasks, it also became clear that some sequences in the application were seemingly without a place in the overall structure of system objectives: they had been included because it was felt that they were a good idea and there was technological support for implementing them in the authoring package.

During the post-mortem after the evaluation, it was decided that perhaps too much time had been spent on trivial components of the system such as graphics and animation sequences, and too little time had been devoted to the overall system focus and concepts.

At this stage, all the technical personnel associated with the product were put to work on another project for the meantime, and a month was spent on doing a 'concept wall', a paper prototype, and later a series of storyboards.

When the low-level prototypes had been developed sufficiently to demonstrate an overall system concept and an effective coherence, the technical staff were put back in the project. A lot of low level code was re-usable, and experience gained in the authoring package was invaluable. However, the appearance of the total system was radically changed, and work to the next prototype proceeded rapidly.

The moment at which the HCI evaluator had been called in, although late, was sufficiently timely to enable revision without a critical loss of development effort. The slippage in schedule was nevertheless considerable, and could have been avoided had the company decided to adopt a more user-centric design philosophy from the start.

16.5   A Guide to Available Tools and Methods

The BASELINE project IE 2013 is most easily accessed through the project Web-site, at http://www.ucc.ie/hfrg/baseline Several public-domain collections of documents are present on this Web-site in a form suitable for downloading via ftp, including the User-based Validation Assistant mentioned in Section 16.2, above.

A description of the Context Analysis process is contained in *'Usability Context Analysis: a Practical Guide'*, available from the National Physical Laboratory Usability Services, National Physical Laboratory, Teddington, Middlesex, TW11 0LW, England. This guide is particularly useful in that it has stood the test of numerous applications in commercial software environments.

The *'Handbook of User-Centered Design'* (current version 1.1 as of July, 1997) was produced by members of the European Usability Support Centres network, as part of the EC-funded INUSE Project IE 2016, and is also available from the above address at the National Physical Laboratory. This handbook gives sources and some commentary on a wide variety of usability evaluation techniques, all of which have satisfied the criterion of evidence of successful use in commercial environments. See the INUSE project Web-site at http://www.npl.co.uk/inuse.

A particular technique mentioned in this chapter is the *'Software Usability Measurement Inventory'* which is at time of writing, the only internationally standardised and validated usability questionnaire, available in a variety of languages, supported by an extensive normative database. It has been used to evaluate a number of learning systems for user perceived quality of use. It is available from the Human Factors Research Group, University College Cork, Cork, Ireland, and details can be found at:

http://www.ucc.ie/hfrg/questionnaires/sumi.

The reader may also wish to look at other questionnaires produced by this group of relevance to the present chapter pointed to by the 'questionnaires' Web page.

The *'RESPECT User-Requirements Framework Handbook'* (preliminary version 2.2 for feedback, as of April, 1997) was produced by members of the European Usability Support Centres network, as part of the EC-funded RESPECT Project TE 2010. It presents a framework for user requirements engineering within a user-centered design methodology such as suggested by ISO 13 407, and it references a number of user requirements and prototyping techniques which have been well validated in industrial use. The handbook is available from the HUSAT Research Institute, the Elms, Elms Grove, Loughborough, Leics LE11 1RG, England. Documents from this project are available from the project Web-site at http://www.npl.co.uk/respect. A collection of methods for user-based requirements engineering is publicly available at:

http://www.ucc.ie/hfrg/projects/respect/urmethods.

Published standards and Draft International Standards (DIS) can be obtained from the Inernational Standards Organisation in Geneva, Switzerland. Committee Drafts (CD) circulated for national vote are difficult to obtain. Until this situation changes, copies for review purposes may be obtained from your national ISO contact point: for more information, contact the National Physical Laboratory at the address given above.

References

Mention has been made in this chapter of two ISO/DIS standards. They are:

ISO/DIS 9241-11: Guidance on Usability (ISO, 1997)

ISO/DIS 13 407: Human-centered design processes for interactive systems (ISO, 1997).

Chapter 17

Groupware and Software Engineering Criteria for Success

Linda Macaulay, A N Shaikh and Roger Young[*]

Groupware presents a new challenge for both business and universities. It provides support for collaboration between people and as such potentially offers many benefits.

Potential benefits include improving the quality of and access to shared information, improving the speed and accuracy of group decision making, and reducing the need for time-consuming face-to-face meetings. However, as with all new technologies, with every benefit there is also a risk. Potential risks include overuse of communication tools not allowing enough time for thinking, reduced access to information for people who do not have adequate technology, and variable reliability of shared data.

Success in the use of groupware will depend on recognising not only the potential benefits but also the risks. In this chapter we begin to examine the criteria for groupware success. In particular we are concerned with our own subject area, that of software engineering, and how we might successfully introduce groupware into the university curriculum. We seek to learn from experiences in business and to learn from case studies of actual use of groupware within the university.

Two case studies are presented, the first uses a shared workspace for document sharing, threaded discussion and email for a group of fifteen final year software engineering students throughout an entire module. The second case study uses video conferencing with whiteboard, chat, video and audio for undertaking a specific software engineering task. In this case eighteen 'in-house' students from

[*] Department of Computation, UMIST, Sackville Street, Manchester, M60 1QD, U.K.
Email: Lindam@sna.co.umict.ac.uk

UMIST undertook the task in groups of three, and a further twelve 'distributed' students from UMIST, Keele University and Durham University Computer Science departments. The distributed groups were organised in teams of three, one student from each university.

17.1   Introduction

Software engineering is a generic term that refers to the process of establishing the requirements for designing, building, testing and maintaining software. This process may involve a number of generic activities such as writing documents, brainstorming, prioritisation and diagramming.

A number of recent studies have highlighted the importance of group working within software engineering. For example, Perry *et al* [1] report on experiments designed to identify how programmers spend their time, they conclude, inter alia, that software development is not an isolated activity. Over half the studied time was spent in interactive activities other than coding , and a significant part of the programmers' day was spent interacting in various ways with co-workers.

Kinney and Panko [2] have developed a profile of project teams based on a series of questionnaire surveys in which 165 managers and professionals each described a single recent project. They found that over half the projects had at least one member from another site, and many had several. Thus project teams are already characterised by a good deal of distributed work. In addition, they found that projects had a mean duration of 6.1 months with an average of 16.5 meetings per project. Thus each project has, on average, about 3 meetings of the project team each month.

This limited evidence, already points to the fact that much of the work within software development involves interpersonal communication, team meetings and distributed working.

This chapter has five main sections. Section two provides an overview of the main activities of the software engineer and suggests how groupware might support them. Section three discusses research into criteria for successful adoption of groupware in industry. Sections four and five present the two case studies of practical use of shared workspaces and video conferencing with software engineering students. Section six draws out the lessons learned from the case studies and the authors suggest additional criteria for success in a university setting over and above that of industry.

17.2   Groupware and its Potential in SE

Software engineering in simple terms can be thought of as the process of specifying, designing, building, testing and maintaining software. It could also be described as a collection of activities, many of which are common to other areas of team working.

For example software engineers:

* formulate and exchange ideas

* allocate work among team members

* hold meetings

* develop and edit graphical designs

* develop shared documents and reports

* track the progress of jobs

* chat to each other about the work in hand

* mount presentations and demonstrations and elicit feedback.

Groupware can support most of these activities. Classes of groupware are described briefly below together with an indication of how they can be used within software engineering.

1. *Shared whiteboards.* As well as talking to and seeing other users, it may be necessary for software engineers to view and edit documents or diagrams together. This can be achieved by the use of whiteboards. These are tools that allow two or more users to create and edit documents, by the use of text boxes, freehand drawing and diagramming tools. Most are similar to simple graphics packages, for example Paintbrush. Such tools are useful when editing a document or diagram, or just brainstorming a problem, they can be coupled with video, audio or text conferencing to create a virtual environment for synchronous collaboration. Examples of whiteboards are: TalkShow and Internet TalkShow (Future Labs), Internet Conference (Vocaltec), Microsoft NetMeeting, WhitePine Whiteboard.

2. *Group document handling.* Group document handling systems support group editing of documents through use of a shared screen, group document management and document databases. A typical application might be to obtain comments on draft documents in a more effective way than using a simple circulation list. Typical products include: Mark-Up (Mainstay Software), OnGo Document Management (Uniplex).

3. *Meeting room systems.* Meeting room systems support face-to-face meeting activities such as brainstorming, prioritisation, categorisation, voting, minute taking and action review. These systems are reported to significantly improve the productivity of meetings. Typical products include: GroupSystems (Ventana), Works2 (Enterprise Solutions).

4. *Video conferencing.* Desktop real-time video conferencing enables two or more geographically distant software engineers to inter-work using a common screen display, video images of other engineers in separate windows on the

screen, and an integrated voice connection. A typical application might be to save travel time by holding a video conference instead of a face-to-face meeting. Typical products include: ShowMe (Sun Solutions), NetMeeting (Microsoft), CoolTalk (Netscape).

5. *Procedure processing or work flow technology.* Procedure processing or work flow technology can automate paper-based forms, handling and, at the same time, provide summary information about status, whereabouts and over-runs. A typical application might be to reduce the amount of 'memo passing' in a project while still keeping the team well informed. Typical products include: Flowmark (IBM), Formflow (Symantec), Open Workflow (Wang).

6. *Group Memory Management.* Some CSCW systems will provide support for helping the team to remember statements made, actions taken or decisions reached by the group. A typical scenario might be "I remember it was an idea we had a couple of days ago. I think it was Susan and it has something to do with 'program optimisation'." Systems can contain notes from team meetings, with links between the words and concepts. Various paths through words, data and people can be tried in order to locate the lost idea. Emerging products include: Raison D'Etre (University of Virginia).

7. *Shared workspaces (incl. threaded discussion databases).* Any collaborative project needs a way of sharing files, and this allows users to create and edit group documents or diagrams. With group documentation there has always been a problem when two users try editing the same file, and some of the new conferencing tools are now addressing this. As well as sharing and editing files, collaborating software engineers need a discussion forum where arguments and ideas can be developed. This ties in with the need for a shared repository, most shared workspace tools also provide areas for this type of discussion, recording all entries and some allow text searching of the resultant database. Examples of tools that allow sharing and management of group files are: Lotus Notes, BSCW , Novell GroupWise, Microsoft Exchange.

8. *Shared Drawing Tools.* Co-ordination and control of design diagrams and other drawings is important for a number of reasons. For example, consider a software engineering team attempting to develop a hierarchy diagram. If the diagram is maintained on paper, time can be wasted drawing and re-drawing the diagram. There may be delays in circulating amendments within the team, a number of versions of the diagram can accumulate and become difficult to manage. More than one person may be modifying the diagram at the same time and there may be a proliferation of associated notes, papers and diagrams that become difficult to maintain. The team needs support such that changes are immediately available to all team members; versions of the diagram and cross-referenced documents are effectively maintained, and multiple amendments can be prevented or controlled. Emerging products include: GroupSystems (Ventana).

It is evident from the above discussion that groupware has a great deal to offer software engineers. There is potential to improve both the quality of the decision making processes and the performance and productivity of the team. The table below illustrates which of the available technologies support typical software engineering activities.

Software Engineering Activity	Groupware
formulate and exchange ideas	shared workspaces, memory management meeting room systems, video conferencing
allocate work among team members	workflow technology
hold meetings	video-conferencing, meeting room systems
develop and edit graphical designs	shared drawing tools
develop shared documents and reports	group document handling
track the progress of jobs	workflow technology
chat to each other about the work in hand	shared whiteboards, video-conferencing
mount presentations and demonstrations	video-conferencing

Table 17.1. The potential groupware support for software engineering activities.

It appears that groupware does exist which has the potential to support software engineering teams. However, what is not clear is whether software engineers will adopt the new technology and if they do adopt it, if it will lead to achieving the benefits promised. In the next section the authors examine some of the current thinking on groupware success criteria.

17.3 Groupware Success Criteria for Business

Achieving success with groupware, as with any other technology, is dependent on there being a real economic benefit to be accrued. It is also dependent on the willingness of people to change the way they work, in addition, there has to be a corporate and political will to change [3].

In his latest book Coleman suggests a formula for groupware success[3]:

Groupware success = technology + culture + economics + politics

In the context of software engineering, the technology for groupware does exist although there are certainly areas where it can be improved. The culture of collaboration exists particularly at the early stages of a software engineering project when meetings are held to sort out ideas and develop the specification. Later in the detailed design and coding phases much of the work is individual and collaboration may not be appropriate or desirable. Software engineers are likely to be resistant to change, especially if the groupware does not have a 'seamless' integration with their current software. A particular problem with groupware is that the whole team has to use it or else it becomes ineffective. Thus significant investment in technology and training may be needed. The economic justification for this investment will need to be clear, thus in turn there must be corporate desire for change.

The politics of change relate not only to the willingness of people to use the technology but also to the changes in power and influence that might ensue. A software engineer may have design artifacts or information that are his or her own and as such represent a way of differentiating his or her work from others. Groupware may present a threat to such a person by making previously 'private' information available to others. Further problems of a political nature refer to the career and promotion prospects of the individual. Groupware may have the effect of blurring the individual contribution to a project by increasing the focus on joint documents, joint designs and so on. It may be more difficult to assess or measure the individual contribution.

Success in the use of groupware requires attention to many issues. Coleman [3] suggests nineteen 'rules' for success when attempting to introduce groupware into an organisation. These embody good advice based on his own experiences of introducing groupware into organisations. Below is a summary of the main points:

- *Choice of project*
- Choose a pilot project rather than trying to roll groupware out to the whole organisation
- Choose a bounded project with a group that is supportive of both technology and innovation
- Choose a project with visibility and financial impact
- Choose a project where there is a specific problem to be solved.
- *Technology*
- No single groupware product will be adequate, don't expect it to be!
- Don't expect software vendors to offer you all the services you need for groupware. Internal people or consultants may be needed
- Try to pick software that fits with existing systems.
- *Culture*
- Groupware changes the corporate culture. Plan for it!

- You can't change people overnight. Be prepared for resistance!

- People take time to change. Organisations take even longer!

- It takes time to change corporate culture. Applaud those who are willing to change.

- *Economics*

- Realise that training, maintenance, and support will be the majority of the cost

- Measure productivity factors before and after the project has started.

- Groupware is not a quick fix! As part of a re-engineering effort, it may take 2 to 4 years to see results.

- *Politics*

- Find a groupware champion! The higher in the hierarchy the better. Get management's hands on the keyboard. By getting top management involved, they see benefits, and you get a lot more support!

In this chapter we report upon the results of using groupware in a university setting and speculate whether the success criteria for university are the same as they are for business.

The case studies involve software engineering students in the use of a subset of groupware technologies namely shared workspaces, shared whiteboards and video conferencing.

17.4   Case One: Use of Shared Workspace

The first case study is concerned with the use of a shared Web-based workspace, called BSCW [4]. BSCW was used to support information sharing and provide a platform for collaboration among fifteen final year students and the lecturer on a course called 'CSCW and Software Engineering'.

The shared workspace was used in three main ways:

1. *as a repository for course documents*

   For the lecture notes and course schedule, for advertising jobs from employers who were recruiting in CSCW and for details of research papers that the students were expected to read, and class tests.

2. *as a platform for threaded discussion*

   This was used as follows: students were asked to read a research paper prior to a class and to consider four or five questions set by the lecturer. In class the students were divided into small groups and each group was given one of the questions to answer. One member of the group made a short presentation on the result of the group discussion. After class a second member of group then 'posted' the answer to the question on the shared workspace. Thus on BSCW the lecturer had set the question, a student then gave an answer, then other students and the lecturer responded to the answer and so on, thus an on-line threaded discussion took place. In this way the discussion on particular topics continued throughout the week and indeed throughout the course.

3.   *as a means of communication through email*

The shared workspace was set up specifically for the students and lecturer on this course. Entry was by password and a directory of valid email addresses and passwords was maintained. This restricted access by anyone outside the course but also made it easier for contact within the course.

17.4.1 Evaluation Techniques

In evaluating the use of the shared workspace we wanted to answer three questions:

1.   Was a shared workspace the right groupware tool to use for this group?

2.   Did the students know how to use it?

3.   To what extent did they actually use it?

1) To answer the question: was a shared workspace the right tool?, the authors used some of the work of Roberts [5]. He has developed a technique for assessing the characteristics of a group and the properties of the information being processed. The actual characteristics of the group are compared with the ideal characteristics for using a particular type of groupware. The technique takes the form of a questionnaire, see Appendix 17.A. The questionnaire is in four parts. The first considers the attributes of the group itself generally assessing the 'groupness' in terms of cohesiveness, sharing, location, adaptability and intelligence. The second part assesses the type of activity being carried out by the group in terms of autonomy, variability, interaction and thought. The third part is concerned with the properties of the information being processed in terms of quantity, type, confidentiality, sources and flow. The fourth and final part asks questions related to the acceptance and take-up of the technology and classed as 'business issues'.

2) To answer the question: did the students know how to use the shared workspace, BSCW?, we devised a BSCW feature checklist, see Appendix 17.B. For each feature available on BSCW we asked whether the student was aware of the feature, did they use it, how many times and did they find it easy to use.

3) To answer the question: to what extent did the students actually use BSCW?, we used the log of usage actually generated by BSCW. Each time a user reads a message, replies to a message, creates a document, cut or deletes from a document, logs in or off an entry is made in a transactions log. This was accessed at various points on the course and analysed.

17.4.2 Evaluation Results

1) The fifteen students were asked to complete the questionnaire (Appendix 17.A) and as recommended by Roberts [5] the average score for each question was plotted onto a 'spider diagram'. Appendix 17.3 shows the result. The continuous lines are the actual results from the CSCW and SE course, the dotted lines are the ideal results as derived by Roberts [5]. The top spider diagram in Appendix 17.3 shows the "groupness" of the group and the group activities (the first two parts of the questionnaire). The CSCW student group appear to lack cohesiveness and interaction with each other when compared with the ideal for using a shared workspace. The bottom spider diagram in Appendix 17.C shows the properties of the information being shared and the business issues. Here there is a very good match between the ideal and the actual particularly in terms of the shape of the diagram. The values on the right-hand side of the diagram are lower than the ideal but still follow the same overall shape.

The spider diagrams suggest that the use of shared workspaces was on the whole an appropriate choice for the CSCW course. However, the lack of cohesiveness within the group and low level of interaction between students may point to some problems. There are also some indications that the quantity of information the students have to share is insufficient.

2) The feature checklist was completed by students towards the end of the course. The results indicated that students were only aware of 41% of the features offered by BSCW. However they felt that those features they did use were easy to use.

3) The BSCW log analysis, undertaken part way through the course, Appendix 17.D, indicates that only about half on the students used BSCW regularly. However, when students were shown the analysis by the lecturer, the number of accesses increased considerably.

17.4.3 Discussion

A shared workspace is an appropriate tool to use for the course, however it appears that some work is needed to make the group more cohesive and more communicative with each other prior to its use. Students found the features they tried easy to use but it appears that they would have benefited from a period of more formal training in its use. (Students were given a quick demo of the main features and then left to learn the rest themselves.) The analysis of the usage log is helpful for the lecturer in seeing who is participating in discussions outside formal class time. Once students know that their work is being monitored in this way they apparently increase their amount of usage. However, an increase in quantity does not necessarily represent an increase in quality and may be misleading for the lecturer.

17.5   Case Two: Use of Video Conferencing

The second case study relates to the software engineering activity of formulating and exchanging ideas. In particular, a collaborative task was specifically designed which involved students in brainstorming and evaluating ideas. The task was carried out using CUSeeMe with whiteboard, chat, video and audio. The task was created for groups of three software engineering students, each at a different geographical location. The task was carried out by four groups whose members were from three different universities, and by 6 in-house (UMIST only) groups. The in-house groups were treated in the same way as the 'distributed' groups, with only collaboration through the computer possible.

17.5.1   The Brainstorming and Evaluation Task

The task consisted of each student having a different part of a case study to read on the current manual accounting system of a small bookshop. The first stage was to share this information with the other group members, and represent this information of the system by a simple diagram. The second stage was to brainstorm for possible features of an automated system for the bookshop. The third stage was to prioritise this list into 3 releases, with the most important features going in the first release. The task was two hours long, including some practice and tuition on using the tools, and the completion of questionnaires.

17.5.2   Evaluation Techniques

Three questionnaires were designed, the first taking the personal details of the test users, the second an anonymous questionnaire to find out the level of computing experience and group working background of each user. These two questionnaires were both completed before the task was started. The final questionnaire was an evaluation of usability of the tools for completing the task, the user scoring (on a scale of 1-5) how often they used a component of the tool, how easy they were to use and whether they found them useful for the task in hand.

17.5.3   Evaluation Results

All the students filled in an evaluation questionnaire, the distributed and in-house questionnaires varied slightly and are not summarised together.

For the 'distributed' groups (from Keele, Durham and UMIST) 12 students in total:

Tools Overall:

- 7 out of 12 thought the environment as a whole was easy to start-up
- 9 out of 12 thought the tools easy to use
- 10 out of 12 thought the tools were useful for doing the task.

Tool Usage:

- The easiest to use (easiest first) were Chat, Video, Whiteboard, Audio
- The most useful to do the task (most useful first) were Whiteboard, Chat, Audio, Video
- The most frequently used to do the task (most frequent first) were Whiteboard, Chat, Audio / Video.

For the 'in-house' groups (UMIST only) 18 students in total:

Video:

- 14 out of 18 thought it was easy to use
- 9 out of 18 thought it was necessary for SE students working in this way
- 7 out of 18 thought it helped the group complete the task.

Audio:

- 6 out of 18 thought it was easy to use
- 13 out of 18 thought it necessary for SE students working in this way
- 8 out of 18 thought it helped the group complete the task.

Chat:

- 13 out of 18 thought it was easy to use
- 9 out of 18 thought it was necessary for SE students working in this way
- 9 out of 18 thought it helped the group complete the task.

Whiteboard:

- 16 out of 18 thought it was easy to use
- 14 out of 18 thought it was necessary for SE students working in this way
- 18 out of 18 thought it helped the group complete the task.

17.5.4 Discussion

On the whole the students got on well with the tools and the task. Each of the tools is summarised below.

Video The students on the whole did not rate this as very useful, but it would be interesting to see if they acted the same without it. The video provides a cue as to what the other users are doing i.e. typing, talking, reading, (or even if they are there). Some said it was helpful to put a name to a face.

Audio Some difficulty was experienced with the audio, some students using the chat tool or whiteboard instead. This could be down to the expectation level of the users (expecting telephone quality), not using the microphone properly, or just not talking to the other members. Some groups do not communicate well, it often depended on the make up of the group. On the whole the in-house groups communicated more, probably as some of them of them already knew each other, none of the distributed group members knew each other.

Chat Most found this very useful and reliable, although rather slow. Those who used the audio a lot, hardly used the chat at all. Those who were experienced Internet chat users, but not video conferencing users used this tool too much.

Whiteboards All students found this easy to use and very useful. For this task it was considered to be the most useful and essential tool.

The next section draws together the experiences from the two case studies and considers what lessons have been learned about criteria for groupware success.

17.6   Groupware Success Criteria for Universities

In this section we revisit Coleman's success criteria and discuss the extent to which the same criteria apply in a university setting.

From the limited work reported here it is the authors' view that Coleman's success criteria (Groupware success = technology + culture + economics + politics) provide a useful starting point. However, a number of additional factors should be considered which relate directly to the teaching and learning objectives of the university. Some of the points drawn from the case studies including not only the student feedback but also the lecturer experience and the experience of the technical support staff. The technical support staff played a vital role in setting up and supporting the groupware technology and in developing the social protocols for group working.

Technology:

- There must be equal availability of systems among group members
- Groupware is not an 'off-the-shelf' technology and therefore must be configured to meet the specific needs of the group.

Culture:

- For software engineers there needs to be an integration of CASE (Computer Aided Software Engineering) tools and groupware

- The lecturer needs to be educated to accept a different relationship with students. More of an equal participant in learning

- The groupware facilitator is needed to work with the lecturer and the student to devise and review the social protocols for using the groupware.

Economics:

- There must be infrastructure investment, all students must have access to similar computer systems. The worst system will limit the whole groups performance

- Financial support from the department needs to be justified.

Politics:

- Students need to be motivated to use the technology, for example, by making its use part of the assessed coursework

- Support for the use of the new technologies is needed at the highest level within a university department.

In-course assessment and learning objectives:

- It must be clear what you are trying to achieve by using groupware

- Metrics of user performance are often available in groupware. These should be used with extreme caution

- Problems of assessing group work in this context are not fully understood.

Training:

- Groups need to learn how to collaborate using the specific technology. Existing person to person collaboration skills do not necessarily transfer

- There needs to be a period of 'confidence building' in using the technology before any serious (assessed) task is undertaken

- Students and lecturers need training in the effective use of the technology.

Technical support:

- A 'technical' groupware facilitator is needed who can set up the groupware environment, organise and manage its use and monitor student usage

- Students and lecturers need ongoing support.

Thus success criteria in a university setting suggests an extension to Coleman's formula:

Groupware success = technology + culture + economics + politics + learning + training + support

The introduction of groupware into the university teaching and learning programme is gathering pace. This chapter contributes to the rightful reflection as to how, where and why it should be used. The next section indicates future work in progress that will help to strengthen our understanding of the success criteria.

17.7   Conclusions and Future Work

The case studies in this chapter refer only to a subset of the activities of the software engineer, those of idea generation and information sharing. Further work is in progress to examine the effectiveness of groupware in supporting shared drawing of design diagrams and typical software maintenance tasks. In addition, the three universities, Keele, Durham and UMIST, are undertaking one year study of the use of groupware for final year projects. Students from the three universities are working together in teams of three, one student from each university. The students will collaborate to establish requirements for, design, build and test an information system. Eighteen students are presently involved in six teams. This longitudinal study should provide further insights into the risks and benefits of adopting groupware and of student-based collaboration across universities.

In conclusion, this chapter indicates that the success of groupware in a university setting depends upon a number of key factors:

- Groupware technology of the same quality must be equally available to all group members.

- Lecturers must be willing to accept a different, more equal, relationship with students.

- Social protocols for group behaviour and groupware usage will need to be developed.

- Students need to be motivated to use the technology, for example, by making its use part of the assessed coursework.

- It must be clear what you are trying to achieve by using groupware.

- Groups need to learn how to collaborate using the specific technology. Existing person to person collaboration skills do not necessarily transfer.

- Students and lecturers need training in the effective use of the technology.

- A 'technical' groupware facilitator is needed who can set up the groupware environment, organise and manage its use and monitor student usage.

Acknowledgements

Case study two was undertaken as part of the UK JTAP (Joint Information Systems Committee Technology Application Programme) project number JTAP-2/140 'Developing a Virtual Community for Student Groupwork'. The authors wish to acknowledge the contribution of Matt Gumbley, Pearl Brereton and Sue Lees at Keele University, Sarah Drummond and Cornelia Boldeyreff at Durham University, and of the project co-ordinator Paul Layzell at UMIST. The project Web site can be found at: http:\\cssec.umist.ac.uk

References

1. Perry D.E. et al. (1994) People, Organisations and Process Improvement. *IEEE Software*, 11, 4 (July), 36-45.

2. Panko, R.R. and Kinney, S.T. (1996) Project Teams: Profiles and Member Perceptions, Implications for Group System Support System Research and Products. *Proceedings of the 29th Hawaii International Conference on System Sciences.* Maui, Hawaii, January 2-5.

4. Coleman D. (1997) *Groupware – Collaborative Strategies for Corporate LANs and Intranets.* Prentice Hall Inc.

5. Bentley R., Appelt, W., Busbach, U., Hinrichs, E., Kerr, D., Sikkel, S., Trevor, J., and Woetzel, G. (1997) Basic Support for Co-operative Work on the World Wide Web. *The International Journal of Human-Computer Studies: Special Issue on Innovative Applications of the World Wide Web.* Spring. Academic Press.

6. Roberts M. (1994) Creating a Human Technology Partnership. *Groupware.* St. John Bate J. and N. Travell, Alfred Waller Ltd.

Appendix 17.A: Questionnaire "To Assess Work Group Characteristics"

[Note: Information Sharing Characteristics = Bold + Italics CSCW'97 Course Characteristics = Bold + Underline]

Attributes of the Work group:

1   Was the team operating as a cohesive unit? (**Cohesiveness**)

         Acting as individuals [(1) (*2*) (3) (*4*) (5)] Cohesive Unit

2   How adaptable were the team members to change? (**Adaptability**)

         Did not welcome change [(1) (2) (*3*) (4) (5)] Welcome change

3   How intelligent or IT literate were members of the team? (**Intelligence**)

         No IT awareness [(1) (2) (*3*) (*4*) (5)] IT awareness

4   To what extent did the team members share their information? (**Sharing**)

         No information sharing [(1) (2) (3) (4) (*5*)] Total information sharing

5   Were the team members located locally or dispersed across diverse locations? (**Location**)

         Located in the same office [(1) (2) (*3*) (*4*) (5)] Spread over diverse locations

Analysis of Work group Activities:

1   Did the process carried out by the work group require much thought? (**Thought**)

         Easy, repetitive tasks [(1) (2) (*3*) (4) (5)] Complex tasks

2   How much autonomy did the team members have? (**Autonomy**)

         Conformed to prescriptive rules [(1) (2) (*3*) (4) (5)] Adapt working environment

3   To what extent were the team members required to interact with their colleagues? (**Interaction**)

         Can work in Isolation [(1) (2) (*3*) (*4*) (5)] Must interact to complete task

4   Did work group activities vary from day-to-day or were they stable? (**Variability**)

         Same daily activities [(1) (2) (*3*) (4) (5)] Unpredictable daily tasks

Properties of the Information being processed:

1.   Did the information arrive from number of sources? (**Sources**)

         Sole source [(1) (2) (3) (*4*) (5)] Wide range of sources

2.   Was the information of a variety of types? (**Types**)

         Same type [(1) (2) (*3*) (*4*) (5)] Complex range of data types

3.   Was the information being handled of a private or confidential nature? (**Confidentiality**)

Public Information [(1) (*2*) (*3*) (4) (5)] Strictly confidential information

4.   Were vast quantities of information processed by the work group? (**Quantity**)

Small amount [(1) (2) (*3*) (4) (*5*)] Large amount

5.   Was the information held for long periods of time? (**Time**)

Held for hours [(1) (2) (3) (*4*) (*5*)] Held for Months/ Years

6.   Is there a recognised path for the flow of information amongst the work group? (**Flow**)

Rigid information flows [(1) (2) (*3*) (4) (5)] Information takes varying paths

Business Issues:

1.   Was the process being carried out critical to business success? (**Criticality**)

Internal, non-critical process [(1) (2) (3) (*4*) (5)] Critical to business success

2.   Did the activities of work group evolve? (**Evolution**)

Static processes [(1) (2) (3) (*4*) (5)] Continually evolving area

3.   Was management committed to the introduction / development of work group computing? (**Commitment**)

Reluctant to change [(1) (2) (3) (*4*) (5)] Strongly committed to change

4.   How knowledgeable was the work force to the benefits of BSCW? (**Knowledge**)

No knowledge of concepts [(1) (2) (*3*) (4) (5)] Fully understand the benefits

Appendix 17.B: BSCW Feature Checklist

Features	Were you aware of this feature?		Did you use it?		How many times have you used it?			Did you find it easy to use?	
	Yes	No	Yes	No	Less than 5	5 to 10	More than 10	Yes	No
Access									
Add article									
Add doc									
Add folder									
Add member									
Add url									
Add version									
Add ws									
Attach note									
Catch up									
Change pwd									
Change type									
Cut									
Delete									
Destroy									
Drop									
Edit									
Edit banner									
Edit desc.									
Edit details									
Edit prefs									
Edit url									
Mail									
Move									
Next									
Previous									
Rename									
Replace									
Reply									
Undelete									
Version									

Appendix 17.C: Spider Diagrams

Appendix 3: Spider Diagrams

<u>Note:</u>
Dotted Lines = Information Sharing Characteristics
Continuous Lines = CSCW Course Characteristics

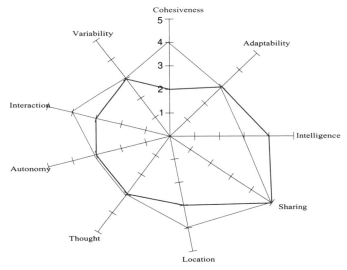

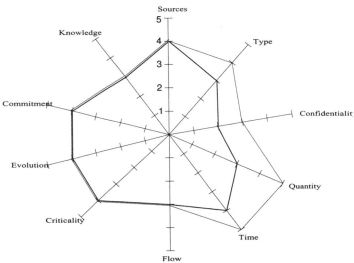

Appendix 17.D: Log of BSCW Usage

Name	Log date	Read Papers	Read Comments	Read Weekwise Plan	Read Jobs	Reply Papers	Reply Comments	Created Papers	Created Comments	Cut Papers	Cut Comments	Delete Papers	Delete Comments
Sanjay	16/03/97	11	5			1	2						
	13/04/97												
	17/06/97	1											
	Total	17				3							
Paul	16/03/97	3	6	2	1		1		1		1		
	13/04/97												
	17/06/97												
	Total	12				1		1		1			
Jon	16/03/97	16	10	2	3	1	2	4	1	3			
	13/04/97												
	17/06/97	20	3	1	3								
	Total	58				3		5		3			
Nick	16/03/97	13	9	2		4	1	1					
	13/04/97												
	17/06/97	4			1								
	Total	28				5		1					
Wong	16/03/97	9	14	2	2			2	1				
	13/04/97		1										
	17/06/97	5	2										
	Total	35						3					
John	16/03/97		14	1				2					
	13/04/97												
	17/06/97												
	Total	15						2					

Name	Log date	Read				Reply		Created		Cut		Delete	
		Papers	Comments	Weekwise Plan	Jobs	Papers	Comments	Papers	Comments	Papers	Comments	Papers	Comments
Ali	16/03/97	5	14		3		2	2				1	
	13/04/97		1										
	17/06/97	3	10		2								
	Total		**38**				**2**	**2**					
Azhan	16/03/97	4	10	1	2		1		1		1		
	13/04/97												
	17/06/97												
	Total		**17**				**1**		**1**		**1**		
Andrew	16/03/97		9		3		2						
	13/04/97												
	17/06/97												
	Total		**12**				**2**						
Mark	16/03/97	1						1					
	13/04/97												
	17/06/97												
	Total		**1**					**1**					
Susan	16/03/97												
	13/04/97												
	17/06/97	13	6	2									
	Total		**21**										
Josh	16/03/97				1								
	13/04/97												
	17/06/97	20		1	2								
	Total		**24**										

Chapter 18

The Application of Intranet and Business Groupware Technologies to Support Collaborative Learning with Face-to-Face Students

Clive Holtham, Mark D'Cruz and Ashok Tiwari[*]

This chapter reviews the support of asynchronous teams, initially utilising Intranet-based mini-case study publication with Web-based conferencing. There was subsequent use of Lotus Notes within the same context. The specific situation relates to large groups of one-year full time MBA students. The chapter reports on this exercise from both pedagogic and groupware perspectives. Implications, and planned future developments of this approach, are reviewed.

The key pedagogic assumptions behind this exercise were based on theories of collaborative or cooperative learning, particularly peer tutoring, discussion in learning, and learning from case studies.

The exercises involved students preparing work individually, then publishing that work to a groupware or Intranet database. Small groups then had to work asynchronously on group tasks, using the groupware, and drawing on their individual material. Students were assessed wholly on an individual basis.

As a result of the use of both Intranet and commercial groupware technologies, it was possible to reach a number of conclusions relating to their relative advantages and disadvantages. A great deal was learnt about the academic issues arising from this type of work, as well as technical issues. Very considerable emphasis needs to

[*] City University Business School, Frobisher Crescent, Barbican Centre, London, EC2Y 8HB, U.K.
Email: C.W.Holtham@city.ac.uk

be placed on clear pedagogic goals. It is also essential to have confidence both in the computer network and in the technical support facilities available.

The overall feedback from the exercise was very positive, but the clear academic benefits need to be assessed alongside the relatively greater actual and opportunity costs of running this type of intensive exercise.

18.1   Educational Context

The key pedagogic assumptions behind this exercise were based on theories of collaborative or cooperative learning, as outlined in [1] and [2]. There is a sub-set of this theory which focuses on peer teaching or tutoring [3]. [4, 5] define this as "the system of instruction in which learners help each other and learn by teaching. These authors examine the specific topic of tutorless groups, which "aim to motivate students to become more involved with their own learning, so that they become more active and self-directed in their work."

There is also closely related theory to be derived from the role of discussion in learning [6] and from the use of syndicates and small groups in higher education [7]. There is in addition a specific concern with learning from case studies, a method which was refined at the Harvard Business School using relatively substantial, teacher-led cases [8]. Six different types of skills that can be developed through cases [4] analytical, application, creative, communication, social, self-analysis. In this exercise, the skills of particular relevance were:

- *Analytical*: Basic research of a case; analysis of the whole set of cases created by team members

- *Application*: Students need to be able to apply basic information management concepts e.g. the McFarlan Grid and the Balanced Business Scorecard

- *Communication*: Ability to edit and present a mini-case in an unfamiliar structured format, published to a large group electronically

- *Social*: Development of social skills in asynchronous computer supported communications.

18.2   Computer Supported Collaborative Learning

Even though the term CSCW was not used at that time, the first generation of CSCW application and research was during the 1960's arising from Englebart's work at Stanford [9]. The second generation began during the 1970's and was primarily based around innovations in higher education. One major centre was at the University of Illinois where PLATO was developed [10]. PLATO involved both a multimedia intelligent tutoring system, as well as groupware-style conferencing and shared databases. Another major centre was at the New Jersey Institute of Technology (NJIT) where the pioneers Murray Turoff and Starr Roxanne Hiltz [11] still continue to evolve what they call the Virtual Classroom [12, 13].

As networked technology has become widely available in higher education, the related concept of Computer Supported Collaborative Learning (CSCL) has been developed. It is worth noticing that much of the historic evolution of CSCL has been rooted in the needs of distance education [14]. There has been relatively less research concerning the use of CSCL with students who are otherwise wholly face-to-face. This imbalance can be expected to change, both as conventional teaching resources become more constrained, and as face-to-face institutions seek to enrich the range of learning experiences available [15].

18.3   Other Relevant MBA Experiences

Apart from the general use of case studies there have in the last decade been a wide variety of experiments, pilots and implementations of collaborative learning approaches within Business Schools and specifically MBA programmes. Many examples relate to distance education e.g. Henley Management College, New York University's Virtual College and the University of Texas executive MBA programme.

The largest single initiative has been taken at the University of St. Gallen, Switzerland where for some time the whole academic and administrative infrastructure is conducted through a Lotus Notes-based environment. The example with the most similar context to that of City University is probably that of the University of Ohio MBA programme [16].

One of the most sophisticated approaches to date developed for MBA work was the CATT (Computerised Argumentation Based Teaching Tool) prototype [5]. This was "built around the concept of asynchronous, distributed, multi-party interaction". It used a specific argumentation methodology - IBIS. Its developers argued that "the creation of a truly global classroom environment requires the development of groupware-based systems to support the case discussion method...that spans the boundaries of time and space."

18.4   Specific Context

At City University Business School, the Day MBA course has five specialisms, - Finance, Marketing, Human Resource Management, International Business and Export, and Information Technology and Management. This chapter specifically describes the utilisation of groupware technologies during the 1995/96 academic year on the "Information Management Core Course". This is taken by four of the above groups, the IT and Management students being exempt from the course, with 137 students participating in 1995/96. The average age of students is 29, with almost all having good previous business experience.

Since 1989, use of the Internet on the course has been compulsory, and has evolved from email only, through telnet and ftp to gopher. As soon as the World Wide Web became available it was incorporated in the course. Hands-on skills in these technologies are provided at the beginning of term one, with the Information Management course itself provided over nine weeks in term 2. All MBA students are expected to have PC facilities at home. Only a small but increasing minority have also had modems. The university IT facilities are based around central Unix servers, with clusters of modern PCs linked to the core via Novell LANs.

The Business School has been researching the use of groupware in business since the late 1980's (e.g. [17]). It has also been developing network-based educational use since 1989 [18, 19]. This has particularly involved use of 'virtual teams' of both MBA and undergraduate students based at business schools in France, USA, Finland and Ireland. They are given a management case study which they need to discuss and resolve electronically via email, closed usenet groups, and customised conferencing facilities provided by the COMCONF consortium in the USA.

There has been use of Lotus Notes and a wide range of other groupware tools in researching executive's business use of groupware [20], and to support this Lotus Notes was available since 1993 on a research LAN under OS/2. It was also provided on the University's Unix servers for student use since 1994. As a result of other groupware research and development work, the Business School had by the start of the academic year 1995/96 also developed a Web-based conferencing system. This required a Netscape client, and drew on CGI and PERL-based facilities.

18.5 Specific Pedagogic Objectives

The Information Management Core Course is concerned not with the mechanics of business IT, but rather with its strategic application. It is taken for granted that students will make practical use of IT during the course, but all hands-on technologies are taught ahead of time so the Core Course syllabus is entirely academic and business-based. Once the Web conferencing software had been successfully developed in 1995, and used extensively in a major international research project, it became clear that it could then be used in term two from January onwards. Three formal objectives were set for the core course exercise:

1. The software should be used to prepare MBA students for experiences they were certain to face on returning to work, and which benefitted from an experiential approach. The theme chosen was "working in global virtual teams". Only three of the 137 students had prior experience of using conferencing software for this purpose in their business careers.

2. It should directly familiarise students with key business issues they needed to be aware of, for example the social and process dimensions of technology-supported virtual teams.

3. There was a need to apply information management theories covered in lectures and reading.

Other objectives that were set were:

4. The exercise should involve creating particular types of pressures on students, especially those relating to timeliness and to timing.

5. The exercise should not only be challenging, but enjoyable and even fun.

6. If possible external moderators from business should be involved.

7. It was decided early on that this exercise would comprise a major part of the coursework for the course. Explicit criteria for student assessment were therefore set, and published in advance. This importance of compulsion had been learnt from earlier year's use of groupware with MBA students [21].

18.6 Design Considerations

During the period before January 1996 when the exercise was being finalised, it was discovered that ICI had just completed an exercise using Lotus Notes to support a global virtual team of over 40 fast-track middle managers [22]. The concept which had actually been used by ICI was unexpectedly close to that already envisaged for the MBA students. This involved the participants researching, and writing up in a structured format, a mini-case study concerning the strategic use of IT in business. The ICI case studies were input and published via Lotus Notes, which then provided the platform for subsequent discussions among the virtual team.

The Business School had a difficult decision to make between using Lotus Notes or its own proprietary Web-conferencing software. The decision was eventually taken to use the Web conferencing primarily because there was no time in the MBA schedule in term 2 to run even the brief training sessions necessary for Lotus Notes. But the intention always was to reverse-engineer the content into a Notes database both for marking and for research purposes. So the Web-conferencing system was customised in a format largely indistinguishable from Lotus Notes in its input forms. The database and 'viewing' functionality of Notes was not, however, easy to reproduce economically, so a bulletin board type of output was used.

18.7   The Exercise

The objectives of the exercise were published in the course handbook in week one of term two, and explained at the week one lecture. The basic stages were as follows, and relevant statistics are shown in Table 18.1:

1. Students 'bid' for subject of mini-case study; bids submitted were immediately published to the respective virtual teams.

2. Students research case and input mini case via Web forms. There was an immense variety of topics covered both within and across specialisms.

3. After deadline, the mini cases are published to the four virtual teams. Teams were organised by specialism, ranging in size from 18 to 45 participants.

4. First discussion phase in virtual teams, responding to a topic set by the virtual MD.

5. Feedback from MD on first discussion.

6. Second discussion phase in virtual teams, responding to a second topic.

7. Feedback from MD on second discussion.

8. Assessment of students' individual performances.

Groups	A	B	C	D	All
Nos. Male	33	7	31	17	88
Nos. Female	12	11	10	16	49
Total Participants	45	18	41	33	137
No of comments for discussion 1	133	84	120	249	586
No of comments for discussion 2	148	67	86	87	388
Range of comments per participant discussion 1	1-21	2-8	1-12	0-29	1-29
Range of comments per participant discussion 2	0-10	0-9	0-5	0-11	0-11
Range of comments per participant for both discussions	2-24	4-15	1-16	4-29	1-29

Table 18.1. Statistics of the MBA discussion database.

18.8   Post-exercise Phase

After the discussions were completed, the reverse-engineering of the content into a Lotus Notes database was carried out. There were three aims in this reverse engineering. The first was a research objective - to be able to compare the informational value of data held in Lotus Notes contrasted with the identical data held in Web conferencing software. Secondly, there was a need to prototype a Notes database for potential use in the 1996/97 Information Management Core Course. Thirdly, it was essential to be able to assemble all the contributions of students into a single easily-viewable location, to enable marking to take place.

18.9   Practical Problems

As with any novel approach there were both unexpected problems and unexpected benefits. Starting with the problems, there was little doubt that the tight weekly deadlines ran counter to the preferred modus operandi of a minority of students who tend to hand in material at or near deadlines. In this exercise, there were either advantages (as in the bidding phase) or desirabilities from participating other than at the very last moment.

Secondly, since most students did not have modems at home, and since all inputs had to be made electronically via Netscape, the great majority had to make their inputs via the university's computer laboratories. Given the inevitable time pressures on an intensive MBA programme, this placed strains on students who naturally wanted to make inputs at a time convenient to them, regardless of whether that was a time laboratory space was generally actually free.

Thirdly, again because students did not have electronic access at home, many more than expected decided to print out their virtual team case studies (up to 45), and also the discussion lists. This put, during certain time periods, the normally good printing facilities into very heavy overload, causing frustration to many students.

The rather basic navigational interface available on the bulletin-board style presentation of the electronic discussions was found by many students to be clumsy if not time wasting. This was a relatively serious criticism given that time is a precious commodity to the MBA student. The largest virtual team had 45 participants and given some of the overload problems identified above, with the benefit of hindsight this should in the event has been split into two groups.

18.10   Benefits

In the assessment of the exercise by students, it received very positive feedback by the majority of students despite the logistical problems. The ability to use collaboration technology, becoming common in many businesses, was very positively rated. It also has to be said that there was a novelty element for face-to-face students in carrying out group interactions via this asynchronous method. For a highly rated MBA course there is a very substantial amount of group work, which can be both energising and frustrating (especially in synchronising meetings). Carrying out parts of the coursework via quite large asynchronous teams did not place the students under even further pressures to have meetings. This was generally welcomed, although a small minority of students strongly disliked the lack of face to face contact even where they recognised the inevitability of use of the asynchronous approach in many businesses.

There is little doubt that from the Course Leader's point of view, asynchronous course work offers one great benefit, namely that the contributions being assessed are all physically visible, and group work can be marked on a wholly individual basis. There was nothing to prevent students discussing matters face-to-face but there could be no marks allocated for such discussions. Our impression was that the time pressures involved meant that there was little scope for off-line discussion - the nearest we could observe was where a group of students were working on individual input at the same time in the same laboratory.

Students were asked to comment on the advantages and disadvantages of collaborative technologies generally. From their answers it was clear that overall, even in the short time available, there were mostly sound insights achieved out of the student's own experiences.

18.11 Generic Team Skills

[7] provides a checklist for effective small group work. In our experience these valuable guidelines developed for face to face syndicate work in higher education apply almost directly to groupware-based interactions. Most of these were followed in the MBA exercise:

1. *Exchange Information* Make sure the students know what it is all about; Teach them how people work in groups; Hold a preliminary procedural meeting.

2. *Engineer Cooperation* Insist on participation; Anticipate conflict; Use subgroups; Encourage any moves to assume responsibility for their own learning.

3. *Playing Roles* Certain roles must be filled if the group is to function efficiently; Variations in roles of individuals fits wider educational objectives.

4. *Controlled Informality* Make time specifically for less formal chat.

18.12 Roles of Asynchronous Participants

For the purposes of the exercise, instructions were issued to students in the name of the Managing Director of the company they were working for. The MD also reviewed the performance of teams overall at the end of each of the electronic conferences. The

MD assessed teams in business language in much the same way as any senior executive would do. At the same time, performance of teams was reviewed by the Course Leader in both process and academic terms.

The exercise was directed by the Course Leader, with input and advice from a departmental colleague with considerable experience of mail-based simulations. Technical support was provided by a "technographer" [5]. The individual involved was already expert in HTML, CGI, and PERL, as well as being an experienced Lotus Notes developer. When using innovative technologies the importance of a highly qualified technographer cannot be over-stated.

No explicit briefing was given to students on roles. Teams found the first week of discussion quite difficult as they had to learn by experience how to function in this unfamiliar environment. The most critical roles needed were for participants who could shape the discussions towards convergence on the questions set by the MD. Not all groups appeared to have equal shares of individuals with these skills in Week 1. Explicit reminders were given at the end of Week 1 concerning the need for convergent behaviour. The teams who were better skilled at convergence in Week 1 still performed relatively better at convergence in Week 2. In the future much more explicit advice will be provided in this area of roles and skills.

18.13 Groupware Issues - Web and Notes Facilities

The Business Schools' groupware strategy has been based around use of Lotus Notes for electronic publishing and discussion conferencing. Since Notes was introduced in the early 1990's, there has been growth in the business use of the Internet, plus the availability of new forms of groupware based on the Intranet. The exercise as undertaken by the MBA students was effectively an Intranet exercise, with the exception that external moderators were able to access the system and the servers were not physically isolated from the Internet, protection being via a basic ID and password system.

The Business School strategy has envisaged active use of the Internet as a window on the outside world, with the its groupware being a parallel internal world. This strategy is now being revised as a result of the release of Lotus Domino. This software enables a Notes server also to be a Web server. Notes databases (within certain constraints) can then be accessed by any standard Web browser client, as well as by the proprietary Lotus Notes client. The revised strategy now envisages Lotus Notes as, additionally, the standard Web publishing environment for the School. It can also particularly serve as the underlying architecture for future Web-based conferencing.

The comments made here should be placed in a context of being written in the summer of 1996, and particularly in relation to the skills available to the City University Business School in 1995/96 - an individual equally capable in Notes and HTML/CGI/PERL. The decision to use Web conferencing for the exercise was essentially pragmatic for reasons given earlier, and the eventual transition to a Notes environment was in little doubt. Had there been a long term commitment to a Web-server solution, effort would have been put firstly into devising a more sophisticated discussion conferencing system. Secondly, there would have been the development of a database architecture to enable some Notes-like facilities to be emulated via Intranet software.

Allowing for all these provisos, some comparison of non-Domino Notes and Web-based environments as gleaned from this exercise can be summarised in Table 18.2.

Feature	Notes	Web
Client-availability	Additional client needed	Client widely available already
Client-user skills	Additional training	Usually present already
Client-standardisation	Standard; multi-platform	Non-standard; multi-platform
Development Environment	Fully Integrated	Additional
Database Functionality	Fully Integrated	Additional
Development skills	Much can be achieved with minimal expertise	Expertise essential
Internet Hyper-links	Not directly available	Immediately available
Bi-directional Replication - remote clients and servers	Fully Integrated	Additional and non-standard
Discussion Conferencing	Fully integrated	Custom
Security	8 user levels; Field-level protection	Custom
System Administration	Expertise essential	Use existing expert

Table 18.2. Notes and Web features.

Given the availability of existing Notes expertise within the business school, and the existence of both Notes clients and servers on the business school network, the main barrier to future Notes use was the additional training need. Based on a pilot with MBA students in Summer 1996 this is not expected to exceed a 60 to 90 minute hands-on session. A second barrier is the ready availability of Notes clients on student home machines at reasonable cost. With a new CHEST deal in the Summer of 1996, this cost is now set at a modest level.

Assuming these two barriers are removed, Notes has all the in-built functionality needed for the particular approach used in this exercise. Our experience with Intranet tools is that considerable custom effort is necessary even to achieve emulation of basic Notes features. By 1997 the questions and answers about Notes and the Intranet will both have moved on, so this is only a snapshot perspective at the time of writing.

18.14 Were the Educational Objectives Achieved?

Referring back to the 7 objectives originally set:

1. *Prepare for work in asynchronous teams* In general met; students who did not enjoy the exercise mostly stated it was a valuable experience.

2. *Key business aspects e.g. social/process* This was partly met, but more effort needs to be given to achieve insight into the roles and phases of asynchronous work.

3. *Apply information management theories* This was achieved well overall. Students had the opportunity not only to apply methods but to discuss their use and face discussion and criticism practicalities.

4. *Creating pressures* This was achieved in relation to timeliness.

5. *Challenging, enjoyable and fun* It was challenging and a large minority of students found it enjoyable. As a result of the logistical problems and a hard-learning experience in discussion 1, a significant minority unfortunately did not find it fun.

6. *External moderators* Worked in some cases, but not consistently well.

7. *Coursework achievement* The high level of collaborative learning reached was a major benefit. But much greater student effort than planned for, was needed to achieve this.

18.15 Future

In 1996/97 the whole exercise will be carried out in Lotus Notes. Training in Notes will take place at the end of Term 1, and this will also be the time when students can prepare for bidding for the case study. The topics covered in 1995/96 will be listed and will not be allowed to be covered again. At the appropriate time the 1995/96 mini-cases will be made available to 1996/97 teams, in addition to their own list. Students have already been recommended to purchase Notes for their home machines so they can take copies of their databases home and work on them there. Printouts simply cannot provide the richness of navigation and search available via the Notes interface. Consideration is being given to use of a Domino server to enable remote and local access via the Netscape browser for those who prefer it.

A major addition planned for 1996/97 is to add a radio button panel to each discussion conference form. Completion of this panel will be mandatory. The panel will require the student to consider the conversational categorisation of their particular input. The categorisation methods currently under consideration are firstly the action language perspective [23]. Secondly would be a more general purpose approach such as found in [24].

The intention here is to introduce some element of self-diagnostic for both individuals and teams. Participants will be able to view the conversational nature of their own inputs, and the teams will be able to do the same for the group as a whole. Our assumption is that if we are able to provide some kind of conversational role model for the different phases of a discussion, groups will have a way of comparing their actual overall approach with this role model. They will perhaps need to review their behaviour if, for example, they are in the final phase of discussions and relatively little convergent activity has taken place.

18.16 Conclusions

In a generally critical perspective of the current application of CSCL in UK Higher Education, [15] it was concluded:

"What we need are computer tools to support educationally proven group learning techniques, based on best practice and educational research, not a programmer's (limited) imagination. Much can be done by extending existing technologies."

Our own experiences would fully endorse this conclusion.

References

1. Collier, K.G. (1980) Peer Group Learning in Higher Education: the Development of Higher Order Skills. *Studies in Higher Education* 5, 1, 55-61.

2. Murray, Frank B. (1990) Cooperative Learning. *Handbook of Educational Ideas and Practices*, Entwistle, Noel (Ed.). Routledge, London. 859-864.

3. Goodlad, Sinclair (Ed) (1995) *Students as Tutors and Mentors*. Kogan Page, London in Association with BP.

4. Easton, Geoff (1982) *Learning from Case Studies*. Prentice Hall International, Englewood Cliffs, New Jersey.

5. Hashim, Safaa; Rathnam, Sukumar and Whinston, Andrew B. (1991) CATT: An Argumentation Based Groupware System for Enhancing Case Discussions in Business Schools. *Proceedings of the 12th International Conference on Information Systems*, DeGross, Janice et al. (Eds.) ACM, Baltimore, MD, 371-385.

6. Van Mentis, Morry (1990) *Active Talk - The Effective Use of Discussion in Learning*. Kogan Page, London.

7. Cockburn, Barbara and Ross, Alec (1978) Working Together. *Group Work in Education*. University of Lancaster, Lancaster.

8. McNair, Malcolm D. (Ed.) (1954) *The Case Method at the Harvard Business School*. McGraw-Hill, New York.

9. Engelbart, D. and English, W. (1969) A Research Center for Augmenting Human Intellect. *Proceedings of FJCC*. AFIPS Press, Montvale, NY. 33, 1, 395-410.

10. Alpert, D. (1975) The PLATO IV system in use - A Progress Report. *Computers in Education*. Lecarme, O. and Lewis, R. (Eds.) North-Holland, Amsterdam.

11. Hiltz, S.R. and Turoff, M. (1978) *The Network Nation: Human Communication via Computer*. MIT Press, Cambridge, MA.

12. Hiltz, S.R. (1995) Impacts of college level courses via asynchronous learning networks -focus on students. *Sloan Conference on Asynchronous Learning Networks*, Philadelphia, PA.

13. Turoff, Murray (1996) Teaching Computer Systems Management in the Virtual Classroom Environment. *Report for the Sloan Foundation Virtual Classroom Project*, NJIT.

14. Mason, Robin, and Kaye, Anthony (1989) *Mind Weave - Communication, Computers and Distance Education*. Pergamon Press, Oxford.

15. Newman, David (1994) Computer Supported Cooperative Learning. *Groupware for the 21st Century*. Lloyd, Peter (Ed), Adamantine Press, London.

16. Stinson, John E and Milter, Richard G. (1995) The Enabling Impact of Information Technology: the case of the Ohio University DMBA. Ohio University, Working Paper.

17. Holtham, Clive (1993) Improving the performance of work groups through information technology. City University Business School. Working Paper.

18. Rich, M. (1993) The use of Electronic Mail and Conferencing Systems in Management Education. City University Business School. Working Paper.

19. Rich, M. (1995) Supporting a Case Study Exercise on the World Wide Web. *Proceedings of International Conference on Computers in Education*, Singapore, 1995.

20. Holtham, Clive (1995) Integrating Technologies to Support Action. *Interacting With Computers*, 7, 1 (March), 91-107.

21. Rich, M. (1994) Building Computer Supported Group Work into an MBA Programme. *International Journal of Computers in Adult Education and Training* 4, 1/2.

22. Sykes, R. (1996) The IS Function in New ICI. *Information Management: People, Performance and Profit Conference*; Elan Group, London.

23. Winograd, T. and Flores, F. (1985) *Understanding Computers and Cognition: A New Foundation for Design*. Ablex, Norwood, NJ.

24. Crowston, K., Malone, T. and Lin, F. (1988) Cognitive Science and Organizational Design: A Case Study of Computer Conferencing. *Human Computer Interaction* 3, 1, 59-85.

25. DeKoven, B. (1990) The Connected Executive. *Institute for Better Meetings*, Palo Alto.

26. Goodlad, Sinclair and Hirst, Beverley (1989*) Peer Tutoring - A Guide to Learning by Teaching*. Kogan Page, London.

27. Hiltz, Starr Roxanne (1994) *The Virtual Classroom - Learning without Limits Via Computer Networks*. Ablex Publishing, Norwood, NY.

28. O'Shea, Tim and Self, John (1983) *Learning and Teaching with Computers*. Harvester Press, Brighton.

Chapter 19

The Relevance and Impact of Collaborative Working for Management in a Digital University

*Brian R Mitchell**

This chapter seeks to explore the impact and relevance of formal collaborative working on the management of Universities. As a result of increased competition for students, staff and funds, HE institutions are being subjected to pressures for continuous improvements in academic and financial performance. The thesis of this chapter is that a formal development of collaborative working practices, supported by appropriate technology, can make a substantial contribution to the effective running of a modern university. The chapter also attempts to place current university management practices in the broader context of commercial management practice in the Twentieth Century.

One critical point of principle: there is NO assumption that the human relationship between teacher and student should be replaced in whole or in part by electronic means of communication. For some institutions, an increase in electronic communication in teaching and learning may be desirable and appropriate, but the perceptive use of collaborative working for **management processes**, supported by technology, has a contribution to make to academic activities by releasing academic staff time for person-to-person contact with students and colleagues. Technology has now created the opportunity for HE institutions to choose how their management processes are to be managed. By "management" we mean all those administrative processes which provide the resources and facilities to support academic staff in teaching and research, and support students in the process of learning.

* Director, Management Systems Division, University Collage London, Gower Street, London, WC1E 6BT, U.K. Email: B.Mitchell@ucl.ac.uk

19.1 Management Issues

On 7th September 1997, the headline in the Independent on Sunday read "A farewell to form-filling as the State goes electronic." The article defined Ministers' objectives:

"They plan a technological revolution to cut down form-filling and eventually to enable people to collect government allowances and benefits 24 hours a day from cash-point machines. The technology will allow people to file tax returns, pay vehicle duty or apply for licences at the touch of a button."

David Clark, the Chancellor of the Duchy of Lancaster, who is in charge of the project, told the newspaper:

"This will be a massive reform of the system of government, started by looking at things from the citizen's point of view. When people think of government, they think of forms and queues. We must put an end to that."

Those sentiments could be the manifesto for a programme to create a Digital University which could be defined as:

- To look at the institution's management processes primarily from the point of view of those teaching, learning and researching.

- To put an end to - or at least significantly reduce - the management and administrative work-load of academic staff, by reducing form-filling and delays.

- To enable the institution to be seen, in appropriate areas, as a whole rather than as an assembly of separate units.

This aim can only be achieved in a large institution by means of an appropriate technological infrastructure - networks, desktop facilities, coherent information - and a cultural shift towards willingness to share information. This will involve a trade-off some degree of personal and departmental independence and self-determination in the interests of easier sharing of information and a reduction in the duplication and reconciliation of data. The underlying cultural change is to move towards more "collaborative" or "asynchronous" working.

From the outset, it must be made clear that the views expressed here do not derive from any formal research. They are the considerations of an experienced IS manager, recently recruited from industry, who is required to manage the continuous delivery of administrative systems to a large College within the University of London and, more specifically, to manage practical and effective systems projects.

19.2   A View on the Development of Management Thinking

19.2.1 The Balance of Power Between Competition and Cooperation

The view that collaboration is a normal or desirable method of working is not universally held. Throughout history, indeed throughout the whole process of evolution, there has been conflict between the forces of collaboration and co-operation and the forces of competition.

The truth of the matter is that there is no absolute: in some situations a competitive response is appropriate, in others a collaborative response is likely to be more effective. Individuals operate in both modes without much difficulty. They cooperate with members of their own family or club or country (in time of war) as the most effective strategy for Life, Liberty and the pursuit of Happiness. The same individuals will compete vigorously against an anti-social neighbour, an opposing team or the enemy.

The history of management presents a specific and more localised case of the same diversity of opinion. Generally, the prevailing philosophy of commerce is that of competition. Most managers would hold that view that what is good for their own organisation must be bad for other organisations with which they are in competition. This is clearly not an absolute: trade associations are living examples of structures set up to exploit the benefits of cooperation with the very institutions with which they compete in other arenas. Universities compete to attract the best students, best staff and most research funding, but they still find overall benefit when cooperating in their dealings with government.

The process of management shows a similar dichotomy. Some - many - managers see themselves as being in competition with their colleagues and staff as well as other divisions in the same enterprise. This type of manager sees commercial life as nasty, brutish and short, and acts accordingly. But there are other types of manager: the work of W. Edwards Deming, for example, has shown that collaboration with one's colleagues, suppliers, customers, local communities and even with other suppliers in the same industry actually is more effective than competition. Given his success in the development of the Japanese electronic and motor industries since the war, such views are very compelling. Maybe the recent cold winds blowing through the Pacific tiger economies might have been less traumatic had Deming also been invited to apply his philosophies to the property and financial sectors.

What is certainly true is that the maturing of electronic communication has introduced a new dimension into the collaboration/competition equation that we ignore at our peril. At first sight, this could look like a war-winning weapon for the forces of competition. But electronic communication, effectively used, can profoundly improve the effectiveness of the collaborative approach. My two key hypotheses are:

1. That it is possible to manage even large enterprises which exploit the benefits is size but without creating a bureaucratic monster, subject to the development of a cooperative culture, and supported by a suitable means of inter-personal communication. In any large organisation, this must mean electronic communication.

2. That Universities could particularly profit from this concept. HE institutions must resolve two conflicting cultural pressures: to maintain their traditional liberal role as teachers and employers, while at the same time responding to governmental demands for tighter cost control, more accountability expressed in statistical terms and more responsiveness to the "market".

19.3   Demands on Universities

19.3.1 The Problems of Managing HE in the Late 20th Century

This is not the place to describe the pressures on the management of HE; enough has already been written. However, the increase in the size of institutions from both organic growth and mergers, reduced unit funding, additional government involvement, student expectations, litigation and funded research has created major problems to which formal management responses are needed.

It is here that the parallel between HE and commercial organisations can be instructive. Until recently, most UK Universities could have been usefully described as operating in the "proprietorial" phase of development: individual members of academic staff operated rather as proprietors of particular courses or leaders of unique research teams. It is this highly organic relationship between staff and students that characterises much of HE in the UK. But Universities then began to suffer the same kind of pressures from growing scale and complexity that the commercial proprietors saw, but the commercial solutions did not fit Universities well, at least in the UK.

There are good reasons why this should be so:

•   UK Universities do not operate in a free market: the role of the funding councils makes Universities feel much more like nationalised institutions.

•   Universities are very complex organisms. They do not have the clear definitions of products, shareholders, directors, managers, customers that even large commercial organisations can define.

•   The notion of "management authority" lies much less easily in HE than in commerce. There tends to be a far higher percentage of inquiring and questioning staff in Universities than in commerce. Indeed, many commercial organisations find difficulty in "managing" knowledge workers - such employers as stockbrokers, investment houses and the media go to extreme lengths in salaries and bonuses to retain and direct key knowledge workers.

19.3.2 Asynchronous Working Requires a Culture Shift in Management Thinking

The development of electronic information systems has both caused and facilitated dramatic changes to the way in which institutions - commercial, industrial, public as well as educational - operate. By facilitating the rapid creation and communication of information, and its interlinking with administrative processes, it has created the opportunity for a revolution in management thinking. The benefits could be especially relevant in Higher Education, which is fundamentally knowledge-based and needs to achieve a fine balance between academic freedom and administrative efficiency. Unfortunately, collaborative working has not so far been a readily adopted concept among the Western population at large, and especially not as a management approach.

The creation of a digital university will not be an easy, or cheap, exercise, but in the increasingly commercial culture in which universities operate, the degree of collaboration which it permits should improve both the effectiveness and efficiency of the institution while improving the quality of life which it provides for its students and staff. The need to move in this direction has been recognised by Sir Ron Dearing, whose recommendations include the exploitation of Communication and Information technology, the development of a new Institute for Teaching and Learning, covering among other things the "management of teaching and learning."

Electronic, collaborative working, may provide the answer to a whole family of problems - those related to personal relationships within an enterprise - which a host of management philosophies (or fashions) have sought to resolve by non-technological means. Collaborative working, based on electronic communication, could cause a ground shift in management, organisational and motivational theory.

From this point, this chapter follows three threads:

1. An outline of the way in which **collaborative working might impact a university**.

2. A description of the **process for developing collaborative working** using electronic information systems.

3. A short perusal of where **previous management theories** might be absorbed within the broader concept of collaborative working.

19.4   The Way in which Collaborative Working Might Impact a University

19.4.1   Features of a "Collaborative University"

There are situations for which the collaborative approach is particularly appropriate:

- **Knowledge Workers**. The collaborative approach works especially well where the deliverable is intangible, as it is more difficult to specify in advance the nature, time and cost of the result of the work.

- **Research**. Development work with an external requirement for a specific outcome at a specific time may need more mechanistic management. However, the exploratory stages of projects of this type can be ideal for a collaborative approach.

- **Distance Working**. The costs of the traditional structured meeting (i.e. of getting everyone together in one place at one time) are becoming widely recognised. Eliminating such meetings appears to be in opposition to the concept of collaborative working; however, once the dimension of full electronic communication has been built into the management style from the beginning, arms-length operation becomes the norm.

Under all the above criteria, Universities seem an ideal ground for exploiting the opportunities offered by collaboration based on electronics. Assuming that a university has decided to adopt the collaborative model, it will demonstrate a number of features:

- A set of shared values that permeate the whole Institution. These values will inevitably and desirably differ between Institutions. Each will settle on its own balance between research and teaching; between covering all faculties and academic specialisations; between high technology and human chemistry as the main teaching techniques; between metropolitan and remote campus site; between centralised and department structures; between fixed courses and flexible inter-disciplinary programmes; between traditional formality and inventive anarchy. It may of course be a value not to have a single value, but to encourage cultural diversity. However, a university will experience problems if its academics are designing inter-disciplinary programmes of study, but its administrators are unable to provide staff and students with the means to generate, publicise, present and examine such courses.

- The purposeful blurring of the established distinction between "administrative" and "academic" roles. All administrative procedures, whether undertaken by academic members of staff or not, must support the teaching, learning and research activities which the university undertakes. This is easier said than done: the university has legal obligations which cannot be evaded but which do not obviously support academic endeavour.

- Widely distributed decision-making at the point closest to the activity. Only major decisions are routed to or initiated by the senior management. Responsibility for financial decisions are delegated as far as possible to departmental level and beyond, but using electronic communication to monitor compliance with budgeting authority and the institution-wide situation.

- Collaborative structures therefore tend to be wide rather than deep. There are the fewest number of organisational levels.

- Very good lines of communication particularly across, as opposed to up and down, the institution. Communication is a two-way process, not just broadcasting.

- Elimination of fear: individuals are expected to contribute their views even if these are against the prevailing preference, and to do this requires widely disseminated information. The concept of information on a "need-to-know" basis is not collaborative, as it is not possible to predict when an item of information will be useful or by whom it will be used. A collaborative institution will establish a policy of open communication, up to the point where further communication would jeopardise personal or institutional confidentiality. Hidden agendas are seen as damaging and are exposed by peer pressure. Uncertainty is seen not as a weakness but as part of a genuine seeking for good solutions. Errors and mistakes are seen as stimuli to identify the causes and to do better next time: exploration and experimentation are encouraged and supported.

- The structure is dynamic and flexible: new groupings of individuals are created for new problems. Interfunctional steering groups, working groups, quality circles and workshops are established where each is the optimum solution to a problem. Such groupings have clear, although different, life cycles. They are created, developed, maintained and then terminated once their objectives have been met.

- There is the minimum of social stratification: individuals are valued and used because of their potential contribution and not because of their seniority or status.

- Quality is seen as something which is built into any procedure and sought by all those involved: it is not a subsequent phase of inspection and rejection of below-standard examples. Quality is a process of continuous improvement based upon an objective review of variation and not as deviation from a fixed set of norms.

19.5 Characteristics of a Digital University

A collaborative university showing the above characteristics is not an easy thing to create, and without electronic communication it would be impossible. I suggest that the following type of electronic information infrastructure is going to be a necessary prerequisite to such an institution:

19.5.1 Information must be Accurate, Appropriate and Available

There are countless examples in commerce as well as HE where information is not adequate for the task of supporting a collaborative institution. The information may be flawed in many respects:

- It may be just plain wrong - from being invalid or not up to date.

- It may be inappropriate - it may be designed for one purpose but used for another.

- It may be at the wrong level of detail and either swamp the receiver with masses of detail without summary features, or may give bland generalisations without the ability to drill down to locate the really significant detail.

- It may be unreliable - it may be available for a period but then cease, when the individual champion who created the system moved on or got bored. It may have been written to inadequate design standards. This has become a particular problem with do-it-yourself database software. Conversely, systems for the creation and distribution of information may have been quoted by the IS professional which are so expensive or which will take so long to deliver that there would not be hope of approval for such a project.

- A system which works fine for one or two users may fail as the number of users increases beyond the capability of the initiating enthusiast - systems should be designed for appropriate scalability.

- It may not be consistent - different definitions of critical items of information may prevent consolidation into useful higher-order reports. This may cause an associated problem: that the information cannot be shared.

- The medium may be inappropriate - a screen-based view does not help the receiver trying to work on the train home or at a research site. It may be too structured - only possible to locate the required data if the full 34-character ID code is known and is entered flawlessly every time. It may be too unstructured - a long sequence of helpful menu items to home in on a record that the receiver could have identified by a simple known code.

- It may be inconvenient - it may be protected by so many levels of security that only Houdini or an enthusiastic hacker is likely to use it. It may take an inordinate length of time to retrieve the data.

- It may be inflexible - like it would take months to create a related report for even a slightly different purpose.

19.5.2 Contribution of the Internet

No discussion of collaborative working would be complete without a few views on the Internet. The role of the Internet is so obvious that it can be taken for granted:

* It is virtually universal, relatively free of constraining technical monopolies or standards, the subject of rapid growth and acceptance.

* It is already accessible to the overwhelming majority of those likely to be involved in HE collaborative projects. It can be accessed on-campus and anywhere a telephone line exists.

* It is the subject of great development effort. Organisations from the size of the Microsoft and Oracle Corporations down are investing large sums of money in enabling technologies.

Notwithstanding the above eulogies, I have some concerns, even though there may be no alternative:

* The nature of information exchange can be misunderstood; simply "putting up information" on the Web, may be of little help. If the resulting portfolio is a random mixture of personalised views, not presented and edited for wide consumption, the results can be downright confusing to those seeking to share the data.

* Information exchange is not sufficiently secure. Although both commercial and free security products are available, their use is not particularly widespread and is often viewed as psychologically unacceptable. Furthermore, to provide good security requires more than simplistic application of boxed solutions, as the banking and military communities can attest from experience.

19.5.3 Example of a Process Based on Collaborative Working: No 1 Staff Recruitment

Staff recruitment is an example of a process of something that should be very simple: all organisations, from all commercial and public sectors, undertake such processes and it would have been thought that there were no special contributions that collaborative working could make. However, there are some particular problems which Universities face:

* Universities are relatively large organisations but their staff cannot be mass-produced. The contribution of an individual to a research team can be unique. This requires a recruitment process which can deal with large numbers of potential recruits, but with many unique jobs.

* Individual employment contracts may be relatively short - especially for research posts: in some cases there is one unique candidate. The recruitment

process must set up effective milestones to ensure that the progress of every post must be monitored very closely and efficiently.

- Universities, in the UK at least, are running under tight budgets: there is usually no room for lavish recruitment procedures involving external agencies. On the other hand, the system has to be very effective as there may be competition with other institutions to attract and retain key individuals. Every post has to be checked against available funds, provided by Funding Council, research sponsor and so on.

What is required is a system that provides rapid and effective communication between all the parties involved: the employing department, the personnel function, and the budgeting function. It must also involve numerous supporting agencies: the advertising media; the interview team; pensions; health and safety; providers of references; estates and providers of accommodation and office or laboratory facilities; security; telephones; computing services… the list is extensive. If each of these agencies must be involved serially, the recruitment process will take so long that the best candidates will be long gone by the time an offer can be assembled.

It is critical here that all possible actions are undertaken in parallel, and each step that is serially dependent on another is triggered automatically as soon as the preceding step is complete. Paper-based systems cannot be that responsive: the only effective approach is electronic communication, with all parties able to access and, in appropriate cases update, a coherent pool of information.

Note that there is no distinction between "administrative" and "academic" activities here. Academic and administrative skills are needed to interact seamlessly if the whole process is going to appear efficient and sympathetic to the new member of staff .

19.5.4 Example of a Process Based on Collaborative Working: No 2 Course Development

The development of courses may sound initially like a purely academic process; however, this is an over-simplification. There are a variety of skills to be involved, and again here, collaborative working is needed. The process is likely to involve the following steps:

- Identification of the need or opportunity for a new course, by responding to demand from students, or by identifying a gap in the market. The idea will need to be discussed with academic colleagues and a concept developed. The review process may involve a number of colleagues, in one or more departments or institutions, and may need to incorporate existing modules. This will involve communication with academic colleagues.

- The idea will need to be assessed for costs, for materials, equipment and so on, and departmental or institutional budgets earmarked. This will require communication with departmental and financial staff, usually requiring the interchange of financial models and their progressive refinement.

- The content will be developed and refined and drafts prepared. Information will need to be presented in a variety of formats - text, graphics, plans, physical and conceptual models, reference material, slides, programmes, brochures, etc. - and all formats should be able to be exchanged and refined in collaboration with colleagues in a variety of locations.

- The course will no doubt require institutional approval, based on a demonstrated opportunity in the market, on accurately predicted costs and potential income. It must then be added to the institution's portfolio of courses. This too requires the exchange of information across space and between individuals with special contributions to make.

- Potential students will need to be given information about the course, and details added to the registration and examination processes.

With the advent of Sir Ron Dearing's proposals, the process could be more complex still: a pricing structure may need to be created for individual courses or modules, for different types of student, at different times. Attempting to navigate through this process without electronic communication and shared local and institutional data would seem to be a hopelessly slow and tortuous task.

19.5.5 Example of a Process Based on Collaborative Working: No 3 Research Management

Research is one of those university processes which show up most clearly the apparent conflict between administrative and academic processes. However, for many universities, the effective management of all aspects of research is critical to their ability to flourish, or even simply to survive. The problems are legion:

- Research is a process which is fundamentally collaborative. However, there are contradictory aspects: at the simplest level, there are needs for confidentiality and also for publicity. The very existence of a research project may be considered confidential, but to be first with published results has been a key objective for researchers since time immemorial. As research is based upon the interchange of results between team members, secure but convenient methods of exchange are necessary. This applies to the process of seeking funding as well as undertaking the research itself.

- Establishing a research project requires acquiring and funding of some or all of: staff; office or laboratory accommodation; access to information; authority and licences. It also requires control procedures to be in place to handle some or all of: costing and budgeting; the flow of funds; meeting research deadlines; monitoring the activities of each member of the team; preparing results for publishing in a variety of formats for in-house and external use; developing a product and its marketing; copyright; patents; and so on.

This process requires rapid communication between the research team and almost every administrative service in the institution. Electronic communication can achieve rapidity and reliability of information flow that would make a contribution to all but the smallest research projects.

19.6   The Process for Developing Collaborative Working Using Electronic Information Systems

19.6.1 How to Build Information Structures for Collaborative Institutions

It could be argued that collaborative working cannot be "built", that it is fundamentally an organic, cultural process, and that any attempt to implement would be a contradiction in terms. I have heard it argued that it should emerge rather as did the Internet itself. I am not persuaded by that argument: were that case to be valid there would be more cases of fully-fledged collaborative working in operation, and fewer instances of staff asking for the facilities to work collaboratively.

- Given that it requires at least some degree of pump-priming, if not fully managed implementation, the starting point is an institutional policy to develop a culture of collaborative working: this will require supporting strategies in a number of areas:

  - A commitment from the Vice-Chancellor supported by the most senior individuals and departments.

  - An organisation - steering group - to direct the development process, and to argue for appropriate levels of investment.

  - Clear objectives and recognition of the benefits - and costs. Costs will be both in financial terms and in the extent to which individuals and departments will need to relinquish some degree of freedom of choice.

  - A formal plan with details of phases of work, responsibilities and schedules.

  - The group steering the development of collaborative working must be privy to the innermost plans of the institution. Systems take time to develop, and it is highly wasteful for work to be progressing into areas which are incompatible with the institution's plans.

- An educational and communication plan, which must be based on wide, if not universal, participation by all major units in the institution, in developing and accepting the plans. A vision imposed by a few enthusiasts may act as a starting point but must develop to achieve widespread ownership by the institution's staff.

- All future systems must conform to the concept that critical information must derive as by-products from properly structured administrative processes. Institution-level information about, say, staff should be captured at source throughout the recruitment **process** and then be made available to using departments. The supporting system should permit information of more local use to be added. It is a sign of very unhealthy systems if users of information have to create their own pools of localised data simply to compensate for inadequacies in the institutional data. Such local pools are convenient in the short term, but effectively prevent such information being shared. This inability to share can severely damage collaborative processes.

- The Institution requires a high-level data model to achieve consistent definitions of the key data entities. A single definition of such an entity as "department" should be applied across all potential uses, including financial, student, personnel, estates and course administration. This high-level model should start at the level of a simple process/information matrix. It is then available as a top-level information and process model.

19.6.2 Technical Infrastructure for Collaborative Management

Collaborative working requires a core infrastructure of common technology. Even quite simple commonality would help: one only has to consider the problems of routing text documents widely across a diversity of mail systems to be aware of the problems of technical diversity.

Very few institutions will be in a position to start from a green field in terms of technology. It is very likely that there will be a variety of hardware, operating systems, application software and development methods in place. It will rarely be possible to replace all the infrastructure at a stroke, but a progressive move towards conformity in some areas will be crucial. There are a number of strategies by which this may be achieved:

- A series of policy statements on the future direction of the institution, such that each unit will convert to products within the standard portfolio at the next major upgrade. This will be much helped by central funding and site-licensing agreements, central technical support during the conversion process, wide consultation before the standards are established, and the selection of stable, high quality, widely available products.

- The establishment of a limited number of ideal solutions among champions of the preferred standards. The message of the benefits of conformity should then be encouraged to permeate organically across the user population.

- The definition, not of standard products, but of standard interfaces between a number of feasible products.

The following elements are required:

- A high-performance, high-reliability network, right up to the socket in the wall. This should be all-pervasive, cover data, telephones and video and be the responsibility of a single coordinating function. This same function must have the right to certify all networking equipment and protocols downstream of the socket. This must be the physical link to all external networks.

- An institution-wide provision of the hardware and operating system to support all the Institutional databases, including back-up.

- An institution-wide standard for desktop facilities to be used by any member of staff who participates in the collaborative process with other members of staff. This must be managed at the institution-level such that all client software can be delivered concurrently to all users. This standard may be expressed as specific products or as industry standards, as appropriate. With time the nature of such a standard is becoming less onerous; as the Web interface matures it will no doubt provide the level of universality, platform independence, security and functionality that will provide the required degree of interoperability.

- The adoption of a limited range of application software: this must cover all desktop and database applications:

  - Word processing and text management.

  - Spreadsheet and numerical management.

  - Graphics and presentation products.

  - Web and Email development and access tools.

  - Network access tools, for on-site, at-home and mobile communication.

  - Database software for use on institutional databases.

  - Desktop database software, able to interface to the institutional database, and permit the development of local applications.

  - Screen and report generation products, for use by development professionals, and by users. The range should be sufficient to cater for the needs for power and functionality by systems professionals and sufficiently user-friendly for users.

  - Systems development methodologies used for creating all the institutional systems. These may be simply standard procedures, or specific development products, CASE for example.

- A well-equipped and staffed support centre, offering Helpdesk, training and consultancy. This unit must be staffed to carry out both routine support of line-of-business, as well as research into pertinent developments in the market and trials of promising products. This research and development function must not be squeezed out of the odd spare moments in the work of routine support.

- The technology must support some critical facilities:

    - Reliable and recoverable file stores.

    - Sound security standards to provide known level of protection against hacking, and unauthorised use of the institution's facilities.

19.7   Where Previous Management Theories Might be Absorbed Within the Broader Concept of Collaborative Working

The last fifty-or-so years have seen a plethora of management philosophies or methodologies which have, in their various ways, sought to deal with the problems of how best to create coordination between individuals to achieve consolidated institutional direction. Management thinking in the first half of the Twentieth Century could be characterised as an initial move towards the adoption of the practices of industry to management and to knowledge working. The work of a number of key management thinkers developed and refined the concept that management could be explained in objective, scientific terms:

- Frederick Taylor (who defined management in scientific time-and-motion-study terms in "Scientific Management", 1947, Harper and Row)

- Max Weber (who applauded the role of charismatic authority in "The Theory of Social and Economic Organisation", 1947, The Free Press)

- Peter Drucker (who is credited by Tom Peters with the creation of the discipline of management) represented management as a "hard science" in such works as "The Practice of Management", 1954, Harper & Row).

These works predated the opportunities for degrees of distributed operation and joint participation offered by electronic communication. The following section provides the merest hint of the theories of more recent writers and the suggests ways in which their philosophies can contribute to the development of a model for collaborative working.

19.7.1 Relationship with Representative Management Philosophies

Business Process Re-engineering ("Reengineering the Corporation", Michael Hammer and James Champy, 1993, Harper Collins)

Hammer and Champy demonstrate the value of seeing tasks as being performed by identifiable and continuous processes. These processes should be simplified and rationalised, or preferably eliminated entirely, with resulting savings in cost and time. One key contributor to this improvement is electronic communication which enables barriers between organisational functions to be broken down to the point where clients are provided with a single point of contact and where tasks are performed as a coherent process and not as a series of disjointed sequential steps. They outline examples where tasks have been restructured: serial tasks each performed by an expert in that task - as would be the case before the advent of robotics in vehicle mass-production - are replaced with single individuals performing all tasks related to a single process but with access to a limited number of specialists to provide collaborative advice on complex individual cases.

Empowerment (Rosabeth Moss Kanter, "Men and Women of the Corporation", 1997, Basic Books)

Rosabeth Moss Kanter describes the "post-entrepreneurial enterprise" by empowering all staff with the ability to make decisions without the constant need for control from their seniors. This concept is encapsulated in the acronym: PAL. *Pool* resources, *Ally* to exploit an opportunity and *Link* systems in partnerships. This could be a definition of asynchronous collaborative working, in which the most admired characteristics of management move from outdated "predictability" to the ability to take executive decisions based on an understanding of corporate policies as well as local situations.

Hierarchy of Needs (Abraham Maslow, "Motivation and Personality", 1970, Harper & Row)

Maslow provided the academic justification that individuals come to work for more than just the need to earn money and gain security. He was an optimist who noted the role of personal satisfaction and fulfilment of ambition as a major (if not the sole) source of motivation. This philosophy is widely recognised and practiced among most staff in Universities, if not in many commercial enterprises. Maslow provides the justification for the willingness to trust staff and share responsibility for collaborative endeavours

Lateral Thinking (Edward De Bono, "The Use of Lateral Thinking", 1967, McGraw Hill and others)

Edward de Bono's concept of thinking differentiates lateral thinking from vertical - i.e. from traditional sequential thinking. Vertical thinking is a step-by-step process; lateral thinking operates by innovative leaps into uncharted waters. This disparity between thinking styles mirrors the difference between traditional hierarchical organisations, and inter-functional ad-hoc collaborative groups.

Theory X vs. Theory Y (Douglas McGregor, "The Human Side of Enterprise", 1960, McGraw-Hill)

McGregor formalised the distinction between authoritarian and participative (i.e. collaborative) management into Theory X and Theory Y. Theory X is based on the assumption that staff are all lazy and antipathetic to work: only the stick can motivate them. Theory Y assumes that people need to work and that they actively seek responsibility and the satisfaction that comes from achievement. Theory Y has been refined in more recent years as experiments have shown that even individuals inclined to a theory Y approach, still value some structure and predictability in the work-place. Theory Y is facilitated by collaborative approaches.

The Prototyping or Rapid Application Development (RAD) Concept

The IT industry itself has explored the problems of developing systems to time, cost and functionality. Since the mid 1950s many practitioners (Martin, Jackson, Yourdon, Gane and Sarson) have sought to tackle the problem of delivering systems effectively. Particularly in the early years, they mostly involved a structured, engineered approach. This was appropriate where vast teams of specialists were required before the days of development tools with high functionality. The RAD concept not only exploits the capabilities of new software tools, it also exploits the concept of collaborative working between small teams.

Management Teams (R Meredith Belbin, "Management Teams", 1981, Butterworth-Heinemann)

Belbin extends the concept of multi-discipline teams. He identifies multi-personality teams where the personal and cultural styles of participants are also balanced to form a coherent whole. His view would be that a team with all the right technical skills can fail if everyone wants to be boss, or if internal personality conflicts emerge. This is a crucial consideration for collaborative ventures: a team comprising all egomaniacs or all subservient servants is not likely to achieve. [22]

---

[22] I can recommend a slim volume which has routed me to becoming acquainted with some of the major writers on management thinking: Kennedy, Carol (1991), *Guide to the Management Gurus*, Business Books Limited.

19.8 Conclusions

The purpose of this chapter has been to explore the impact and relevance of formal collaborative working on the management of universities, especially in an increasingly commerce-like environment. It is my conclusion that formal collaborative working could have a major role to play in making HE institutions more efficient without imposing draconian controls over financial administration, enforcing robotic management processes or impinging upon academic freedom on teaching and research.

However, there are some critical messages:

- *Implementation:* some formal planning and management of the development of collaborative working is required. A solely organic approach to development is unlikely to produce the required results in the time or to the quality needed.

- *Culture:* a greater willingness genuinely to share information and trust teamwork is required. This may be an Elysian ambition; it would be totally unrealistic to C. P. Snow. But such defensive strategies - hidden agendas and so on - are inimical to the collaborative approach.

- *Management:* a greater willingness to accept formal management thinking is required. I have found formal management training and practice very helpful in actually getting things done. There is too great a willingness in universities to condemn all formal management thinking as pretentious self-indulgent. There are some very attractive babies in with the bathwater.

- *Technology:* this must be seen as the infrastructure upon which the new types of cultural relationships can be built. However seductive some of the technology is, it is a means not an end. The Web is a case in point. For all the potential, and many valuable contributions by the Web to genuine collaboration, I can see it also as a hindrance. Far too often self-proclaimed exponents of collaborative working respond to accusations that they have not actually shared anything, with "but it's on the Web." The Web can be a defence against the need to collaborate.

While some degree of collaborative working has emerged in UK Universities, there remain many unexploited opportunities for improving the management processes. This will need a formal institutional will, acceptance of cultural change and a major management project to develop and fund. The continued competitiveness and effectiveness of the UK HE sector requires such a commitment.

Index